WISDOM

Also by Dr. Larry Lea
from Thomas Nelson Publishers

Releasing the Prayer Anointing

The bestselling author of *Could You Not Tarry One Hour?* reveals exciting new insights into Jesus' model prayer that will create a newfound joy in personal prayer. *Releasing the Prayer Anointing* offers you proven steps for a more consistent prayer life and shows you how to experience the miracle of answered prayer on a daily basis through personal prayer, power prayer, and prevailing prayer.

WISDOM

THE GIFT WORTH SEEKING

DR. LARRY LEA

OLIVER
NELSON

Thomas Nelson Publishers
Nashville • Atlanta • London • Vancouver

Published in Nashville, Tennessee, by Thomas Nelson, Inc., Publishers, and distributed in Canada by Word Communications, Ltd., Richmond, British Columbia.

Unless otherwise noted, the Bible version used in this publication is THE NEW KING JAMES VERSION. Copyright © 1979, 1980, 1982, Thomas Nelson, Inc., Publishers. Verses marked TLB are taken from *The Living Bible,* copyright 1971 by Tyndale House Publishers, Wheaton IL. Used by permission. Scripture quotations noted KJV are from The King James Version of the Holy Bible. Scripture quotations noted J. B. Phillips are from J. B. Phillips: THE NEW TESTAMENT IN MODERN ENGLISH, Revised Edition. © J. B. Phillips 1958, 1960, 1972. Used by permission of Macmillan Publishing Co., Inc.

Printed in the United States of America.

Library of Congress Cataloging-in-Publication Data

Lea, Larry.
    Wisdom : the gift worth seeking / Larry Lea.
      p.   cm.
    ISBN 0-8407-9019-8 (hardcover)
    ISBN 0-7852-7350-6 (paperback)
    1. Christian life—1960–   2. Wisdom—Religious aspects—
Christianity. I. Title.
BV4501.2.L38   1990
241'.4—dc20   90-35652
                                          CIP

2 3 4 5 6 7 8 9 10 — 03 02 01 00 99 98 97 96

To my dad and my mother,
Harold Joe and Tommie Jean Lea,
whose prayers and godly advice
have guided my life
and my ministry.

Debra Young
1/13/04

Northwestern
Book Store

Contents

Preface

A few weeks ago a man came to me after I had preached my Sunday sermon and said, "Larry, that was a great sermon. How long did it take you to develop that one?"

Without hesitation I looked at him and said, "Twenty years."

Some messages aren't "studied" messages. They are life messages.

That is the case with the message you hold in your hand.

My college roommate will attest to you that during our early days in college we often got on our knees to pray and that my number one prayer was for wisdom. That's really all I ever prayed for in any consistent, enduring manner. I didn't know why at the time. But I know today without a doubt that it is the very best prayer that I could have ever prayed or could ever pray . . . or that any person can ever pray.

Wisdom flows from your prayer life. It comes as a result of making wisdom your number one prayer request. "God, give me wisdom!" must become your heart's cry.

To have God's wisdom is to enter the heart of God.

To have God's wisdom is to hold the keys to the unspeakable riches from His glory that He desires for you to have.

To have God's wisdom is to take the first step toward anything—and everything—you need in life.

The good news to you today is that you CAN experience God's wisdom. It's available to YOU. It's available NOW!

LARRY LEA

Introduction

We don't hear a lot about wisdom at parties. It isn't the juicy topic of the day.

We don't hear a lot about wisdom by the drinking fountain at work. It isn't the buzzword of commerce.

We don't hear a lot about wisdom at the dinner table. It isn't the day's news.

We don't even hear a lot about wisdom in our churches. It isn't a hot topic.

Most of us rarely give wisdom a second thought.

Furthermore, most of us don't think of ourselves as being wise or, sadder still, as ever being capable of becoming wise. The wise person is too often thought of as a guru sitting atop a mountain in a faraway culture or as the "wise guy"—either the local smart aleck or a person's drug connection.

Few of us long to be wise.

We don't seek wisdom the same way that we set our affections on a new car or work for a promotion in our careers. We don't long for it the same way we long for loved ones we haven't seen in a while. We don't ask for it the same way we ask God for miracles of healing or the salvation of lost souls.

And yet . . .

Wisdom is THE most important topic of the Bible.

Gain wisdom and you'll learn how to become a truly whole, fulfilled, purposeful, contented man or woman.

Get wisdom and you'll learn how to raise your children and have a happy marriage.

Possess wisdom and you'll know how to lead a church . . . or a business . . . or a practice . . . or an organization.

Obtain wisdom and you'll learn how to become healthy and whole.

Wisdom is the foremost key to having everything you need and desire in life.

And the converse is also true. . . .

Without wisdom you may marry and have children, but you'll be in danger of losing them. Without wisdom you may establish a church, a business, a professional practice, or an organization, but you'll struggle constantly to keep it. Without wisdom you are in danger of losing your health and your life. Without wisdom you may experience temporary happiness, but you will never know lasting contentment, joy, or satisfaction.

The Bible says, "Trust in the Lord with all your heart, and lean not on your own understanding; in all your ways acknowledge Him, and He shall direct your paths" (Prov. 3:5–6).

Those verses are a challenge to seek and to gain WISDOM. They are God's challenge to you now. Seek His wisdom. There's no substitute for it. There's no genuine success without it.

Make a decision today—you won't live your life without it!

Part One

Wisdom and the Wise Person

For this reason we also, since the day we heard it,
do not cease to pray for you, and to ask that
you may be filled with the knowledge of His will
in all wisdom and spiritual understanding;
that you may have a walk worthy of the Lord,
fully pleasing Him,
being fruitful in every good work and
increasing in the knowledge of God.

—Colossians 1:9–10

Chapter 1

The Five Most Important Questions You Can Ask about Wisdom

For the Lord gives wisdom;
From His mouth come knowledge and understanding;
He stores up sound wisdom for the upright.
—Proverbs 2:6–7

We need wisdom more than we've ever needed wisdom before. Just look around.

The drug problem is totally out of control, despite what our government officials—and government officials in other nations—have tried to do. The sexual revolution has resulted in disease evolution. The national debt is in such high figures that the average person cannot comprehend that amount of money. Gangs roam our city streets. Abortionists are killing more than 1.5 million babies a year in the United States alone. One in every two marriages ends in divorce. Crime rates are up—especially crimes against children and young people. The homeless rate is up. Things are out of control! Never have we needed wisdom more than we need it today.

When you look at the world situation, the problems are compounded. Everything that is wrong in America is wrong in other nations, and sometimes in far greater proportion. One out of four children will go to bed hungry tonight. One out of ten children will not have a roof over his or her head tonight. The problems seem beyond solution and, in many cases, even beyond accurate definition. Never has the need for wisdom been greater.

And . . .

The best news I can share with you today is that God wants to give you His wisdom more than you want to have it. He longs for you to have His wisdom, to experience it fully in all areas of your life, and to walk in it day by day.

I challenge you to ask yourself five key questions about wisdom. . . .

Question 1:
What Is Wisdom?

Wisdom is the God-given ability to perceive the true nature of a matter and to implement the will of God in that matter.

Wisdom has two facets to it. First, it is the God-given ability to perceive the truth of a matter. What is real? What is true? And furthermore, what is real and true from God's perspective?

Man's reality and God's reality are often very different.

Consider for a moment the story of the three young Hebrew men—Shadrach, Meshach, and Abed-Nego—and the situation they faced when the king said, "I'm going to throw you into this fiery furnace if you don't bow down to my image" (see Dan. 3).

Natural wisdom would say, "I'd better bow down. What good am I going to do for God on this earth if I don't bow and am burned alive?" Natural wisdom looks at the facts and makes a choice that seems right for the welfare of the person (or persons) involved.

Spiritual wisdom, however, says, "Take your stand. You are commanded by God not to bow down to any idol at any time. Trust God in this. If you die, you die. The consequences are up to God. Your entire life is under God's control. So trust God and obey." Spiritual wisdom makes a decision based on the absolutes of God.

Nearly every situation or circumstance you face in life can be approached from these two angles: natural wisdom and spiritual wisdom.

You need to know not only WHAT it is that God desires in a situation but also HOW to implement God's will. Specifically, you need to find God's methods and His perfect timing.

Some months ago the word of the Lord came very strongly to me that I was to resign a position I had held for nearly two years, the deanship of the seminary at Oral Roberts University.

I had accepted that position after considerable prayer on my part and on the part of the elders of my church. When Oral Roberts first approached me about taking the deanship, he said that he thought my stay at Oral Roberts University might be a minimum of from twenty-four to thirty-six months. That was a considerable time commitment, especially since I felt no leading of God to resign my position at the Church on the Rock. Still, I felt impressed in my spirit that I was to go, and when I discussed it with the elders, they had responded, "Yes, this is the will of God. We don't completely understand it, but you are to go." They laid hands on me and sent me to accomplish a certain task.

When the day came that the Lord said, "Your work there is done," I had no doubt as to *what* God wanted me to do. His word to me was very certain. But I prayed, "Lord, I need and want Your wisdom as to *how* I am to resign and *when*."

Natural wisdom would have said, "Do this over a period of months. Make plans for a transition. Don't resign in November. Wait until the end of the school year."

But God had said, "Your time is completed."

I felt an immediacy in my spirit. Again, I consulted the elders of my church. I told them that the Lord had spoken in my heart and that I felt an urgency in my spirit. They prayed about it and said to me, "Larry, we sent you there. We knew it was right. Now we know that it is the time for you to resign."

So I went to Tulsa the next week and resigned. And there was such a sense of peace and joy over that. Often when you resign a position, there are conflict and a lack of understanding. That wasn't at all the case this time. We parted in the full fellowship of the Holy Spirit.

You need to know WHAT God wants you to do in a certain situation. It is a God-given ability. It is the ability to perceive what is real and true from God's perspective.

You also need to know HOW and WHEN to implement what God wants you to do.

That's wisdom.

Question 2: What Does Wisdom Have to Do with ME?

Wisdom has everything to do with YOU. God does not desire that He alone possess wisdom. If so, He never would have made wisdom available to you or have challenged you to obtain it. If wisdom were impossible to find, He never would have challenged men and women to seek it.

Furthermore, God does not withhold His wisdom from those who desire it. He hasn't set aside one class of people, one race, one nationality, one sex, one age group, or one socioeconomic segment of society to possess wisdom.

Wisdom is God's desire for you . . . yes, YOU.

Let me share with you four ways God's wisdom relates specifically to YOUR life.

Wisdom is the vehicle for getting you to the place you want to go.

Most everyone I know today travels by car. It's the vehicle most people choose for getting to work, school, shopping, church, and recreation. When I look out at a group of people gathered for a service at the Church on the Rock, I know that every one of those people arrived by some type of automobile. The Church on the Rock is so far from anywhere that you simply can't get there by public bus. No trains go by. The church has no landing strip. And I don't know anybody who travels by foot.

Those who attend could wish all day that they might be transported directly to the Church on the Rock. But that isn't likely to happen. They could want to come, but wanting wouldn't get them to the church. No. They must get in their automobiles and drive. Their cars are the vehicles that make church attendance possible. Similarly, wisdom is your vehicle for getting from where you are to the place you want to be in life.

Now if I asked you face-to-face what you need most in life right now, I suspect you would answer, "I need financial stability."

I would respond to you, "No. You need WISDOM to know how to get financial stability."

Some of you might say, "I need for my children to obey me. My home is so unsettled and in turmoil. Things would be perfect if only my children would obey."

I would say to you, "No. That isn't what you really need. You need WISDOM to know how to be a good parent and to know how to lead your family."

Some might say, "I need for my spouse to start loving me."

I would say to you, "What you really need is the WISDOM to know how to be a good spouse yourself."

You might say, "I need a friend—someone to talk to."

My response? "No. You need the WISDOM to know how to be a good friend to someone first."

Wisdom is the single, greatest, primary need of your life. It is the first principle for your daily existence.

Wisdom is an absolute.

Most people I know believe that everyone has some degree of wisdom. Some have a lot of it; some, a little; some, almost none. And just about everyone believes that no matter how much you have, you can use more of it.

But the Bible doesn't talk about wisdom in terms of degree. It establishes wisdom as an absolute. Either you are wise, or you are foolish. Search the Scriptures and you'll find time and again these words: "the wise person" does thus and so, and "the foolish person" does thus and so.

God recognizes only two categories. You are wise, or you are not.

Wisdom is a commandment.

Matthew 10:16 says, "Be wise as serpents."

That's an imperative command from God. Wisdom is not an option for your life. It's a requirement.

Proverbs 1:20–29 tells us what wisdom would say if wisdom were a person who could talk.

Wisdom calls aloud outside; she raises her voice in the open squares. She cries out in the chief concourses, at the openings of the gates in the city she speaks her words: "How long, you simple ones, will you love simplicity? For scorners delight in their scorning, and fools hate knowledge. Turn at my reproof; surely I will pour out my spirit on you. I will make my words known to you. Because I have called and you refused, I have stretched out my hand and no one regarded, because you disdained all my counsel, and would have none of my reproof, I also will laugh at your calamity; I will mock when your terror comes. When your terror comes like a storm, and your destruction comes like a whirlwind, when distress and anguish come upon you. Then they will call on me, but I will not answer; they will seek me diligently, but they will not find me. Because they hated knowledge And did not choose the fear of the Lord."

Like all commandments, the commandment to be wise is a commandment that you will choose to obey or disobey. It is subject to your free will, as established by God. Wisdom, therefore, is a choice—and more specifically, YOUR choice. You can choose to be wise. If you don't choose wisdom, you are, in effect, choosing destruction.

Proverbs 1:30–33 goes on to say:

They would have none of my counsel and despised all my reproof, therefore they shall eat the fruit of their own way, and be filled to the full with their own fancies. For the turning away of the simple will slay them, and the complacency of fools will destroy them; but whoever listens to me will dwell safely, and will be secure, without fear of evil.

God's wisdom doesn't fail. You can count on it. It is your key to arriving at a place where you are safe, secure, and assured.

Wisdom extends to every area of your life.

The enemy of your soul will try to bring great strongholds against you, your family, your business, and your church. He is continually seeking ways to shackle your progress; to bind you up with fear; to cause you to turn away from your first love; and to fall into the pits of error, despair, and sin.

But I want to assure you that God has a WAY for you to defeat the enemy at every turn and on every front of your life. God has WISDOM for you that can reveal how you can overcome every negative circumstance, situation, or problem you face.

Wisdom is available to YOU.

Question 3:
Who, Then, Is Wise?

When Paul wrote his final benediction to the church in Rome, he used these words: "To God, alone wise, be glory through Jesus Christ forever. Amen" (Rom. 16:27).

Only God has wisdom. He alone is the Source of all wisdom.

In 1 Corinthians 1:30 we read: "Of Him you are in Christ Jesus, *who became for us wisdom from God*—and righteousness and sanctification and redemption" (emphasis added).

Man, in his natural state, does not have supernatural wisdom. Now a person may have natural logic. He or she may have natural wisdom. But logic and wisdom err in that they will always put the individual person first. They are not supernatural wisdom.

Supernatural wisdom comes only from God, and it comes through Jesus Christ, who "became for us wisdom from God." Jesus was the personification of God's wisdom to us. That's a key point.

The entire book of Job tells us how to gain wisdom. In Job 28 we find Job answering his friends Eliphaz, Bildad, and Zophar. Each of these three friends had come to Job with a distinct type of wisdom. Each had approached wisdom from a unique perspective.

Eliphaz came to Job and said, in essence, "Wisdom is gained by observing and experiencing life." He based his advice to Job on his own competent, firsthand knowledge of the way life works. He said, "You get wisdom by experience. Let me tell you about my experiences and what they taught me." Eliphaz believed that he had observed how God works and thus had "figured out" God. He believed that he had found wisdom.

Bildad came to Job with this view of wisdom: "It is inherited from the past." To Bildad, wisdom came secondhand through traditional proverbs and the sayings of others. In other words, to get wisdom according to Bildad's method, you must learn everything everyone else has ever said about wisdom, as well as every wise saying that has ever been spoken. He spoke to Job in quotations from others.

Zophar took yet a different approach. He said to Job, "Wisdom comes from the wise." Wisdom was inherent to the self. It was a personal characteristic. He believed that only a few elite people possessed wisdom and that Job should listen to them. To get wisdom by Zophar's method, you would need first to determine who the wise people are of this age and then sit only at their feet, picking up the pearls of wisdom that drop from their mouths.

What do YOU believe to be the source of wisdom?

Where does wisdom come from?

Those three positions—embodied by Eliphaz, Bildad, and Zophar—are not unlike the major positions we find today. Most people fit into one of those three categories when they talk about the source of wisdom. They think that it comes through firsthand experience; or that it is passed along from previous generations; or that it is an inherited character trait, which a few elite people have and most people don't.

But Job, in chapter 28, responded to his friends by stating clearly and forthrightly that God is the only true Source of wisdom and that the first step toward gaining wisdom is to fear God. His attitude was this: "God reveals His wisdom to those who humbly trust Him."

Read Job 28:12–13: "Though men can do all these things, they don't know where to find wisdom and understanding. They not only don't know how to get it, but, in fact, it is not to be found among the living" (TLB).

In the natural world, to natural persons, supernatural wisdom does not exist. Job recognized this belief in others. In the first part of Job 28 we find Job's list of things that man CAN do in his limited natural ability:

• Man can find metal ores and precious stones from the earth, mine them, and make things from them.

• Man can put an end to darkness—in other words, create artificial light necessary for mining.

• In the process of mining, man can turn over mountains and cut deep channels through the rocks. He can search out precious things and use them.

• Furthermore, man alone has this ability. Even the falcon, with its great eyesight, or the fierce lion, with its great power, cannot mine the riches of God's earth.

Now that it true for knowledge too. Man can find the information that is important, mining through a mountain of facts to discover principles and rules, and create wonderful theories and analogies and stories from them. Man can use education to bring light into the darkness of myth. In the process man can create many things, even as he destroys other things. Man alone has that ability among God's creation.

But only God is WISE.

And only those plugged into God can become WISE.

Job said,

"It's not here," the oceans say; and the seas reply, "Nor is it here." It cannot be bought for gold or silver, nor for all the gold of Ophir, or precious onyx stones or sapphires. Wisdom is far more valuable than gold and glass. It cannot be bought for jewels mounted in fine gold. Coral or crystal is worthless in trying to get it; its price is far above rubies. Topaz from Ethopia cannot purchase it, nor even the purest gold.

Then where can we get it? Where can it be found? For it is hid from the eyes of all mankind; even the sharp-eyed birds in the sky cannot discover it.

But Destruction and Death speak of knowing something about it! And God surely knows where it is to be found, for He looks throughout the whole earth, under all the heavens. He makes the winds blow and sets the boundaries of the oceans. He makes the laws of the rain and a path for the lightning. He knows where wisdom is and declares it to all who will listen. He established it and examined it thoroughly. And this is what He says to all mankind: "Look, to fear the Lord is true wisdom; to forsake evil is real understanding" (Job 28:14–28 TLB).

Who is wise?
Who only has wisdom?
Recall when the rich young ruler came to Jesus and asked, "Good Teacher, what shall I do to inherit eternal life?" Jesus said, "Why do you call Me good? No one is good but One, that is, God" (Luke 18:18–19).
Jesus committed all goodness to His heavenly Father.
Let me assure you today that no one is wise in and of himself, no not one.
What, then, keeps us from seeking the wisdom of God?
Is it because we believe that only God is wise, and, therefore, we can never be? Frankly, I don't know anyone who takes that position.
No . . . the foremost reason I see for us NOT to seek the wisdom of God is that we think we're pretty smart in our own mental strength. We don't perceive that we NEED wisdom from God.
Jeremiah 9:23–24 warns us,

"Let not the wise man glory in his wisdom, let not the mighty man glory in his might, nor let the rich man glory in his riches; but let him who glories glory in this, that he understands and knows Me, that I am the Lord, exercising lovingkindness, judgment, and righteousness in the earth. For in these I delight," says the Lord.

In other words, don't trust in your own education, your own knowledge, your own natural logic and wisdom. You have no wisdom in and of yourself. What little you have came from God!
Don't trust in your strength. The degree of fitness and health and strength you have is a gift from God!
Don't trust in your riches. It is God who gives you the power to get wealth!

Just as God is the Source of strength, ability, and wealth, He is the Source of WISDOM. You will never move into God's supernatural wisdom until you recognize that fact.

To plug into God's wisdom, we must first come to God humbly and state, "God, I'm going to seek You with all my might. I have no wisdom. I need YOUR wisdom in my life."

In all their endeavors God's people should be the most successful people in all the world. The reason that the opposite is true is because God's people, for the most part, do not perceive that God's wisdom is important or that they NEED God's wisdom to live their lives successfully in the natural world.

Ask yourself . . .

Do *you* believe that if you had God's wisdom on health, you would be healthy? Do you feel a *need* for God's wisdom on health?

Do you believe that if you had God's wisdom on finances, you would have all of your financial needs met? Do you feel a *need* for God's wisdom on finances?

Do you believe that if you had God's wisdom on prayer, you would be a prayer warrior who sees victories in the spiritual realm daily? Do you feel a *need* for God's wisdom on prayer?

We generally are not seeking GOD'S WISDOM on these things because we don't perceive our NEED of His wisdom.

Friend, let me assure you today that you NEED God's wisdom. God alone is wise. He makes His wisdom available to you, but you must first want it . . . feel a need of it . . . yes, REQUIRE it as essential in your life. Then, and only then, are you putting yourself in a position to partake of God's wisdom and become wise.

Question 4: Where Do You Begin in Your Search for Wisdom?

You go to God.

What will happen if you seek God for wisdom? What will happen if you go to God and say, "I need Your wisdom. I don't know what to do. I've got to have Your wisdom, not my wisdom"?

You will receive God's wisdom! You won't be denied it. God wants you to have His wisdom.

Read what the writer of Proverbs said about this.

My son, if you receive my words, and treasure my commands within you, so that you incline your ear to wisdom, and apply your heart to understanding; yes, if you cry out for discernment, and lift up your voice for understanding, if you seek her as silver, and search for her as for hidden treasures; then you will understand the fear of the Lord, and find the knowledge of God. For the Lord gives wisdom; from His mouth come knowledge and understanding; He stores up sound wisdom for the upright (Prov. 2:1–7).

This is one of those great if-then passages in the Bible. If you do certain things—in this case, if you truly WANT to know God's wants, if you truly WANT to understand God's commandments, if you truly WANT God's wisdom, if you truly cry out to God for it—then God is going to respond. This passage says, "Then you will [. . . you WILL . . .] understand the fear of the Lord, and find the knowledge of God" (emphasis added). Note especially that phrase, "the Lord gives wisdom." God doesn't withhold it from those who diligently seek it. It is a free gift given graciously and fully to those who earnestly desire it.

Where do you begin in your search for wisdom?

You begin with God!

Question 5:
How Do You Begin?

You begin with "the fear of the Lord."

In Proverbs 1:7 we read, "The fear of the Lord is the beginning of knowledge, but fools despise wisdom and instruction."

Where did Solomon, who is credited with writing Proverbs, learn this lesson? From his father, King David, who was the first to say it. In Psalm 111:10 we read, "The fear of the Lord is the beginning of wisdom; a good understanding have all those who do His commandments."

What is "the fear of the Lord?" Why is that the beginning point for wisdom?

Here is my own definition of "the fear of the Lord." It is the awesome respect for the person of the Lord Jesus and His authority, which, when we understand it, excludes evil from our lives and ensures righteousness in our lives.

Have you ever been stopped by a police officer for speeding? As the police officer stopped you, was your heart beating fast? Do you recall that sinking feeling in the pit of your stomach when you first saw the light flashing in your rearview mirror and heard the siren wailing?

That feeling was a healthy respect for the authority of that officer over your life.

Are you aware of the difference between power and authority?

The authority of that police officer says, "I'm going to give you a ticket; and if you comply, you may go free with the proviso that you pay your fine and that you speed no more."

Power, however, is reflected in the Scriptures by the word *dunamis*, the root word for *dynamite*. The power of the police officer is such that should you fail to submit to his authority, he has a weapon and the right to remove you from your car and take you to the police station.

The fear of the Lord is not fear of the frightening, scared variety. It refers to an awesome respect for God, our Father—so much so that we don't want to do anything that would harm Him or hurt Him. It is that fear that causes us to shut out evil from our lives, to exclude it completely, and to birth God's righteousness in our lives.

In Proverbs 8:13 we read, "The fear of the Lord is to hate evil; pride and arrogance and the evil way and the perverse mouth I hate."

The fear of the Lord, therefore, is to hate evil. It's to hate the pride, arrogance, malicious methods, and perversity that create evil.

Do you hear a person backbiting and constantly critical or skeptical of the things of God? That person's perverse mouth reflects the fact that he or she doesn't fear God.

Do you hear a person saying that he or she doesn't need God or the church or the things of God? That person's pride reflects the fact that he or she doesn't fear God.

Do you hear a person planning his or her own life without regard to God? That person's arrogance reflects the fact that he or she doesn't fear God.

Do you hear a person scheming and plotting ways of getting his or her own way to the detriment of others? That person's malicious ways reflect the fact that he or she doesn't fear God.

We all have pride in our lives. There are always times when we say, "I want to do it my way." We all have moments when we trust in our own ability or plan things to go our way. We all have moments when we say things about others, or about ourselves, that we should not say . . . even when we don't want to have those thoughts inside us.

What must be our response when we recognize evil?

First, we must HATE that tendency in our lives. We must loathe and despise the evil that erupts in our lives. And second, we must turn to God with an awesome respect for His authority and repent and cry out to God, "I don't want to do this thing. I don't want to have this pride. I don't want to say these things. I don't want to feel this way. Forgive me. Help me never to do these things again. Help me never to think or feel this way again. I hate this evil in me, and I need Your help, O God!"

As a young boy, I wouldn't have dreamed of doing a number of things because I had such an awesome respect for my father and his authority over my life. He looked about nine feet tall to me, and he had huge, strong, hairy arms. I respected the authority of his size and strength over my life!

When I was in the first grade, however, I played hooky one day. My mother had purchased a baseball glove for me but would not allow me to take it to school because she thought I would lose it. I became extremely angry at her and threw a fit. When my mother drove me to school and let me out, I suddenly was struck with the fact that everybody at school probably knew that I had thrown a fit and had cried over that baseball glove. After all, my sister knew what I had done, and I thought surely she would have told everybody at school before I got there. So I hid behind the door, and after the bell rang, I ran and hid in the bushes. As soon as I got up my nerve to leave those bushes, I spent the rest of the day walking around Kilgore, Texas.

It was a hot May day, so I went to several homes and asked for a drink. My line was that I was only five years old, was visiting my grandmother in Kilgore, and needed a little drink of water. Those women were sure nice to me. But finally, I realized that I had better go back to those bushes and wait for the 3:30 P.M. bell to ring. I planned to hide there until my mother came and then get in the car as if nothing had happened.

As I was hiding there in the bushes, I looked up into that hot glare of sun, and I had a vision of my father's big ol' hairy arms reaching out to me, and I could hear him say, "Son, I told you never to do that." I truly felt an awesome respect for my father in that moment.

When my mother arrived, she said to me as I got in the car, "I need to go in and talk to your teacher today."

That was about the last thing in the world I had thought might happen! Why did she need to talk to my teacher on *that* particular day? My worst fears began to become a reality as I sat in the car and waited for my mother.

Inside the classroom the teacher asked my mother, "What was wrong with Larry today?"

My mother said, "What do you mean?"

"Well, he wasn't in class today."

My mother had no idea what was going on. "He was here," she said. "No, he wasn't," the teacher responded. And they put two and two together and figured out my evil deed.

My mother finally came out to the car, and after she got in and we had started home, she said sweetly to me, "Larry, how was school today?"

"Oh, it was great. It was wonderful." I made up a tremendous story about all that happened in class that day.

When my dad got home, I had another great tale for him. But then I heard those fateful words: "Go into the bathroom." I knew exactly what that meant. The hair still stands up on the back of my neck today when I recall the tone of voice my daddy used, and, believe me, I remember that particular spanking to this day!

But after my dad had spanked me, we went back to the kitchen table, and he took my in his arms and told me that he loved me and that he wasn't nearly as disappointed in me for playing hooky as he was for the lies I had told. I knew in that moment that I had truly disappointed my father. I had hurt him.

You see, I had a knowledge that my father COULD and would punish me for disobedience. But I also had a knowledge that my father could be hurt by my actions. He could be wounded by me. And I didn't want to do anything harmful to my daddy, who loved me.

That twofold knowledge—that my father had authority over me and that my father loved me—created a tremendous foundation of respect for my father. As I entered my teen years, I didn't want to do anything that might disgrace my father or bring reproach to him or to my family. I didn't want to disappoint him. I didn't want to hurt him.

The fear of the Lord is rooted in our not wanting to disappoint our heavenly Father. We act not from a knowledge that God might give us some type of sovereign spanking—although we know that God is capable of doing that—but from a respect for who God is and who we are in relationship to God!

Psalm 112 defines the fear of the Lord in a positive manner. The fear of the Lord is not defined here as hating evil but as delighting in the things of God. "Praise the LORD! Blessed is the man who fears the LORD, who delights greatly in His commandments." And just observe such a person's rewards as you continue to read!

• *His descendants will be mighty on earth; the generation of the upright will be blessed.* [They'll not only be strong . . . they'll be happy!]

• *Wealth and riches will be in his house.* [They'll not only HAVE wealth and riches, but they'll have the righteousness of God that will let them know what to DO with wealth and riches!]

• *And his righteousness endures forever.*

• *Unto the upright there arises light in the darkness; he is gracious, and full of compassion, and righteous.*

• *A good man deals graciously and lends; he will guide his affairs with discretion. Surely he will never be shaken; the righteous will be in everlasting remembrance.* [They'll have revelations and be gracious givers. And their struggles (problems) won't last forever! Some people

I know go from one catastrophe to the next. What a wonderful thing to be in a position where nothing can ever shake you up!]

• *He will not be afraid of evil tidings; his heart is steadfast, trusting in the LORD. His heart is established; he will not be afraid, until he sees his desire upon his enemies.* [They'll not live in fear or panic or be swayed by rumors!]

• *He has dispersed abroad, he has given to the poor; his righteousness endures forever; his horn will be exalted with honor. The wicked will see it and be grieved; he will gnash his teeth and melt away; the desire of the wicked shall perish.* [They'll have influence around the world and be held in such high regard that good things will continually flow their way. Their enemies will hate them for it!]

Persons who fear the Lord are persons who can hardly wait to do the commandments of God. They are a delight to Him, not a chore. They are exciting, not boring. They are thrilling, not devastating. When God says something to persons who fear the Lord, they are EAGER to jump into action and get the job done! They have a sense of holy excitement.

As you grow in your fear of the Lord, you also grow in your delight at following the Lord's commands.

When Melva Jo and I were first married, we tithed out of obligation. We did it because we were commanded to do it. We determined that we were going to tithe even if it killed us. And most Christians I know have that sense of obligation about their giving—in fact, about their entire Christian walk. They are following God because they are commanded to do it, not because they truly delight in it. They have a sense of obligation or duty, not joy.

How can you move from obligation into joy as you seek to fulfill the commandments of God? Here's how. . . .

Every time the Holy Spirit comes to you and says, "I want you to do a certain thing"—and you know it's real and it's the word of God and it's applied to your life, but you don't have joy about it—recognize your unwillingness for what it is. It's a lack of fear of the Lord. Pray, "God, I'm doing this because I believe I'm supposed to do it, but I don't have joy in it. I want to be joyful. Show me what your higher purposes are in this for me. Show me the reward. Show me the final result of my doing this. Give me an insight that will give me JOY."

When it came to tithing, I began to study the Scriptures about what happens to those who give and give generously. I began to study God's methods for rewarding His people. I discovered that tithing isn't losing; it's gaining a greater benefit.

Today, when the offering plate is passed, I can hardly wait to give! I have a great thrill in my soul.

A couple of years ago God told me to give the full salary I had been receiving as pastor of the Church on the Rock back to the church and to give a significant contribution beyond that. In other words, I wasn't to receive any remuneration from the church I was pastoring. Instead, I was to make a contribution to it! When that word from the Lord came to me, I felt fear start to grow inside me, and I said, "God, if I give that much, how will we make it financially? How will we live?"

The Holy Spirit spoke in my spirit, "Fear Me."

Those were the only words He spoke to my human fear. He told me to replace my human fear with a supernatural fear—a holy awe of Him. I said, "Lord, I'm going to be happy about this and obey You. Give me the wisdom to know how to take care of my family."

And He did! The Lord has made a way for us step-by-step as we have followed His word. Plus . . . we have had a degree of joy in our spirits that I can hardly describe.

Do you hate evil today?

Recognize that any time you see evil but don't feel hatred toward it, you are not experiencing the fear of the Lord in your life.

Is there one thing in your life that you know you ought to hate, but you don't? You just let it ride? It's easier to continue to do it than to stop it?

That's recognizing evil and not hating it.

When you sin—or you see sin—and you know that you are condoning it or embracing it or allowing it—and you do not hate evil, then you must—

• begin to acknowledge to the Lord that you do not have enough of the fear of the Lord in your life;

• ask God to give you a fear of the Lord every day of your life.

Don't get into self-flagellation. Don't get down on yourself and try to whip yourself into shape. Confess it to God. Recognize it for what it is, an attempt of the devil to get you out of the flow of God's wisdom. Ask God to fill you with a holy and awesome respect for Him.

Are you aware that you are constantly being bombarded by all manner of evil? Sensuality. Materialism. Pride. That's all that the world really has to give you. "The lust of the flesh, the lust of the eyes, and the pride of life" are being poured on your daily by the enemy (1 John 2:16). These things of the world are being poured on you to stop God's flow of wisdom in your life. You see, if the devil can keep you from getting wisdom, he can keep you in mediocrity all of your life. But if you come to the point that you CHOOSE to fear the Lord, to hate evil, and to love righteousness, then you are in a position to receive God's wisdom.

Now you must make a distinction between evil and the people who do evil. As followers of the Lord Jesus Christ, we are called to love people. We are also called to hate evil. What is our response, then?

We cannot be passive in the face of evil. We must speak up. We cannot be casual about it or pretend to ignore it. We must acknowledge it and take a stand against it.

Now I am not talking about an external form of godliness. I'm *not* talking about doing something or NOT doing something just because society declares that to be the proper way. I'm talking about hating evil and loving the commandments of God that are deep inside you, motivating your actions.

If you recognize that you do not have these in your life, I encourage you to seek God today and cry out, "God, I don't have enough respect for You. I don't fear You. Forgive me and cause me to hate evil and experience joy in doing Your commandments!"

A fear of the Lord. A love of His commandments. That's HOW you begin seeking God's wisdom.

When the pastor says, "Let's take up the offering," do you find yourself saying, "Oh, no, not again. I'll do it, but only because I have to"? That's an obligation that isn't rooted in a true fear of the Lord or in a love for His commandments!

When the pastor says, "Be faithful to your wife. No cheating allowed," do you find yourself saying, "I'll do it, but I won't like it"? That's an obligation, and it isn't rooted in a true fear of the Lord or in a love for His commandments!

Do you have joy in doing the commandments of God?

If you don't, realize that you don't have a genuine fear of the Lord and ask Him today, "God, fill me with a holy awesome respect for You!"

He'll do it!

_____*Let's pray about it.*_____

Father, I recognize my need for wisdom today. I acknowledge to You that I am NOT wise and that I have NOT pursued wisdom as I should have pursued it. Forgive me!

Father, I recognize that You are the only Source of wisdom and that I must have Your wisdom if I am ever going to see the truth of any situation.

Father, I believe that You want me to have Your wisdom, and I pray that You will fill me today with a holy respect for You so that I might fear You in every area of my life. I want to fear You. I want to hate evil. I want to love Your commandments and have joy in doing them. I WANT to get into the flow of Your wisdom!

Give me Your strength today, God. Set my feet on the path toward YOUR wisdom and, in that, Your highest and best for me. In the name of Jesus, I pray. Amen.

Chapter 2

How to Discern the Wisdom of God

The wisdom that is from above
is first pure, then peaceable, gentle,
willing to yield, full of mercy and
good fruits, without partiality
and without hypocrisy.

—James 3:17

How do you tell the difference between natural wisdom and true spiritual wisdom from God?

When faced with information, inspiration, an idea . . . how do you tell if it's truly God's wisdom?

It is critically important that you be able to test within your spirit whether the revelation and insights you receive are from the Spirit of God or from false spirits or the spirit of this world, including your own human spirit.

Let's begin with a very basic presumption. You and I and every other human being on this earth are confronted daily by two kingdoms: the kingdom of heaven—which is characterized by joy, peace, and righteousness—and the kingdom of Satan, the enemy of our souls—which is characterized by loss, destruction, and death. We are faced with choices—to walk in the light or to dwell in darkness. We cannot maintain a neutral stance. We cannot simply ignore life and hope it will go away. We must make choices.

Daily we face an onslaught of input from the enemy camp. Sometimes it comes from what we perceive with our senses—what we see, feel, taste, hear, and so forth. Other input comes from our inner selves—how we feel, what we think. As John wrote in his first letter, this input from Satan generally manifests itself in our lives in the form of "the lust of the flesh" (our sensual desires), "the lust of the eyes" (our materialistic desires), and "the pride of life" (our desires for fame or power) (1 John 2:16).

Furthermore, our enemy is a master of deception. He calls bad that which is good. He calls good that which is bad. Paul said that Satan can transform himself into "an angel of light" (2 Cor. 11:14). John said, "Do not believe every spirit, but test the spirits, whether they are of God" (1 John 4:1).

How do we make that test between what is eternally true and what is eternally false? The book of James tells us how to differentiate between godly wisdom and the natural wisdom of the world and of the devil.

> Who is wise and understanding among you? Let him show by good conduct that his works are done in the meekness of wisdom. But if you have bitter envy and self-seeking in your hearts, do not boast and lie against the truth. This wisdom does not descend from above, but is earthly, sensual, demonic. For where envy and self-seeking exist, confusion and every evil thing will be there. But the wisdom that is from above is first pure, then peaceable, gentle, willing to yield, full of mercy and good fruits, without partiality and without hypocrisy. Now the fruit of righteousness is sown in peace by those who make peace (James 3:13–18).

In this passage we see seven hallmarks of "wisdom" that is NOT of God:
- bitter envying
- selfish ambition
- confusion
- every evil thing
- earthly—for earthly purposes

- sensual
- demonic

On the other hand, godly wisdom has nine attributes in this passage, and they correspond directly to the characteristics of ungodly wisdom. In other words, godly wisdom operates directly opposite natural wisdom, according to the categorization provided by James. Let's discuss this further. . . .

For example, James said that *bitter envying* is natural wisdom. But godly wisdom is characterized by *meekness*. *Selfish ambition* is a characteristic of natural wisdom, but God's wisdom is characterized by a *willingness to yield*. Natural wisdom results in *confusion*, but godly wisdom is *peaceable*. Natural wisdom produces *evil fruit*, but God's wisdom produces *good fruit*.

Natural wisdom is that which produces success only for the *short term*, but God's wisdom produces fruit that is without partiality and is for the *long haul*. God's wisdom is good today, and it's good tomorrow, and it's good forever.

Natural wisdom produces only that which is sensual, or for temporary physical pleasure on this earth. Godly wisdom is pure.

Natural wisdom is aimed at the destruction of your soul—which is the work of Satan and his demons. Godly wisdom results in mercy. (Demons are never merciful, and they are never gentle!)

The categories break down this way for easy reference.

NATURAL WISDOM	GODLY WISDOM
bitter envying	meek
selfish ambition	willing to yield
confusion	peaceable
every evil thing	good fruits
earthly—for earthly purposes and the temporary short haul	without partiality and without hypocrisy—for the long haul
sensual	pure
demonic—for destruction	merciful and gentle—for growth and wholeness

James said, in conclusion, that God's wisdom is always—always, *always*, ALWAYS, *ALWAYS*—going to bring forth peace.

Have you ever been deceived? Have you prayed and asked God

for wisdom and then started to act on the first thoughts that came into your mind? Don't do it! TEST them against the criterion that the Bible provides for testing the spirit realm.

It's time today for the church to wake up and stop believing everything it hears. It's time for each of us to realize that when we open ourselves to the spirit realm, we are open to the ENTIRE spirit realm. It's time to TEST, or to "try" the spirits, and to determine which are of God and which are of the devil.

I can just hear some of you saying to yourself, "Oh, my, if that's the case, I'd just better not open myself up to the spirit realm."

Friend, that's fear at work in your life. You don't need to be AFRAID of false spirits. You just need to be DISCERNING.

Furthermore, you had better realize that you are subject to the activities of the entire spirit realm, regardless of whether you open yourself to receiving spiritual wisdom. You are under attack day and night by the enemy of your soul. That doesn't change. The only thing that changes is your ability to be ARMED against the attacks of the enemy and to have the wisdom of God so you can withstand the wiles of the devil.

The Bible says that Satan goes around *constantly* seeking whom he may devour. He and his demons are after you continually with their chief methods of the lust of the flesh (earthly, physical desires), the lust of the eye (materialism and greed), and the pride of life (your ego and your sense of self-importance). Satan and his demons have a plan for your life, and, let me assure you, it isn't a good plan. Their plan for you is death, destruction, and loss (John 10:10 reveals that the lines are clearly drawn). The devil is out to steal from you, destroy you, and kill you. Jesus makes available to you life, and life more abundantly. No . . . you won't be immune from the attacks of the enemy spirit realm just because you refuse to open yourself to the spirit realm. By refusing to open yourself to the spirit realm, you will DENY yourself the wisdom of God and access to the fullness of the Holy Spirit's powerful, perfecting work in your life.

Don't be afraid. Be discerning!

The same ability to discern also operates on words that you may receive from others. When someone comes to you and says that he or she has a word from the Lord for you, be discerning. Use the same criterion that you use to try the spirits.

"Well, Larry," you may say, "how can I tell if the person who is giving me advice is wise?"

Concentrate on the advice, not on the person giving it. God's wisdom may very well come to you through some strange methods and means. It is the word of God that is important to your life, not the vessel that carries it. (Consider for a moment Balaam's donkey, which spoke to him in the narrow path as Balaam was on a journey with the princes of Moab!)

It's easy to say, "That person isn't very credible, so why listen to anything he has to say?" You could be missing something important. Don't shut yourself off from what others have to say. Concentrate on the message, not on the person giving it.

The converse also is true. Just because you like certain persons—or admire them or think of them as wise—don't take everything they say to you as wisdom from God. Again, concentrate on the advice, not on the person giving it. Be discerning about WHAT is said to you more than about WHO is saying it.

Is the word to you uplifting, pure, and peaceable and for your edification, exhortation, or instruction? Is it aimed for your eternal good and your earthly blessing? Then it is in keeping with God's desires for your life!

Or does it condemn, pull you down, cause you confusion about God, or cause doubt or fear to spring into your heart? Is it aimed for your eternal damnation and your earthly devastation? Then it is contrary to the will of God for you, and it is a false teaching, false wisdom, or false exhortation from a false spirit!

Now if you shut the door to all prophetic words into your life, you will miss many great blessings. I believe in the prophetic ministry, and I believe that it is for today. I also believe that a number of false prophets can give you a word that can result in your destruction, both now and forever. Don't throw the baby out with the bathwater when it comes to prophecy. Learn to TEST the spirits. Learn to DISCERN between the word of the Lord and the word of the enemy. Learn to HEAR God's voice and to know the voice of the enemy when it whispers in your ear.

Not everyone who says, "Thus saith the Lord" is giving you a true message from the Lord. And it's up to YOU to be able to tell which ones are true words from God.

You must also *not* be deceived into thinking that the Lord will give you only "good words" that you *want* to hear. Just about everybody I know loves to hear "words" from the Lord that result in their wealth, health, and happiness. God has that for you! But be wary of those words when they ACTUALLY mask greed, vanity, and the temporary sensual "highs" of life.

It's easy to get sidetracked or to believe only what we WANT to believe. Because many of us have spent most of our lives living unto ourselves, exclusively for ourselves, all the while trying to please ourselves, when we hear a word that promotes our selfish ambition, our own will, and our own greed, we may automatically choose to believe that it is a word from God. In reality, it is NOT from God. It is a word that leads to selfish ambition and bitter envying!

The way you can really judge whether something is of the Spirit of God or of the enemy is by understanding this criterion in James and by using it as a template for discerning what is and what is not of God for your life. Let's explore further this passage from the book of James. . . .

What Godly Wisdom Is NOT

James described three kinds of natural wisdom: earthly, sensual, and demonic. In all cases, natural wisdom operates contrary to the laws and atmosphere of heaven.

The kingdom of heaven has one motivating factor that rules it, and that is the motivation of love manifested by the servants of the Lord Jesus. The kingdom of heaven is characterized by selflessness and by a willingness to give generously and cheerfully of all that one has—material goods, spiritual gifts, insights into the Scriptures, time, concern, gentle touches, joy, laughter, faith . . . ALL that one has that is of a good and righteous nature.

The kingdom of heaven operates according to divine wisdom—the wisdom of God being shed abroad into the hearts of people to become the template by which a new social order might be created on this earth, a social order based on the teachings and example of Jesus Christ.

The kingdom of the enemy is motivated by personal ambition and personal promotion. There is no acknowledged and agreed-upon "lord" of that kingdom. Each person and each demon is striving to be his own lord. That kingdom is characterized by one giant, unending power struggle. Satan, because he bears the greatest power, is the chief of the demons, but he is not worshiped and adored by the demons under his dominion. He rules by fear.

The kingdom of the enemy operates according to natural wisdom, and it takes the form of earthly, sensual, or demonic.

Earthly Wisdom

The psalmist wrote in the first lines of the first psalm, "Blessed is the man who walks not in the council of the ungodly" (Ps. 1:1). He was referring to earthly wisdom.

This counsel of "wisdom" is not of God but has been created by men and women through the centuries. That wisdom is filled with folk tales and myths and customs. It often has a kernel of divine wisdom in it, but that little bit of divine wisdom is masked or warped by something else so that it is not a pure reflection of God's wisdom.

For example, we often hear the "wise saying" of earthly counsel: "Well, I'll forgive you, but I'll never forget it." That kind of "wisdom" manifests itself in a wide variety of ways: "Fool me once, shame on you. Fool me twice, shame on me. Fool me thrice, a fool I be!" That style of wisdom results in a person's holding a grudge, developing bitterness, and always being suspicious of the other person's motives and actions.

God's wisdom says, "Forgive and forget." How often? When Peter asked Jesus that question, Jesus responded, "Up to seventy times seven" (Matt. 18:22).

My father came to me years ago and said, "Son, I'm going to give you some wisdom. Stay away from people who speak in tongues.

Son, if you don't, you're going to end up out in a pup tent somewhere preaching to people with snaggleteeth." That was good
earthly wisdom. Everything about my father's past experience had
shown this to be good advice. Indeed, if I had followed his advice, I
may well have become the pastor of a very respectable, formal,
downtown church somewhere. But I would have missed God's best
for me because my father's "wisdom" wasn't the wisdom of God.
(And as it turned out, it was advice my father has since repented
of!)

Earthly wisdom arises when people turn to their own common
sense and knowledge to try to discover how to handle life's problems. Believe me, we see plenty of that type of wisdom in our
world!

As good as that type of advice may sound to our natural ears, we
must recognize that it is, indeed, natural wisdom. It is rooted in
humanity's accumulated knowledge and common sense. It is
earthbound, not heavenly.

Sensual Wisdom

The second kind of wisdom described by James is sensual wisdom, the kind we perceive from our own senses. This goes beyond
instinct. It is basically a sensual criterion that says, "If it feels good,
do it." That's the basis for hedonism, and our world is filled with it
today.

Are you aware that a lot of things today feel good, but you had
better not do them for the sake of your eternal soul?

Every day the world discovers a little more about WHY the Lord
has said, "Thou shalt not" to certain things. He wasn't trying to
take all the fun out of life or spoil your good times. He was trying to
keep you and me away from things that would destroy us. He
knows our bodies and our minds and our emotional makeup. He
created us! And He knows what will *destroy* the bodies, minds, and
emotions He created.

God didn't say, "Thou shalt not commit adultery" and "Abstain
from fornication" because He was against sex. Not at all. He was
trying to keep men and women away from venereal disease, AIDS,

the destruction of the family, and the devastation of marriages—all of which result in great mental anguish; emotional turmoil; and, eventually, the death of the body, the death of the family, and the death of an entire culture.

God didn't say, "Thou shalt not eat of certain foods" because He didn't want us to enjoy eating. He knew that certain foods and beverages contain things that poison our bodies and result in everything from cholesterol to iodine poisoning—which, in turn, result in all manner of diseases and terrible physical ailments.

Sensual wisdom does not refer only to sensuality or sexuality. *Sensual wisdom* also refers to the information that you take into your life—and by which you make decisions—based on what you see, feel, taste, and otherwise sense to be true.

It's a what-you-see-is-what-you-get mind-set.

It's trusting that your senses give you accurate information.

It's believing that everything you hear has an element of truth in it, . . . that seeing is believing, . . . that you believe it if you hear it with your own ears.

It's placing feelings on a higher plane than faith.

Faith is never generated in the sensory realm. Certainly, we have to HEAR the word of God in order for our faith to rise up within us, but faith does not come because we *feel* faith. Faith comes only as we choose to believe the promises of God. If you have to feel something to believe something, chances are you'll never experience what you desire from God.

Demonic Wisdom

The demonic realm has a knowledge and understanding of God and about how God works. Demons recognize God's handiwork, and they know Jesus when they see Him at work in people's lives. It is that knowledge we refer to when we say, "demonic wisdom." This knowledge can be tapped into through occult practices. It's a deadly knowledge to have, a deadly course to pursue.

Our world today is under the onslaught of demonic knowledge that is packaged in the form of horoscopes, tarot cards, and fortune-telling. By and large, those who commune with demon spirits to give information to people are wrong 99 percent of the time, but still, an entire movement is being built up by those who long for a "new world" that is ordered by familiar spirits and an adherence to humanistic principles. Believe me, the New Age movement has nothing new about it! Its roots lie in ancient Babylon. Its process is the deification of the self, and its doctrine is a denial of the word of God and of the lordship of Jesus Christ.

How can you tell if something is demonic in its "wisdom"?

Ask, "Does it profess that Jesus Christ is Lord?"

Now a good many of the New Age and occult followers will tell you that Jesus is a lord. Not THE Lord, a lord. I declare to you that there is only way to God, and that is through Jesus Christ. You can't get there through Buddha. You can't get there through a séance. You can't get there through any other medium or method. I declare to you that Jesus Christ is THE way, not a way. He is THE truth, not a truth. He is THE life, and apart from Him you cannot know the full and eternal life God has designed for you.

Oh, you may have spiritual experiences apart from Jesus Christ. But you will not have a spiritual experience with the Holy Spirit of almighty God apart from Jesus Christ.

In Deuteronomy we read this warning from God:

> There shall not be found among you anyone who makes his son or his daughter pass through the fire, or one who practices witchcraft, or a soothsayer, or one who interprets omens, or a sorcerer, or one who conjures spells, or a medium, or a spiritist, or one who calls up the dead. For all who do these things are an abomination to the Lord, and because of these abominations the Lord your God drives them out from before you. You shall be blameless before the Lord your God (Deut. 18:10–13).

Have you ever wondered how the children of God were so successful in their battles against their enemies as they took over the land that God had promised to them? I believe it was, in part, because these enemies were wrapped up in the occult. They were trusting their horoscopes to tell them on which days to fight. They were trusting sorcerers to tell them which weapons to use. They were trusting mediums to tell them who was going to win. The Scriptures say that because of their occult abominations God signed their death warrants. Deuteronomy 18:14 concludes: "These nations which you will dispossess listened to soothsayers and diviners; but as for you, the Lord your God has not appointed such for you." Another way of saying that is, "The Lord your God has not allowed you to do so."

Christian, are you reading your horoscope on a daily basis in the morning newspaper?

"Oh, sure, Larry," you say, "but it's just a casual thing. I read it, but, of course, I don't follow it. I'm just curious to see what it says."

I say to you, in the name of Jehovah God, stop it. Don't do it anymore. Don't be misled into a quasi, friendly relationship with anything that stems from the occult! It is in no way in tune with the Spirit of God and never will be.

Jesus Himself promised us that the Holy Spirit will be our guide into all truth. Jesus said the Holy Spirit will be our helper—our comforter and our counselor—and will give us the information we need to know about the future (see John 14:16–26).

Many of us have depersonalized the Holy Spirit of God, turning Him into a vague sort of impression that comes and goes from our lives. The Holy Spirit is a PERSON of the Trinity. You can have an experience with Him. You can talk to Him. He talks to you, and you can hear Him. You don't need to consult your horoscope or fortune-tellers or mediums. Consult the Holy Spirit. He will gladly tell you everything that you need to know!

"Well," you say, "I'm only a LITTLE curious as to what is going on in the occult realm. Shouldn't I know a little about it so I can speak against it?"

No. You don't need to know ANYTHING about the occult, either experientially or objectively, to please God. In this area you should be as innocent as a dove. Solomon, the wisest man who ever lived, was ruined because he strayed just a little bit.

In 1 Kings 3:3 we read: "Solomon loved the Lord, walking in the statutes of his father David, except that he sacrificed and burned incense at the high places." *EXCEPT THAT*. The rest of the story of Solomon is built around that one phrase. *EXCEPT THAT.* That flaw was the turning point in his life that eventually led to his ruin and personal devastation.

If your decisions, then, are based entirely on your past experiences, good guesses, hunches, feelings, sensory input, or dabbling in the occult, . . . you can rest assured that those decisions are *not* based on the WISDOM OF GOD. They are outgrowths of natural wisdom, derived from earthly, sensual, and demonic knowledge. The wisdom of God points toward very specific attributes and results. You can't miss them if you are looking for them!

God's Wisdom Is Pure

James writes first that the wisdom of God is pure. This means that the wisdom of God is without mixture. It is untainted. It is not an alloy. Nothing of the earthly, sensual, or demonic realm is mixed with it. There are no "except thats" when it comes to God's wisdom.

Many people want their Christian walk to have just a touch of the world to it. They want the best of God, but along the way they also want what THEY want.

God's wisdom doesn't allow for "just a little" earthly, sensual, or demonic wisdom. It's pure.

I learned something recently about the purity of gold that I believe relates to our discussion of wisdom. One of the surprising things I learned is that no gold is truly "pure gold." All gold on the market has a bit of dust or other minerals in it.

We are that way too. We have a physical body and a history of experiences and a culture and an upbringing that influence us. We must constantly be aware of these. We must fight against them. We must SEEK ardently in the spirit the PURE wisdom of God. We must do the work that is necessary to have impurities removed from our lives, layer after layer, dross upon dross.

I also learned that the more "pure" gold is, the more it bears two great characteristics. First, it is softer and more malleable.

The purity of God's wisdom allows God's wisdom to mold to

your life so that you are malleable in God's eyes. You have a softness about your heart that allows God to prick your spiritual con-
science with a still, small voice, not an angry or loud shout. The
more you rely on God's pure wisdom, the LESS you have a stiff
neck, always bent on having your own way and doing your own
thing.

I'm not talking about softness here as a weakness in being able
to stand up to the wiles of the devil or the wicked ways of this
world. Not at all! I'm talking about a wisdom that keeps your heart
available to God. You can become "pure gold" in His sight, easily
molded into His image and into the tool and instrument that He
wants you to be to accomplish a certain work on the earth. You are
a malleable vessel in His sight.

Second, the purest gold, when heated into liquid form, is like
fluid light. It flows with a transparent quality unlike anything I've
ever seen. You can literally SEE through the metal as it flows in its
purity. God's wisdom purifies your own spirit so that you, too, become transparent before God and guileless before men. You have a
see-through-me-and-see-Jesus quality about you.

God's Wisdom Is Peaceable

The wisdom of God never leads to an adversarial relationship.
The man or the woman who is wise never seeks to have his or her
own way. Jesus said, "Blessed are the peacemakers, for they shall
be called sons of God" (Matt. 5:9). The writer of Proverbs said,
"He who loves transgression loves strife" (Prov. 17:19). John wrote,
"He who sins is of the devil" (1 John 3:8). People who love strife,
arguing, and competition always have something in their lives that
they love more than God. They have something that they are holding on to and won't give up. That thing agitates them in their spirits
to the point that they always have to pick on someone else. These
people love to play word games, with innuendos for everything.
They love stirring up the pot behind the scenes, to pit person
against person. John said it plainly: "They love sin."

What does a true peacemaker do? He or she says, "Let's find a way to make this thing right." "Let's find a way to bury the hatchet." "Let's find a way to resolve the conflict." "Let's find a way to be part of the solution and not part of the problem." Those are the peacemakers. And they are the ones who are operating in the wisdom of God, for the wisdom of God always seeks peace.

God's Wisdom Is Gentle

The wisdom of God is not harsh. It is not arrogant. It doesn't have a rough edge to it. Jesus was noted as the Lamb of God. He didn't walk up and down the streets with a bullhorn. He didn't buttonhole people. He didn't demand that His way be accepted.

I believe that the gentleness of God's wisdom makes it most acceptable to those who have teachable spirits. Have you ever met a person who was unyielding, inflexible, unteachable? I met a man like that recently.

We were in a meeting, and I said, "Boy, there seems to be a mistake here. I'm so sorry that happened. God bless you, but let's get this thing together the right way now." And the person I was talking to looked at me and said, "I don't believe one word you're saying."

Was there any wisdom in that statement? Was there any gentleness in seeking God's wisdom? Was there a teachable spirit? Hardly. In fact, I would consider that minus-zero wisdom.

Are you aware that at some point in your life you WILL submit to God's wisdom? It will happen. You may not accept God's wisdom coming to you from your parents. You may not accept it from a schoolteacher or a Sunday school teacher. You may not accept it even from the military. You may not accept it from a police officer, a judge and jury, or a warden in prison. But eventually, someplace and somehow, even standing in the throne room of God's judgment, you WILL find yourself in a position in which you WILL submit to God's wisdom. Having a gentle, yielding, teachable spirit toward God's wisdom now can save you years of turmoil on this earth and eternal damnation, as well.

God's wisdom comes gently, and it is best received by those who have gentle spirits.

By the time I was twenty-one years old, I was married to Melva, had graduated from college, and was the youth director of a church that was growing. I had been enjoying a special anointing from the Spirit for eight months, and, putting it simply, I was "wild" for the things of God. I was knocking on every door I could get to, telling people about Jesus.

One day I felt the Lord say to me, "Go to Israel."

That's all He said. So I went home and said, "Melva, pack your bag. We're going to Israel."

She said, "What are we doing once we get there?"

I said, "I don't know. God just spoke to me and said, 'Go to Israel.' We're moving. I've got to be obedient to what I hear."

So we started packing things to move to Israel. Brother Howard Conatser, the senior pastor of the church where I was the youth pastor, heard about this, came to me, and said, "Larry, I hear that you feel God is calling you to go to Israel."

I said, "Yes, that's right."

He said, "I believe God did tell you to do that, but I don't believe He's telling you to MOVE there. He didn't tell you to take your family there. He didn't tell you to resign your position here. He's telling you to go to Israel because you are going to go to Israel periodically throughout your entire life to be a great blessing to Israel."

Now if I had had an unyielding, unteachable spirit, at that point I would have said, "Hey, who do you think you are? Do you know who you're talking to? I'm twenty-one now. I've got a college degree. I'm married." But I didn't do that. I yielded to that counsel. I agreed that, indeed, I was getting ahead of God and jumping to conclusions about the things God wanted for my life, beyond what He had said for me to do. Indeed, God had said, "GO to Israel." God had not said, "MOVE to Israel." He had not said, "YOU AND MELVA move to Israel." He had not said, "RESIGN FROM YOUR PRESENT POSITION AND GO to Israel."

I learned a great deal through that experience. I learned that we must carefully weigh everything we hear from God. First Corinthians 2:15 gives a one-line definition of the person who is truly spiritual. It's the only place in the Bible that gives a definition of a spiritual person. That verse reads: "He who is spiritual judges all things."

What does it mean to judge something? It means, first of all, to get evidence. You hear all sides. You get as much information as you can get.

Next, you weigh that information against the law. You go to the Word of God and study how it applies to the situation you are facing or the word that you are hearing from God.

Third, get the godly counsel of other spiritual men and women. You'll find some of that guidance in church history. Men and women through the ages have asked the same questions you are asking. They have sought solutions to the same problems you are having. Older men and women in the faith (not necessarily in years but in spiritual maturity) have faced what you are facing. Get their counsel.

And fourth, question God about His words to you. Ask Him with sincerity and openness to elaborate and further define EXACTLY what He means. The Bible says that God gives wisdom *liberally*. He doesn't just give you a few odd-shaped puzzle pieces and then ask you to figure out the rest of the puzzle on your own. He isn't playing a divine treasure-hunt game with you, with clues scattered in sequence all over town. ASK God for further information. Press Him for it. Persevere in His Word and in His presence until you receive it.

That's the process of judging we use in our courts. Attorneys present evidence. The judge and jury also refer to the laws that have been passed and to the court-case precedents that they consider wise counsel. The judge and jury hear witnesses—including expert witnesses—before making a decision.

Now the Scripture doesn't say anything about judging people. It says to judge all THINGS. You judge the words that come to you as "Thus saith the Lord." You judge the ideas that come to your mind. You judge the "voice" you hear in your spirit and the deep impressions you feel in your innermost being. You weigh the message.

Believe me, if it is NOT the wisdom of God you are receiving, you won't have to look very far to see the destruction that will come as a result. It will make itself evident fairly quickly!

God's Wisdom Is Merciful

The wisdom of God always results in forgiveness. When you receive God's wisdom on a matter, you will know exactly and precisely if you need to seek someone's forgiveness. That person's name or face will come looming into your mind! You'll KNOW if you have wronged someone—purposefully or inadvertently—and you'll be eager to find the person and apologize sincerely. You'll see in a flash if you are holding a grudge against someone. You'll be in a hurry to make things right.

And with the ability to forgive will come the ability to forget.

God's Wisdom Bears "Good Fruit"

When the wisdom of God is present, you'll always get a glimpse of how something GOOD can result from the situation. You'll be able to anticipate the fruit of the event or situation or circumstance. God will give you perhaps only a hint of the fullness of the GOOD that He can work, but you'll see enough to know that it is, indeed, the "good fruit" that will come in the fullness of His timing.

Ask yourself this question if you receive a word of direction that you believe is the wisdom of God: Where will this take me three years from now? Does it lead to something that will enlarge and prosper and bless my life and, at the same time, bless all those around me, including my church?

Some time ago I had a vision while I was sitting in my backyard. I saw a large triangle. I asked God what He was revealing to me. The Holy Spirit spoke in my heart, "Son, you are to birth two other churches in the greater Dallas area"—what we call the Metroplex.

Now at that time I had my hands full with ONE church, much less two others. (And by the way, I still do!) Pastoring is a big job.

I said to the Lord, "Really?"

That's the question I always ask the Lord. It isn't an expression of doubt or cynicism but rather an expression of, "Am I hearing you correctly? Do I *really* get to do this?"

My next question was, "How, Lord?"

He said, "I'm going to show you My wisdom in this."

And so I watched God put it together. Over the next weeks and months I stood in amazement as God drew leaders to Rockwall to serve with me.

And the day came when God said, "Birth a church in south Dallas." The natural mind said in natural wisdom, "Hey, that's going to cost a lot of money—in fact, more than you have." Natural wisdom said, "You are going to lose a lot of people. And with them you are going to lose a big percentage of the tithes and offerings you receive each week. How are you going to pay for everything?" Natural wisdom said, "Who is going to replace the people you are sending out to start that church?"

But God's wisdom prevailed. The church in south Dallas was birthed.

The same thing happened a little while later: "Birth a church in north Dallas."

Natural wisdom said, "You've just lost your senior associate pastors. You're giving all your leaders away. You're starting a mission church with 1,132 people on its first Sunday, four full-time paid staff members, and a forty-thousand-square-foot building. Don't you know that a mission church usually starts in a back alley somewhere with a building that rents for about one hundred dollars, and you draw about twenty-five people to the first service? What are you DOING?"

But God's wisdom prevailed. A church was born in north Dallas.

One day one of my leaders, Jeff Wickwire, came to me and said, "Pastor, we want a church in Quitman"—a town about seventy miles away from Rockwall. "About seventy people are driving 140 miles every Sunday just to come to church here."

Natural wisdom said, "You don't want to lose those people."

But God's wisdom prevailed. Today that is the largest church in Quitman, with more than six hundred faithful members, more than one million dollars in property, all bills paid, and a lasting testimony to God almighty and to all of east Texas that Jesus is Lord.

And do you know what has happened in Rockwall? God provided people to fill up the empty chairs that were left behind. The Word is still being preached twice on Sundays and every Wednesday night in Rockwall. Early-morning prayer is still happening at Rockwall. God provided the finances to keep every one of the programs going, and going strong, in Rockwall.

God's wisdom always leads to bearing GOOD fruit. Certainly, the Vine—Jesus Christ—doesn't die. Neither do we, the branches

God's Wisdom Is Without Hypocrisy

Have you ever wondered about that word *hypocrisy*? The word *hypocrite* means "someone who wears a mask." It comes from ancient days when every actor in a theatrical production wore a mask. The actors never revealed their faces. They revealed only the characters of the parts they were playing. One of the foremost ways of identifying the character being played was by a mask.

People today wear masks of all sorts. But when God's wisdom is established in a situation, nobody needs to have a mask. The wisdom of God bears no hidden agenda. It wears no cloak of deception.

The wise person doesn't have a hidden agenda, either. And just about everyone you meet these days seems to have one, doesn't he? I take comfort in the fact that even one of Jesus' chosen twelve disciples had a hidden agenda. That way I'm never surprised when I find someone on my staff who has one. Persons with a hidden agenda are usually looking to promote themselves rather than the name of Jesus. They want their names on the marquee. They want the attention. And, in wanting that, they draw attention away from Jesus.

God's Wisdom Is Approachable

James used the words *easily entreated*. He meant that wisdom can be approached. The wise person is approachable. God doesn't hide His wisdom away in an eternal attic, where you have to hunt and search all the days of your life before you may find it some day.

That's an approach of Eastern religions to truth, not the approach taught by Jesus Christ. Jesus said, "Ask"—and what? You will receive. "Seek"—and what? You will find. "Knock"—and what? You will get an answer.

God's Wisdom in Action BRINGS Peace

Earlier we discussed peace (or meekness) as a trait of God's wisdom in our lives. Peace is also the fruit of wisdom as it works itself out in the reality of our everyday circumstances and situations.

James concluded that "the fruit of righteousness is sown in peace by those who make peace" (James 3:18). He made two points simultaneously about the nature of those who sow the fruit of righteousness. The result will be peace. And the method will be peaceable. Everything about what they do and say will have PEACE as its badge.

That's the watershed statement in determining whether something is of the kingdom of the enemy (with its earthly, sensual, and demonic wisdom) or of the kingdom of heaven. Does it bring peace? Is it done in peace or with peace?

It's very important that you recognize that the peace MUST extend to all who are involved. God does not bring peace to one in a situation and cause others to collapse into turmoil or confusion, pain or suffering. If it's God's answer, it's an all-win answer. Just because the answer makes YOU feel good doesn't mean that it's God's answer. You've got to be honest with yourself and to look at the situation as objectively as you can. Does the answer you believe is coming from the spirit realm bring peace to EVERYONE involved?

Peace. All-around peace. That may sound like a simplistic criterion to you. It isn't. It's simple, but it isn't simplistic. God's wisdom is always clear. It's evident. It's pure. It has an elegant, clear-cut simplicity to it. It works for the good and the peace of all involved. God's wisdom never causes confusion, a wrangling in relationships, or a jangling of the nerves.

When a conclusion, direction, decision, or idea comes to you as revelation or inspiration from the spirit realm, you can ALWAYS tell whether it's from God or from the enemy by applying this four-word question to it: *Does it bring peace?*

If the answer is no, it isn't from God.

If the answer is yes, it is.

You don't have to look very far to see that the wisdom that arises from the earthly, sensual, and demonic realms is wisdom that neither brings peace nor is done in a peaceful manner.

Earthly wisdom says about alcohol and drugs, "Try it; you'll like it." But you don't have to look very far down the road to see addiction, dependency, and destruction.

Sensual wisdom says, "Sexual freedom is OK." But you don't have to look very far down that path to find disease, death, and destroyed lives.

Demonic wisdom says, "The future is going to be all roses." But you don't have to look very far in any direction to see that most of the world is going to hell as fast as it can get there.

God's wisdom always, *always*, ALWAYS, *ALWAYS* results in peace.

"But," you say, "all of this sounds as if I can never have a confrontation with anyone, Larry."

I'm not saying that at all. You can have a confrontation without a combative spirit. Most people don't believe that they can have an argument or a disagreement without having a mean, angry, combative, adversarial spirit.

You can go to someone and say, "I don't like this. Let's find an answer to it that is in God's wisdom" and have a good, healthy conversation about it, pray about it, and end up not only with a wise solution but also with a deeper relationship!

Is someone coming at you today with a combative spirit? Keep smiling. Refuse to let him rob you of your joy. Refuse to let him rob you of your peace. Say in your inner self, "God, I'm not going to let him steal Your presence from my life. Give me wisdom!"

Usually, the Holy Spirit will give you a word, and you can say simply, "Well, this is what I feel about it," and you can speak that word in peace and with a gentleness in your spirit and a smile on your face. And the word you speak will be sown in peace. But UNTIL you can sow that word in peace, it's best to keep your mouth shut, because even though you might have the wisdom of God in your mind and in your mouth, unless you are able to sow it with a GENTLE SPIRIT, you will not be sowing righteousness in peace.

Replacing False Wisdom with God's Wisdom

Again, I encourage you to look at the list of traits provided by James as they stand in juxtaposition to one another.

When you encounter earthly, sensual, or demonic wisdom, you can see immediately and clearly what to do!

Are you bogged down in a solution that offers a quick-fix, for-today-only answer? Seek God's wisdom for the answer that will extend into eternity!

Are you embroiled in a situation that is marked by "bitter envying" on the part of all parties? Seek God's wisdom for the answer that bears meekness, gentleness.

Are you faced with a person who is blinded by selfish ambition? God's wisdom will be marked by a willingness to yield.

The conclusion to be drawn from James is ultimately this: you CAN KNOW God's wisdom on a matter. You CAN discern whether something bears God's wisdom or wisdom that is earthly, sensual, or demonic. You CAN become wise.

Yes . . . YOU can.

_____Let's pray about it._____

Father, I pray today that I might HAVE Your wisdom. I ask You boldly for it. Show me clearly, Lord, when something is not of You. Reveal to me those things that are born of earthly, sensual, or demonic wisdom in my life. Give me the power to resist the devil, to abstain from evil, and to rely on You totally for wisdom.

Father, help me to discern clearly Your wisdom at work. Help me to bear the good fruit of wisdom. Help me to become a peacemaker. Help me to see things from Your eternal vantage point. Help me to become more malleable in Your hands. Help me to exhibit Your wisdom in ways that are marked by gentleness, purity, and accessibility

Father, I desire above all to have Your Wisdom. I need Your Wisdom. I declare to You today that I can't live without it. I ask You for wisdom. I pray this in the name of Jesus. Amen

Chapter 3

A Gift Worth Seeking with All Your Heart

Keep your heart with all diligence,
For out of it spring the issues of life.
Put away from you a deceitful mouth,
And put perverse lips far from you.
—Proverbs 4:23–24

Is wisdom a gift or something to be obtained? Is it fleeting or lasting? Can it grow?

These are vital questions to ask about wisdom.

Wisdom is always a gift. That is to say, it is something bestowed by God freely and from the depths of His own nature and mercy. And as in the case of all gifts from God, we have only one responsibility: to put ourselves into a position to receive His gift.

Can you imagine a Christmas-morning scene, with brightly wrapped presents surrounding a beautiful evergreen—the gifts just waiting to be opened? Imagine, then, that the children never come into the room—that they never see the presents or rip apart the ribbons and wrapping paper to see them, play with them, receive them, enjoy them.

Such a child might say, "My parents didn't give me anything for Christmas." In fact, they did!

Such a child might say, "It isn't a free gift if I have to do something for it. My parents should have brought the gift to me, unwrapped it for me, and forced me to lift it from the box." That's not the way it works, child!

Such a child might say, "I didn't know the gifts were in that room. I didn't know they were for me."

If you are questioning God today about the availability of His gifts to YOU, rest assured, they ARE for you! They do exist. He longs to have you receive them.

It IS possible to walk in wisdom all of the time—every day—because you come to a full understanding about God's principles and how to apply them. It IS possible to have God's wisdom for very specific situations, circumstances, problems, and opportunities. Wisdom is an ongoing gift for your entire life and for every area of your life.

Now there is a special gift of wisdom that is a sovereign act of the Holy Spirit. Paul wrote about this gift to the Corinthians as a "word of wisdom."

> The manifestation of the Spirit is given to each one for the profit of all: for to one is given the word of wisdom through the Spirit, to another the word of knowledge . . . to another faith . . . to another gifts of healings . . . to another the working of miracles, to another prophecy, to another discerning of spirits, to another different kinds of tongues, to another the interpretation of tongues. But one and the same Spirit works all these things, distributing to each one individually as He wills (1 Cor. 12:7–11).

I have always found it interesting that Paul, in writing to the church at Corinth, chose to list the word of wisdom as the *first* gift of the Holy Spirit as he began to describe the diversities of gifts, ministries, and activities of the Holy Spirit to that church body.

When Brother Howard Conatser (my senior pastor at Beverly Hills Baptist Church, where I served as a youth pastor for six years), received the fullness of the Spirit, the only gift of the Spirit that he prayed for was the gift of wisdom.

This gift of a word of wisdom is a distinguishable gift of the Holy

Spirit that I describe in this way: a flash of revelation when we know without doubt what God wants us to do in a certain circumstance or situation.

It is a gift given for a specific place and time and to a specific person. It is not a gift to the one GIVING the word of wisdom as much as a gift to the one RECEIVING the word. Stated a little differently, the Holy Spirit may prompt you to give a word of wisdom. That word is not for YOU. It is for someone else. You are acting as a vehicle for the delivery of that word. You are a vessel being used by the Holy Spirit.

Consider for a moment that wisdom is like a great river, available to each one of us. We each need to draw from it and to be baptized in it. A word of wisdom is like a bucket of water taken from that river and applied directly to the lips of someone dying of thirst. A word of wisdom is the application of wisdom to a specific person, situation, or church at a particular time.

We can view all of the gifts of the Holy Spirit in a similar way. We certainly are to be praying for the sick continually. But some are endued with a distinct gift of healing that is given by the Holy Spirit, and it operates at a particular time for a particular person or a particular ailment through a particular individual chosen by the Holy Spirit for the working of that gift. Several months ago I experienced this gift as I stood before a young man with a brain tumor. Now I pray frequently for the sick; I believe for miracles of healing as I pray; and often we hear reports of those who are experiencing healing from God. But in this particular instance a special endowment of the gift of healing operated through my life for this young man, and the result was that his brain tumor was immediately and completely destroyed by God as we prayed. That was a gift of healing from the Holy Spirit to this young man, and I just happened to be the delivery agent of the hour.

The Ongoing Flow of Wisdom

The broader flow of wisdom to our lives, however, is an ongoing process. It is not limited in time or space. It is a gift imparted TO you, not THROUGH you. It is wisdom flowing from the throne room of God to encompass your entire spirit, soul, and body.

That does not make this broader flow of wisdom any less a gift. It is still very much an act of giving from God to persons. It is, however, a flow of wisdom into which we must position ourselves. We must get in the river and splash around to get wet!

As such, wisdom becomes a PROCESS in our lives. It is not something that we get once and put on a shelf. It is not a onetime experience. It is an ongoing growth process that is simultaneously daily, and eternal.

That ongoing process of gaining wisdom relates directly to our hearts. As the writer of Proverbs stated, "Keep your heart with all diligence, for out of it spring the issues of life. Put away from you a deceitful mouth, and put perverse lips far from you" (Prov. 4:23–24).

It is up to us to "keep our hearts." That is a command to us. And in keeping of our hearts, we position ourselves to experience the ongoing and ever-increasing flow of God's wisdom.

Most of the time when we think about the heart, we think about our emotions. We have all heard the saying "I love you with all my heart." We put our whole heart into it. We play it or say it with heart. The heart is equated with love, feeling, and a fullness of feeling.

Others who are more scientifically or medically inclined think first about the physical organ that pumps blood through our bodies.

To the Hebrew writer of Proverbs, however, the heart was the center of volition, or will. Therefore, when we speak of giving your heart to the Lord or of letting Jesus come into your heart, we are really speaking about letting Jesus be the Master of our will or of yielding our will to the Lord Jesus.

To "keep your heart with all diligence," then, means to keep your ability to choose in line. Out of your choice-making ability come the issues of life.

The Bible has a great deal to say about the heart.

Jeremiah wrote about negative volition. Are you aware that you were born with negative volition? Each one of us was born without a desire to serve God and to yield our will to His.

Just look at your children. Did you ever teach your children to lie or to tell stories or to cheat? Did you ever teach your child to grab a toy and scream, "Mine!" Did you ever take your child on your lap and say, "Well, today, child, I am going to teach you how to be a bad child"?

When I was seven years old, my sister—who was eight—took a can of hair spray and whacked me with it right between the eyes and sent me rolling down the stairs. I guarantee you, my mother never said to my sister, "Dear, when you hit him, hit him right between the eyes so he'll fall down the stairs backward." Nobody had to teach her that!

We are born saying no to God and to every person. We are born with a self-centered will. We are born with a desire and a capacity to see the world from our own perspective and to twist everything we see into a mold that suits us. Jeremiah wrote, "The heart is deceitful above all things, and desperately wicked" (Jer. 17:9).

It is a lifelong struggle to put ourselves into a position in which our will will keep willing to do the will of God.

The minute we no longer ride herd on our heart and keep it in line—as the writer of Proverbs said, "with all diligence"—we automatically revert to our inborn pattern of doing as we please and of living in a self-centered, self-directed way.

Jeremiah went on to say, "Who can know it? I, the LORD, search the heart, I test the mind, Even to give every man according to his ways, and according to the fruit of his doings" (Jer. 17:9–10).

Who can know your heart? Who really knows the condition of your volition or your will? Who really knows your innermost motives and intentions? God does. He searches your will. He tests your thoughts against your motives. And He rewards each person accordingly.

Jesus had a great deal to say about the state of the unregenerated heart. He said,

Do you not yet understand that whatever enters the mouth goes into the stomach and is eliminated? But those things which proceed out of the mouth come from the heart, and they defile a man. For out of the heart proceed evil thoughts, murders, adulteries, fornications, thefts, false witness, blasphemies. These are the things which defile a man, but to eat with unwashed hands does not defile a man (Matt. 15:17–20).

Your spiritual defilement begins within your will, within your "heart."

You Were Born in the Likeness of Adam

Have you ever watched people analyze a newborn baby? "Oh, he has his mother's eyes. His father's chin. His grandmother's fingers." And—usually because the baby is bald—"his grandfather's hairline!"

Spiritually speaking, that baby and every other baby ever born—including you—is born after the similitude of your great-great-great-great-umpteenth-time-great-grandfather Adam.

Adam was a rebel. He rebelled against God. He tried to blame it on Eve, who also rebelled against God. And the woman blamed it on the serpent, who ALSO rebelled against God. The concluding fact is that a spirit of rebellion entered the human race and became a part of the spiritual genetic code handed down through every generation since Adam and Eve.

Jeremiah, who understood the basic nature of our "Adam-and-Eve heart," also prophesied about a new heart that would come from God.

Behold, the days are coming, says the Lord, when I will make a new covenant with the house of Israel and with the house of Judah—not according to the covenant that I made with their fathers in the day that I took them by the hand to bring them out of the land of Egypt, My covenant which they broke, though I was a husband to them, says the Lord. But this is the covenant that I will make with the house of Israel after those days, says the Lord: I will put My law in their minds, and write it on their hearts; and I will be their God, and they shall be My people (Jer. 31:31–33).

God promised that He would put a new law into our minds and write it on our hearts. And in that we would become the children of God!

This new covenant was the blood covenant cut by God with Christ Jesus. It is the covenant we live under today as believers in the Lord Jesus and as followers of the Way He established. We live in the spiritual age, in which God's law can be put into our minds and written on our hearts. We can literally have a new will.

I can prove to you today whether you truly have a new heart or a new volition. You have a new heart if, when you sin, you hate it. On the other hand, if you can live in sin and still love your sin, then you have not yet been born again spiritually. You are still living with your old heart.

That's the criterion established by the apostle John. The entire book of 1 John is committed to that theme. John said that if you habitually practice sin, and sin has become a way of life for you, and you say, "Hey, this is just the way I am, and I love it," . . . then you have not received a new heart. A true Christian cannot habitually commit sin.

Now a Christian may commit sin. But not habitually. John writes, "If anyone sins, we have an Advocate with the Father, Jesus Christ the righteous. And He Himself is the propitiation for our sins, and not for ours only but also for the whole world" (1 John 2:1–2).

A Christian *can* sin, but a Christian does not *have* to sin.

That's an important distinction for you to understand. You *may* commit sin and fall into error. But that's not an automatic certainty. You can develop a new heart to the point that you do *not* sin. And the step for getting from the place where you do sin to the place where you don't sin is to HATE your sin when you commit it. That's the manifestation of your having a new heart.

When you accept the Lord Jesus into your life as your personal Savior and Lord, God puts a new will within your will. He puts a new spirit inside your spirit. This new will is not motivated negatively toward God but positively. This new volition WANTS to do what is pleasing in the sight of God. This new volition wants to live for God and to serve the Lord.

Can you say, "I don't ever want to fail the Lord. I don't want to ever disappoint the Lord again or hurt the heart of God"? If you can say that with all honesty, then you are speaking from a positive volition that has been planted within your heart by the Holy Spirit. A person who has not accepted Jesus Christ as the Son of God and who is not confessing Him as Lord cannot say that and mean it. He cannot honestly say, "I don't want to fail God. I don't want to disappoint the Lord or hurt His heart."

"But, Larry," you say, "I can say that I hate my sin, but the fact of the matter is that I still struggle with sin. It's still hard for me to live in the victory of *not* sinning. How can that be?"

That struggle involves the renewing of your mind.

Wisdom Involves the Ongoing Renewal of Your Mind

Now there's a major difference between renewing your heart and renewing your mind.

Your heart is renewed by God. Your mind is renewed by you.

That is a monumental difference.

Stop to consider for a moment the process by which your heart was renewed. You repented of your sins and asked God's forgiveness, and then you confessed that Jesus is Lord. But it was GOD who renewed your heart. He is the One who sovereignly changed your heart from one of negative volition to one of positive volition.

You had your part to play. I don't make light of that. It was up to you to acknowledge God and to confess to your sins. It was up to you to repent of your sins and to make a decision to turn away from sin. It was up to you to cry out to God and to ask for His forgiveness. It was up to you to accept by faith that God had forgiven you according to His Word and to act on that faith by confessing, "Jesus is the Lord of my life." But there is no way you could change your own heart. There's no way anyone can change his own heart. It simply can't be done by human means.

Changing hearts is a sovereign act of God. It is a gift of His mercy and grace to your life. You can't earn it. You can't deserve it. You can't bring about that change on your own. It is a gift from above.

And what about your mind? How do you keep your mind renewed?

That question is a critical one for me. I grew up in a church that said to me, "Do this and do that," but the pastor never told me HOW. That really frustrated me as a teenager and as a young Christian. I WANTED to do what I was being taught, but I didn't know HOW to do it, and nobody seemed to be able or willing to tell me. I want to share with you what I have learned about HOW to keep your mind renewed and to "keep your heart with all diligence."

When you are born again, you have a desire to please God, a desire to be wise, a desire to experience the purpose of God in your life. The fact is, however, that something works against that positive desire all the time. It is the downward drag of this world and its programming of your mind.

You were subject to that programming throughout your life until you were born again, until your heart was renewed. That programming ruled everything in your mind, and, as a result, there was nothing in your mind that would counteract anything that your negatively motivated will decided to do. There was nothing in your mind to check, thwart, stop, or otherwise impede what your heart wanted to do. Therefore, if it felt good, you did it. If it seemed like a good idea, you pursued it. And the reason was that your MIND was programmed by this world's systems and by your own fleshly instincts to roll over and play dead into the hands of your unregenerated will.

Once you were born again, your heart was renewed, but most of the programming in your mind was the same old programming. Your motivation was different in life, your heartfelt desires were different; but your ideas were still the product of this world's programming. That's why so many Christians struggle with their thought lives, their fantasies, and their daydreams. Their minds are still unrenewed, even though their hearts have been changed. That's why we still find ourselves doing what we don't really want to do and thinking what we don't really want to think.

Furthermore, the ideas and images and impressions that led to the programming of our minds in the first place haven't stopped just because our hearts have been renewed. The world is still unregenerated. It is still pumping out raw sewage for your senses to receive and for your mind to decipher, code, and otherwise deal with. Your mind is continually bombarded with evil. Some of it is directly demonic. Some of it is rooted in this world's systems. Some of it flows from sensuality. It's continuous! It's from all directions!

Are you aware that you are receiving input daily—even hourly and minute by minute—from the systems of this world? All kinds of negative information flood your mind constantly. That is the work of the devil, your enemy, who is seeking continually to find a way to destroy you, steal from you, and kill you. The devil has an agenda regarding you, and it's this: to wipe out your faith and then to wipe you out.

Your challenge, then, is to bring about the renewal of your mind.

And until you learn how to renew your mind, you'll never be able to "keep your heart with all diligence." And until you learn how to keep your heart with all diligence, you'll never really be able to receive or put to use the wisdom of God in your life. That's why renewing your mind is such a critical factor to your having wisdom.

The writer of Proverbs said that out of the heart the issues of life spring forth. Your heart is the wellspring of your life. It is the driving force, the bubbling up of your motivation, your desire, your energy, and your enthusiasm for the things of God and for seeing His kingdom established on this earth. Your mind will either enhance and flow with your spirit, or it will impede your spirit. Your mind can put into effect that which your spirit desires to see accomplished, or your mind can clutter up or pollute the wellspring of your life.

Ecology is a big issue today. I thank God that it is. We are the keepers of this earth, and our commandment from God since the days of Noah has been to replenish and care for this earth, to nurture it, and to bring forth abundance from it. We hear a lot about pollution of the air and water. And most of us have seen pictures of factories spewing filth and chemicals into pure, sparkling rivers.

We've seen the terrible effects in before and after photographs and on television programs.

We can apply that image to the processes of our hearts and minds. Our renewed heart is a pure, unpolluted stream of living water flowing from our innermost beings. It has been purified and cleansed by the Holy Spirit. It gushes forth from us under the power of the Holy Spirit. And then it encounters our minds. It is the mind that will channel that flow of life into work; into productive and fruitful relationships; into action of thought, word, and deed. The unregenerated mind is like a polluting factory. It destroys and muddies the waters and makes them unfruitful and death-producing. The renewed mind, on the other hand, is like a giant turbine that turns the rushing water into something clean and productive and useful that promotes life. The renewed mind is like the tree by the side of the river that soaks up the water and bears fruit.

Renewal is a process of transformation. It isn't instant. It's a process over time. It can be faster or slower, depending on your commitment to renewing your mind. But recognize as we move deeper into this discussion that the renewal of your mind is a process of replacing the old with the new.

Romans 12:1–2 says it this way.

> I beseech you therefore, brethren, by the mercies of God, that you present your bodies· a living sacrifice, holy, acceptable to God, which is your reasonable service. And do not be conformed to this world, but be transformed by the renewing of your mind, that you may prove what is that good and acceptable and perfect will of God.

The phrase "prove what is that good and acceptable and perfect will of God" means the same thing as discerning God's wisdom. The renewal of your mind brings about your ability to discern the wisdom of God in any situation or circumstance.

Note the process described in that second verse.

• *Don't be conformed to this world.* Another translation puts it this way: "Don't press into this world's mold any longer" (J. B. Phillips). Don't be shaped into the image of this world! Instead . . .

• *Be transformed by the renewal of your mind.* Note that we're talking about your mind here and not your heart. Your heart has already been renewed. The word *transformed* literally means to be "metamorphosed," in other words, to "undergo a change."

• *Have a renewed mind so you can prove what is good, acceptable, and perfect in the sight of God.* The purpose of a renewed mind is so you can discern God's wisdom and so this wisdom can permeate your life, change your behavior, and make your entire life a pure, holy, and acceptable sacrifice to God.

"OK, Larry," you say, "HOW do you do it?"

Here's how. . . .

How to Renew Your Mind

The formula for renewing your mind is found in Ephesians 4:21–23, which says: "if indeed you have heard Him and have been taught by Him, as the truth is in Jesus: that you put off, concerning your former conduct, the old man which grows corrupt according to the deceitful lusts, and be renewed in the spirit of your mind."

1. Put off the old person.
2. Change your mind-set.
3. Put on the new person.

That's the formula: put off something old, switch to something better, and put on—or adopt fully as your own—something new.

Ephesians 4:24 goes on to say that "you put on the new man which was created according to God, in righteousness and true holiness."

This means that every time you are confronted with the downward drag of this world's ideas and its sensory onslaught—which includes temptations and negative influences on your walk with God—you stop and say, "I'm not going to take this into my mind. I'm going to be renewed in my mind."

If it's on the television set, you get up and turn off the TV. If it's on the radio as you are driving, you reach over and turn off the radio. If it's around you and you can't get rid of it, you ignore it. You turn your eyes in another direction or close them. You turn your thoughts inward to the things of God. You begin to hum spiritual songs and hymns and choruses of praise to yourself, quietly or even in your mind. You simply REFUSE to let the negative onslaught of this world come into your life. You choose instead to renew your mind. And then you put on thoughts that are pure and lovely and noble before God.

"Well," you say, "what do you think about instead?"

Philippians 4:8 concludes: "Brethren, whatever things are true, whatever things are noble, whatever things are just, whatever things are pure, whatever things are lovely, whatever things are of good report, if there is any virtue and if there is anything praiseworthy—meditate on these things."

Let's consider several examples.

Scenario 1

The enemy comes to you and reminds you of all your unrighteousness. He points up all your shortcomings and your failures. And each one of us has plenty of examples that the devil can draw on. You know your failures. It's far easier to remember the times we made mistakes and messed up than to remember the times when we got it right. If we don't think we have any faults or have ever made any mistakes, just ask our spouses, right?

So the enemy comes and says, "You're a failure. You're never going to amount to anything."

That's one of the devil's favorite lines. "You're never going to succeed. You're never going to amount to a hill of beans."

In one way he's right. In Adam we're nothing. We're fallen, sinful, rebellious, unlovely people. But on the other hand, the devil is eternally dead wrong. In Christ we're everything. We are born again, redeemed from our pasts, and we have the gift of righteousness through Jesus Christ our Lord (see Rom. 5:17). We've already got more than the devil is ever going to get: the promise of an eternal home with God in heaven.

So when the devil comes with that bunch of nonsense, what do you do? You say, "I refuse to listen to you talk about the old person, devil. You have well pointed out my past and even some of my present struggles. But I'm not going to let you pollute my mind with that nonsense. Let me point out my future to you. Let me show you my new spiritual birthright. According to God's Word, the righteousness of God covers my life. I'm now a part of the bloodline of Jesus Christ Himself. I've been born again. I'm redeemed by the blood of the Lamb. And I'm heaven-bound."

You put off the devil's lies. You choose to have a renewed mind. You put on the TRUTH about yourself in Christ Jesus.

When the devil comes to tell you about your past, tell him about his past—that he was cast out of heaven and defeated by the blood of Jesus Christ shed on the cross of Calvary.

When the devil comes to taunt you and to paint a negative picture about your future, tell him about his future—that he will burn in the lake of fire forever and that he will never be allowed back into heaven, where you will be spending all of eternity.

Tell him that you are free from the bondage of sin and guilt.

Tell him that you are destined for eternity and that you are a child of God.

Tell him that you have been delivered from oppression and depression and that you are now into CONFESSION that Jesus Christ is Lord.

Tell him that you are saved and that you are being healed from the inside out all the way to wholeness and perfection in Christ Jesus.

Tell him that you are going to be the head, not the tail, . . . that you are going to experience victory, not defeat, . . . and that you are going to be blessed by God in order to be a blessing!

"Are you telling me, Larry, to ignore the problems of my life as if they aren't there?"

No. You have problems. Many Christians have very serious problems. I'm not telling you to ignore the problems of life. I'm not telling you to deny matter or reality. That is the teaching of Mary Baker Eddy and Christian Science. That is the teaching of Eastern mysticism. That is the teaching that says, "I don't have a toothache," when all the time your jaw is throbbing with pain. I'm not saying to DENY reality or to IGNORE the facts of life. I'm saying that INSTEAD of focusing all of your attention on the problem, choose to place your primary focus on God's promises for your life!

You don't say, "I don't have a toothache" if, in fact, you have one.

Instead, you say, "Jesus Christ has provided healing for my toothache. By His stripes I am healed. He is going to give me the wisdom about what to do for this toothache, and He is going to provide my deliverance from it."

Don't allow the negative input from the devil to dominate your mind. Don't allow the enemy to discredit your birthright in Jesus Christ. Don't allow the enemy to diminish you in any way.

If you hear yourself saying, "Well, I'm no good. I'm not going to make it. I can't win," recognize where that idea is coming from! It's not coming from your renewed heart that's been washed clean by the blood of Jesus. It's coming from an UNrenewed mind. That's garbage you're speaking, and it's coming from the enemy.

By allowing yourself to think ill of yourself and to speak ill of yourself, you are establishing a mind-set that will allow a negative volition to come back to your heart. You're not "keeping your heart with all diligence."

Say instead, "Hey, I've got problems, but I'm not going to concentrate all my energy on them. I'm going to focus on the promise of the Lord Jesus Christ and on the fact that my sins are forgiven and that Jesus said that if I confess my sins, He is faithful to forgive my sins and to cleanse me from all unrighteousness. Therefore, I'm claiming by my faith today that I'm cleansed. I have the gift of righteousness in me, and I am created the righteousness of God in Jesus Christ."

With that kind of thinking and confessing, you are putting on the new person. You are renewing your mind so that your mind will not interfere with your renewed heart. Your positive volition can remain positive because your mind is being CHANGED to match the change that has already occurred in your heart!

Scenario 2

The devil comes to tell you what rotten, lousy parents you had. Your father was a miserable physical abuser. Your mother was a hopeless, helpless emotional abuser. Have you heard the phrase *toxic parent*? It refers to miserable, lousy parents. And at one point or another the devil will probably come to you and say, "You're not going to succeed in this area of your life"—which may be one of any number of areas—"because of your parents."

What do you do?

You say, "Devil, I'm not going to accept this garbage in my mind. I choose instead to renew my mind. Let me tell you about my new Father. He's God almighty. I've got a new heart and a new lineage, and my new older brother is Jesus Christ. I've got new mothers and fathers and sisters and brothers in the church. They are gifts of God to me, and they are my new role models for my life. I will succeed, and my new parent—God my Father—is the REASON I will succeed."

Scenario 3

The devil comes to tell you that you have a deviant life-style because God made you that way.

Several years ago a young man came to my office for counseling. He started our conversation by saying, "I'm a homosexual." He talked about it awhile, describing his behavior and his desires, and finally stopped and waited for me to say something.

I said, "Are you a believer in Jesus Christ?"

He said, "Yes, I am."

I said, "Have you, to the best of your knowledge and ability, asked God to forgive you of your sins and for Jesus to come into your life?"

He said, "Yes, I have. That's why I'm so confused. Why do I still feel the way I feel at times?"

I said, "You've got to realize that in Adam everybody in the world is in some kind of strange mess. In Adam you really could become a homosexual. But God did *not* create you to be that way. In the beginning God created male and female. He created Adam and Eve, not Adam and Bruce. That idea of homosexuality is something that comes from the flesh and, who knows, perhaps from generation upon generation of fleshly influence in your life. But God did not create you to be that way, and He certainly did not re-create you through Jesus Christ to be a homosexual."

He looked at me thoughtfully.

I continued, "When you accepted Jesus Christ into your life, you received a new heart. Your volition and your will were renewed. But you have had years of programming of your mind, and much of that programming—through your friends and even your family—has been to convince you that you are a homosexual. You have to renew your mind to begin to believe about yourself what GOD says you are. And He says that you are a man, created physically to be a man and created to love a woman as a man. Are you following what I am saying?"

He nodded yes, and I went on.

I said, "You have been given a new heart so that you can live an ordinate, righteous, and holy life before God. You have been given a new heart so you can love God and love the things of God. Your challenge now is to renew your MIND so it can help you express in your everyday physical and material acts in this world the true volition of your heart."

"What do I do when these thoughts come?" he asked.

I said, "You say, 'Devil, I will not listen to any more of this. You've been feeding me these lies for years, and I am no longer going to allow my mind to accept these lies. I choose to renew my mind in Christ Jesus. Jesus said that I am forgiven. He said that I am created in the image and likeness of Him. He is calling me to a new life-style, and I'm going to follow it.'"

This young man began to do what I suggested. When he would feel temptation in his flesh, he would stop and quote some verses to himself about the consequences of homosexuality—and about the wages of sin being death. Over a period of time he was renewed in his mind. The temptations became less and less. And today he is married to a beautiful young woman in our church, and they have a lovely child.

His renewed mind has allowed him to act freely from the volition of his renewed heart, and, in so doing, he is living a pure life-style that is an acceptable, holy sacrifice to the Lord.

Scenario 4

Generally, you aren't even aware of the devil's coming with a temptation or a lie. You are too busy worshiping a false idol. For many people it's the idol of money. You want money. You think about money all the time. You worry about money. You adore people who have money, and you aren't happy unless you are surrounded by possessions that cost a lot of money.

I once worshiped golf clubs. I would clean them, doctor them, and sleep with them (yes, I even put golf balls under my pillow before I had a tournament!).

Once I had accepted Jesus Christ into my life, however, I had to realize that He alone is worthy to be worshiped. Have you come to that point with the idol of money and material things in your life? You must come to the point at which you say, "I will not be obsessed with this THING. I will not let material things rule my life and govern my activities. I choose to renew my mind. I choose to make Jesus the Lord of my life. I choose to think about the things of God, not this THING that will pass away."

Scenario 5

The devil comes to say, "You're going to have a problem because you are MADE to have that problem." Either your parents had the problem, or you have a physical predisposition to the problem. So the devil comes to tempt you at that point and say, "You WILL have this problem."

I'm the adult child of an alcoholic. One of the devil's lies against my life for many years was the lie that I was destined to become an alcoholic too. It's a scientific reality that four out of five children of alcoholics have a tendency toward alcoholism. Plus . . .

One of the major scientific hypotheses today is that many children of alcoholics have a certain chromosome in their genetic makeup that predisposes them to depression and various kinds of deviant behavior. A number of scientists and physicians believe that the outgrowth of this depression, caused by Chromosome 11, is a tendency to turn to alcohol or drugs to alleviate the depression. Boy, can the devil use that to lie to a lot of people! He's going to say, "Listen, it's even in your genetic makeup to be this way."

In Christ you may have that chromosome, but you don't HAVE to give in to its influence. Your chromosomes are no longer the overriding factor of your life. They are not an automatic determinant of your existence.

In Christ you are a new creation. You live by a new standard. You have a new power flowing through your life—that of the Holy Spirit—and the Holy Spirit is mightier than any Chromosome 11 in your body or in my body.

So when the devil comes with his lie that you are destined to be a certain way because of your genetic code, you say back to him, "No way. I refuse to accept that old-person thinking in my life. I choose to have a renewed mind. I am a NEW creature in Christ Jesus. I have a new source of strength and direction and power in my life. I choose to rely on the Holy Spirit to help me overcome anything that my genetic code might try to influence me to do!"

And while we are on the subject of alcohol . . .

I exhort you today to abstain from alcohol, but not because it's prohibited by the Scriptures. The Bible never says, "Thou shalt not drink wine." It says, "Do not be drunk with wine" (Eph. 5:18). But here is the basis on which I exhort you not to drink *anything* alcoholic, including wine. We are living in a stressed-out world, and alcohol is actually counterproductive to relieving stress. You may think that alcohol helps you to unwind, but it really doesn't. The biggest trick of alcohol is that it makes you think that you are more relaxed and have everything under control . . . when, in fact, you don't. You actually have less control. Your tension is only masked for the moment. Your relaxation is not a true relaxation of the inner person. You tend not to sleep as well as you would without alcohol, and you wake up feeling worse. Since you feel worse, the next day tends not to go so well, which produces more stress. The cycle becomes a vicious one, as if the tail is chasing the cat. Little by little, you are worn down. You start drinking more and more. And pretty soon you're addicted to it. And addiction to alcohol is a terrible, terrible addiction. It will eventually ruin you, . . . ruin your marriage, . . . ruin your family, . . . ruin your job, . . . and ruin your relationship with Jesus Christ, because eventually you'll begin to trust in alcohol and rely on alcohol more than Jesus.

What is true for alcohol is true for all chemical dependencies.

Choose to renew your mind, and you won't NEED alcohol or drugs.

Proverbs 23 says,

Who has woe? Who has sorrow? Who has contentions? Who has complaints? Who has wounds without cause? Who has redness of eyes? Those who linger long at the wine, those who go in search of mixed wine. Do not look on the wine when it is red, when it sparkles in the cup, when it swirls around smoothly; at the last it bites like a serpent, and stings like a viper. Your eyes will see strange things, and your heart will utter perverse things. Yes, you will be like one who lies down in the midst of the sea, or like one who lies at the top of the mast, saying: "They have struck me, but I was not hurt; they have beaten me, but I did not feel it. When shall I awake, that I may seek another drink?" (Prov. 23:29–35).

Friend, that's the best description of an alcoholic and the path to alcoholism you will ever read!

If you are addicted to alcohol or drugs today or if you are toying with alcohol and drugs, renew your mind. Every time the urge for a drink or a fix comes, quote some of this passage to yourself. Say, "Devil, I won't do this. I'm not in the market for seeing strange things, or feeling the sting of a serpent, or uttering perverse things I won't even remember later. I'm not in the market for getting sick—as if I were seasick on a raging sea. I'm not in the market to be self-deluded. I don't want to be so numb that I don't know what is going on. I don't want to have every waking thought turn to alcohol and a concern for where and when and how I can get my next drink. I refuse it. I choose to renew my mind. I choose to be the new creation that God has made me to be!"

Remember the formula:

1. Put off the old person.
2. Change your mind-set.
3. Put on the new person.

One of the foremost ways I know to put off the old person and to put on the new person is to get a clear image of where you will end up if you lead or continue to lead the life of the old person. Think of yourself lying in your own vomit in the street. Ask yourself if that is where you want to end up in life. No? Then put on the new person. Get an image of yourself living a cleaned-up life! Don't use that drug or take that drink.

Are you a gossiper? The Bible says that a gossiper is like one who takes an ax and throws it into the heart of his friend. Think of yourself holding an ax in your hand. Don't throw it. Refuse to give in to the temptation to spread gossip.

Decide that every time there is a downward pull on your life, you will not give in to it, but you will resist it. You will stop and declare that you choose to renew your mind and form a new image in your mind.

What do you do if you don't know God's response to certain problems? Study your Bible! Find out what the Bible says about the temptation that the devil is presenting to you.

God didn't create you to be a failure or a sinner. He created you in Christ Jesus to be righteousness. He created you to live a life that is more abundant.

Your genetic makeup, your family history, or your past experiences don't dictate your future. God holds your future in His hand, and He has promised to work all things together for your GOOD as long as you love and trust Him.

You weren't created for idol worship. You were created to worship the Lord God.

Get an accurate picture of yourself today! In so doing, you will renew your mind. And in so doing, you will "keep your heart with all diligence" and will put yourself into a position to understand with accuracy the wisdom of God and to receive it and apply it to your life.

You and only you can decide to renew your mind. Nobody else can do it for you.

As you renew your mind, you are able to say to others who are desperate for help and to speak without shame, fear, or doubt, "I once struggled with that thing, but now I'm a new creature. I'm being changed every day. Let me tell you how. What has happened to me can happen to you."

Wisdom and the Renewed Mind

Now what does the renewal of your mind have to do with wisdom? Everything!

The renewed mind blossoms with wisdom. The renewed mind experiences the ever-increasing flow of God's wisdom. The renewed mind can clearly discern God's wisdom. The renewed mind senses a need for more and more of God's wisdom as each day passes. The renewed mind is most readily available to God for manifestation of a word of wisdom.

In the practical realm the renewed mind most readily grasps HOW to apply God's wisdom to the situation, the moment, the circumstance. The renewed mind is uncluttered, unpolluted, and open territory for God's creativity and His new ideas ready to be made manifest on the earth.

You can . . . indeed, you MUST . . . renew your mind to be in a position to receive God's ongoing gift of wisdom to you. It's there for the receiving. WILL you receive it? Will you choose today to RENEW YOUR MIND and thus "keep your heart with all diligence"?

Let's pray about it.

Father, I pray today that You will work within me to change my volition from what I choose to what You choose. I pray today that You will cleanse my thoughts by the power of Your Holy Spirit. I vow to You today that I WILL renew my mind. I now put off the old creature. I CHOOSE to adopt Your mind-set, Your ideas, Your opinions, Your viewpoint, and Your perspective. I put on Your mind—the mind of Christ.

Father, I want to be available to You, O God, for the ever-increasing flow of Your wisdom into my life. Help me, O Lord, in my weakness. Forgive me, O Lord, for my lack of repentance. Give me the courage to believe that Your wisdom is flowing toward me right now. I pray this in the name of Jesus. Amen.

Chapter 4

The Wise Person Wins Souls

*The fruit of the righteous is a tree of life,
and he who wins souls is wise.*

—Proverbs 11:30

Do you want your life today to be a tree of life—not death? A channel of the life of God? One who bears the fruit of the Holy Spirit into this dark and troubled world?

Well, coupled with being a tree of life is this principle: winning souls!

Your first responsibility—your first priority, your number one goal in life—before God is to win souls. That's the number one character trait of a wise person. That's the Great Commission. That's the great race Paul talks about running. That's the goal for your life. That's the ultimate reason for your existence. Everything else is secondary!

Have you ever stopped to wonder why God has put certain people in your life? Have you ever marveled at the friends you have from points across America and around the world—people whom, in another century, you would never have had the opportunity to meet? Have you ever wondered why God gave you the children you have in your family? Have you ever stopped to think about your colleagues on the job? Have you ever wondered about "chance meetings" or people whom you encounter only briefly on planes or in waiting rooms or standing in lines?

Let me tell you the answer! It's so you might testify that Jesus is Lord.

God has no other mouthpiece but your mouth at the precise times and places you walk on this earth.

God holds no one but YOU responsible for the people with whom you come into contact on a daily basis.

That's a sobering thought. It's a challenging thought. I pray that it may become the supreme motivation of your life!

I firmly believe that wisdom will elude you until you recognize that your number one responsibility in this life is to be God's mouthpiece. I also believe that only as you accept this responsibility and are faithful to it will you be established as a "tree of life" on this earth.

When you fail to accept this responsibility, then you are damming up the "rivers of living water" that God wants to flow through your life. When you fail to acknowledge and embrace this responsibility, you are not in a position to bear the fullness of the fruit of the Holy Spirit. When you do not act on this responsibility, you are not in a position to receive the greatest and most rewarding, fulfilling blessings that God desires to pour into every part of your being.

Let me share with you five reasons why you are responsible for winning souls.

Reason 1: You Are Commanded to Win Souls

The number one reason you are responsible for winning souls is that the Lord has commanded you to do it. The final words of Jesus recorded in the book of Matthew are these:

All authority has been given to Me in heaven and on earth. Go therefore and make disciples of all the nations, baptizing them in the name of the Father and of the Son and of the Holy Spirit, teaching them to observe all things that I have commanded you; and lo, I am with you always, even to the end of the age (Matt. 28:18–20).

Note that Jesus said, "Go." That may be translated another way: "as you go." As you go, you are to do certain things. This means making Jesus' command a part of your daily walk of life. *As you go* . . . in other words, as you work as a garbage collector . . . or as an attorney . . . or as a secretary . . . or as a homemaker . . . or as a teacher . . . or in whatever profession or job or work you do every day, Jesus has three very specific things for you to do.

• *Make disciples of all nations.* In other words, be a missionary to every person you encounter. That's a command.

• *Baptize them.* In other words, bring them to repentance and baptize them into newness of life in the name of the Father, and of the Son, and of the Holy Spirit. In other words, immerse them in the knowledge and presence of God the Father. Immerse them in the knowledge and presence of Jesus Christ. Immerse them in the knowledge and presence of the Holy Spirit. Cause them to live in the fullness of God's presence! Don't just cause them to be aware of God's existence and of their own sin, which is the state in which Paul first found twelve men at Ephesus.

> He [Paul] said unto them, Have ye received the Holy Ghost since ye believed? And they said unto him, We have not so much as heard whether there be any Holy Ghost. And he said unto them, Unto what then were ye baptized? And they said, Unto John's baptism. Then said Paul, John verily baptized with the baptism of repentance, saying unto the people, that they should believe on him which should come after him, that is, on Christ Jesus. When they heard this, they were baptized in the name of the Lord Jesus. And when Paul had laid his hand upon them, the Holy Ghost came on them; and they spake with tongues, and prophesied (Acts 19:2–6 KJV).

We are called to baptize men and women in the name of the Father . . . AND of the Son . . . AND of the Holy Spirit. That's a command!

• *Teach them to observe all things that I have commanded you.* In other words, we're not just to bring people into a state of conversion and then abandon them to "sink or swim." We're to teach them, to disciple them, to bring them to maturity in Christ Jesus, first with the milk and then with the meat of the Word (see 1 Cor. 3:2).

And what are we to teach them? We are to say everything that Jesus said to His disciples. We are not to say less—giving only those parts we like or believe to be the high points. We're to tell it all. We aren't to say more than Jesus said, adding our own opinions along the way. We're to say what Jesus said and everything Jesus said and nothing more. That's the essence of our responsibility to teach. And that's a command.

Three commands rolled into one great command! That's our responsibility. It's spelled out plainly. The big question is, *Will we do what Jesus told us to do?*

A number of years ago when we were pastoring at Beverly Hills Baptist Church in Dallas, a little hippie girl named Christi was in our congregation. She had been a drug addict, but after she accepted Jesus as her personal Savior and Lord, she began to read her Bible regularly, and she came across the Great Commission one day. Being a new believer—and someone who hadn't heard all of the excuses people can give for not doing what Jesus said to do— she took these words at face value. Everywhere she went, she would say to those she encountered, "I have to do this." And then she would proceed to tell them that Jesus was the Lord of her life and that He had come to be the Lord of their lives too. Her opening line was always the same: "I have to do this."

And she was right! That's precisely what Jesus said we have to do. It's our responsibility. It's our purpose. It's our number one job on this earth—to tell others about Jesus Christ and what He did on the cross and what He has done in your life and what He can do in the life of their lives.

That little hippie girl brought literally scores of people to Jesus Christ. She simply didn't know that she had any alternatives or options. She did what Jesus said to do, and in her simplicity she became one of the best soul winners I've ever met.

The world is going crazy looking for an answer. The problems are great. The needs are mind-boggling. The odds are overwhelming. People are craving solutions, direction, a definitive answer. They're looking for someone who will open his mouth and tell the truth about what has happened in his life.

What would happen if Jesus literally appeared to you now in the place where you are reading this book? Suppose that you looked up right now and saw Him standing there, corporally, in the flesh, right there before you, and He said to you, "Now when you put that book down, I want you to get up and go out and tell everyone you meet that I'm real." Would you do it?

Well, friend, it's just that real. His Word hasn't changed. His opinion on the subject is the same as when He spoke to the disciples just before He ascended into heaven. Jesus is still saying:

You are my priest.

You are my servant.

You are my ambassador.

You are my mouthpiece.

And you are to go, and as you go, you are to open your mouth, and say to every person you meet, "Jesus is Savior. Jesus is Lord."

The first reason you are responsible for winning souls is because Jesus tells you to do it! He commands you to do it!

Reason 2: You Are Empowered to Win Souls

The second reason you are responsible for winning souls is because you have been empowered to do it. Jesus told His disciples that after He departed from them, they were to stay in Jerusalem and to "wait for the Promise of the Father, 'which,' He said, 'you have heard from Me; for John truly baptized with water, but you shall be baptized with the Holy Spirit not many days from now'" (Acts 1:4–5).

In other words, Jesus said, "Get the power to do the job."

Jesus had told them repeatedly that He would not leave them comfortless, that He would not abandon them without a sense of His presence. And now He told them to stay in Jerusalem until they were baptized with the Holy Spirit.

What was the purpose of this baptism?

It was to give them dynamite power: "You shall receive power when the Holy Spirit has come upon you" (Acts 1:8). The word is *dunamis* in Greek, the root for our word *dynamite*. It's explosive power that can shake this world.

The purpose of the Holy Spirit is not to give you goose bumps every time you go to church. It's not to give you a rush of joy. It's not to give you a good feeling. The purpose of the Holy Spirit in your life is to give you POWER to do what He has commanded you to do—to take His message into every place you go, to be His witness "in Jerusalem, and in all Judea and Samaria, and to the end of the earth" (Acts 1:8).

Note the four levels of your responsibility:

• *In Jerusalem*—those who are closest to you, the inner circle of your life, your family and your closest friends.

• *In Judea*—your circle of friends.

• *In Samaria*—those in the outer circle of your life, your acquaintances.

• *To the end of the earth*—those with whom you have rare, divine encounters as you travel beyond your normal routes and outside your normal routines.

No matter where you go and no matter whom you are with, the reason that the Holy Spirit has come into your life is to EMPOWER you to have the boldness you need to open your mouth and to tell others that "Jesus is Savior and Jesus is Lord" in your life.

Do you really want to see the power of God manifested in and through your life on a daily basis?

I pray that your answer may be a resounding yes, but some of you may say, "I'm not sure, Larry."

If that's your answer today, I want to challenge you to examine your life and to ask yourself if you have *ever* experienced the power of God. The apostle Paul wrote that his heart's desire was to "know Him and the power of His resurrection, and the fellowship of His sufferings" (Phil. 3:10). Paul wrote that after he had known the Lord for many years!

If you have ever really known the power of God in your life . . . if you have ever experienced the power of God flowing through you to others . . . all you can say is, "Give me more. I want more. I want that power to be flowing in and through my life EVERY day, EVERY minute, EVERY second."

How do you receive more and more of this power of the Holy Spirit in your life on a day-by-day basis? By witnessing to the lordship of Jesus Christ and by fulfilling the Great Commission.

Notice that when Jesus gave the Great Commission, He began by saying, "All *power* has been given to Me in heaven and on earth" (KJV). Then He went on to say, "Go. . . ." Jesus arranged for the transfer of His power to us *through* the Holy Spirit as we go to tell others about who Jesus is and what He has done in our lives and what He can do in their lives. The power comes with a purposeful use attached to it; the power does not come without witnessing, and witnessing is more effective with the power. It's like a gun with bullets. One is made for the other. One needs the other to fulfill its purpose. And the purpose for the Holy Spirit's power in your life is so you can be His witness in Jerusalem, Judea, Samaria, and to the end of the earth.

The purpose of the Holy Spirit in your life is not so you can receive a great jolt of blessing as you sit in church. Now you may feel such a jolt as the Holy Spirit lets you know that He is real. But you may never feel a thing. I didn't feel anything special for nearly fifteen years after my conversion experience. But I did get power from the Holy Spirit, and when I opened my mouth to tell others about Jesus, that power was released through my life.

Have you ever heard the phrase "use it or lose it"? Well, the principle holds true for the power of the Holy Spirit. I use the power of the Holy Spirit to witness to others every opportunity I have; and as long as I use the power, I feel the fullness of God's anointing on my life. I believe that holds true for every man, woman, boy, or girl who is rooted and grounded in the Holy Spirit. When you don't use the power of God for its intended purpose of telling others about Jesus, you'll begin to lose that special anointing that God desires for your life.

You are not anointed by God with the Holy Spirit to contain that anointing. You were anointed to open your mouth and let that anointing flow out to others. You were created to be a vessel of God's presence—not to hold that presence within you but to pour out His presence to others.

After I had been saved only for a few months—and was still pretty fresh from the psychiatric center too—I had a bad case of "reading the red and praying for the power." That's all I knew to do—to read the words of Jesus that were printed with red ink in my Bible and to pray for God's presence and power in my life.

Nobody would let me preach in church. My pastor allowed that to happen only one time! No, my "pulpits" in those early days were often at the local Dairy Queens. From time to time I was asked to be a visiting evangelist in a small church along the back roads of Texas.

The first person I led to Jesus Christ was Jerry Howell, who is now my associate at the Church on the Rock in Rockwall, Texas. Jerry was a hippie. He was experimenting with drugs. He played keyboard in a rock band. He often says that the main purpose of his life at that time was "sitting in the backyard counting blades of grass, trying to avoid having a nervous breakdown." All in all, Jerry was in serious trouble in his life.

One day I called Jerry and said, "Jerry, I'm preaching tonight, and I want you to go out with me to the New London Baptist Church and play the organ for the service."

He said, "Man, you want *me* to go out to that church with you?"

I said, "Yes. I need your help."

He said, "I really don't know any songs like that."

I said, "Well, come play 'Amazing Grace.'" ("Amazing Grace" has never been the same since that night!)

Jerry finally agreed, and that night after the service, about midnight, he said, "OK, Larry, tell me about Jesus."

Now I had never led anyone to the Lord. I knew that Jerry was in trouble. I knew what trouble was like because I had experienced the same kinds of trouble not too long before. I felt the burden of his need and his deep and desperate desire for an answer to his life. And I whispered a little prayer: "Jesus, fill my mouth. Give me the right things to say." And at midnight we began to talk about Jesus.

Friend, all the Lord needs is for someone to be sensitive enough to listen to the hurts of another person and to be willing to open his mouth and share the message of Jesus.

When I began to speak, the Spirit of God began to move, and finally at about 4:30 A.M. Jerry said, "Well, how do you get it?" And I realized that I didn't really know how to tell anyone *how* to get saved, and so I said the only thing I knew at the time: "Well, Jerry, you go and get your Bible and read Matthew 5, 6, and 7 and cry and holler out, 'Jesus! Jesus! Jesus!' and when it hits you, then you know you've got it."

Jerry didn't know any better than to do just what I had told him. He got his Bible, read those three chapters in Matthew, began to cry out to God, and the Lord gloriously saved him.

Jerry got up and went immediately to his drummer, Max, who lived down the street. Jerry called me to come and talk to Max too. And within a year Jerry was preaching, and I was singing for *his* services. We saw ninety young people come to the Lord during a three-day meeting and one thousand young people during the next ninety days!

God didn't use us because we were smart or because we knew much about God or the Bible. We knew only enough to be seriously dangerous. You see, we knew that Jesus had done something tremendous in our lives, and we knew that He wanted to do that for other people, and we knew that God had promised to give us the power we needed to tell others just that message!

You are commanded to win souls. You are empowered to win souls. And . . .

Reason 3: You Are Fulfilled
by Winning Souls

The third reason you are to win souls is that you are going to experience true fulfillment in your life only as you win souls. Winning souls is your actual purpose in life as a Christian. You have no other real purpose. Therefore, the only way to be truly fulfilled in this life is to win souls.

Many people think that their purpose in life is to have children. Or to make money. Or to gain weight and lose weight.

I asked a man one day, "What are you living for?"

He said, "I'm living for my job."

I asked, "Why?"

"So I can make money."

"What's that for?"

"So I can pay bills and get food."

"What's that for?"

"So I can eat and have a safe place to sleep."

"What's that for?"

"So I can have strength."

"Why do you want strength?"

"So I can do my job."

Is your job the reason you're living? No! The real reason you are on the earth is so you can influence people and bring them into the kingdom of God.

The reason for your existence is not so you can fight demons. That's part of what you need to do if you are going to be a soul winner, but that's not the real reason for your existence.

The reason for your existence is not so you can build a house and enjoy the finer things of life. You may have that as one of God's blessings added to you when you seek first the kingdom of God and His righteousness (see Matt. 6:33), but that's not your real REASON for living.

Your reason for living is to claim the promises of God, be filled with the power of God, and bring others to God.

Your purpose in life from the moment you meet Jesus until the moment you die is to bring as many people to Jesus as you can.

When you stand before Jesus someday, you won't be surrounded by all of the people you healed (unless those healings brought people to Jesus Christ).

Ask yourself for a moment, Why did Jesus heal people? He

healed them to give them a revelation of who He was. Jesus said, "I am the light of the world" (John 9:5) and simultaneously healed a blind man's eyes as proof of his claim. Jesus said, "I am the bread of life" (John 6:35), and the disciples had only to recall that He had just fed five thousand people to get the point. Jesus said, "I am the resurrection and the life" (John 11:25), and immediately He called forth Lazarus from the grave. The miracles of Jesus were illustrations so that people would know who Jesus was, repent, and receive God's forgiveness. The miracles were not random events. They were rooted and grounded in a purpose, and that purpose was to show the way to God. Their purpose was to win souls!

At the time when my dad was right on the brink of being saved, I went home for a visit and took Melva with me. Now my dad is a pretty rough ol' boy. He is one of those people who can be sweet and rough at the same time. As we entered the house, we found my dad sitting in the kitchen cutting out his own ingrown toenail with his pocket knife. Now that's rough!

At that time I was "reading the red and praying for the power," believing that the Jesus I was reading about was just the same today as He was in Bible times. When I saw my dad whittling away at his toe, I said, "Daddy, Jesus can heal your toes."

When I said those words, we all laughed. Then my dad said, "Well, if you think Jesus can heal my toes, why don't you ask Him to do it."

I said, "All right." And I put my hand on his toe and shouted, "In the name of Jesus . . ." and I commenced to have a real prayer time.

My daddy called me the next week, and he started the conversation by saying, "Larry, you're not going to believe what happened to my big toe. . . ."

Now the rest of the story is that my daddy experienced the power of God through that brief incident at the kitchen table and the healing of his toe. And that awareness of God's power led to his conversion!

The real reason for you to have God's presence and power in your life is so you can lead people to a saving knowledge of Jesus.

You are commanded to win souls. You are empowered to do it. You are fulfilled as a person only when you win souls. And . . .

Reason 4: Your Compassion Is Enlarged When You Win Souls

The fourth reason you need to win souls is to keep the bowels of your compassion from being stopped. Your compassion will stop flowing if you don't witness to others and win souls.

If you don't open your mouth and let the river of God's power flow from your life, you will dam up the river of life (which is the river of the Holy Spirit moving through your being), . . . and, friend, that river is meant to BE a river, not a lake.

You may say, "But, Larry, I thought the reason for the presence and power of God in my life is so I might experience peace."

Let me assure you that when you open your mouth and begin to tell others about Jesus, you'll have so much peace flooding in your soul that you're likely to fall asleep just about any place and time.

You may say, "But, Larry, I thought the purpose for the presence of God is so I might feel more love."

When you start opening your mouth to tell others about Jesus and about what He has done for you and what He wants to do for them, you'll feel more love flowing out of you than you've ever felt at any other time in your life!

We often talk in church about grieving or quenching the Holy Spirit in our lives.

What does that really mean in practical terms?

I believe it means that we have dammed up the Holy Spirit in our lives so He is no longer released to do the work that the Holy Spirit longs to do.

Do you really want to be your own person? You don't want to be anybody else but you because God created you in His image to be a unique individual? And when somebody comes along and tries to put you in someone else's mold, you are uncomfortable? Praise God—He made every snowflake unique. He made us all different.

You can't be me, and I can't be you. Each of us is a one-of-a-kind individual. No two sets of fingerprints are alike. No two voiceprints are alike. We're each from a unique mold.

The Holy Spirit is also distinct and unique and has a specific nature and purpose. The Holy Spirit is perhaps the supreme Person with a purpose.

Now if you were stopped from fulfilling your purpose in life, either because you didn't understand it or because someone thwarted your efforts to fulfill your purpose, wouldn't you feel frustrated and grieved at the loss of your own potential?

Well, the same holds true for the Holy Spirit!

The Holy Spirit within you longs to woo others to Jesus and to see others grow in His nurture and admonition. He longs to see you become the fullness of who God created you to be. That's the purpose of the Holy Spirit. And when we dam up the flow of God's presence in our lives, we stop the Holy Spirit from fulfilling His purpose.

People often call me and say, "I'm depressed." Now they aren't actually experiencing clinical depression. They are experiencing the Holy Spirit grieving in their lives.

A few months ago a dear friend of mine was going through a major change in his life. God was leading him to make a decision about moving his family to another city to accept a new position of service for God. He was deeply grieved. And when he was grieved, I was grieved. I longed for him to fulfill what God was calling him to do and to be all that God wanted him to be.

That's the way the Holy Spirit feels about you, only one hundred million times more so. He's closer to you than any person could be in the natural sphere. He is literally impregnated within your spirit. And when He is saddened, grieved, quenched, . . . guess what happens to you. You may call it depression. Actually, the river inside your spirit is clogged up or squelched.

Do you truly want to experience the righteousness, the peace, the joy, the love, and the wisdom of God in such a way that it overflows your life? That won't happen by learning Bible principles. That won't happen by might or by power—by having a great experience one time somewhere somehow. No. That flow of God's presence will happen only when the Holy Spirit is allowed to flow in your life, to do His work, to be all that He can be within you.

He who wins souls is wise BECAUSE he is delivered from selfishness.

Do you realize the one thing that God has been trying to do in your life since you were a baby is to deliver you from selfishness? Babies live in a world that revolves around them. Feed me. Bathe me. Clean me. Rock me. Hold me. It's a me, me, me, ME world for a baby.

When you decide, however, to obey the purpose of the Holy Spirit in your life, you basically are saying the same thing that Jesus said: "The Son of Man did not come to be served, but to serve, and to give His life a ransom for many" (Matt. 20:28).

Jesus did not have a ME-first attitude. He took the towel and washed the feet of His disciples.

What God is going to do in your life as you allow the Holy Spirit to work through you and in you is to deliver you from the worst "ism" that has ever existed. It's not Communism. It's not socialism. It's not Taoism. It's me-ism.

I long for the day when every Christian I know becomes a gossip teller of the good news about Jesus Christ. I long for the day when people stop talking about themselves and start talking about their Savior. I long for the day when people stop moaning about their problems and start talking about their Lord, who can and will deliver them from all evil!

"But," you say, "witnessing to people is just not my personality, Larry."

Don't you realize that God is trying to deliver you from your little ol' personality a little bit?

Others say to me, "I'm afraid to tell others about Jesus." Or they say, "I'm afraid of what other people will think of me."

Let me tell you what should be the real cause of your fear. Read the words of Jesus:

A disciple is not above his teacher, nor a servant above his master. It is enough for a disciple that he be like his teacher, and a servant like his master. If they have called the master of the house Beelzebub, how much more will they call those of his household! Therefore do not fear them. For there is nothing covered that will not be revealed, and hidden that will not be known. Whatever I tell you in the dark, speak in the light; and what you hear in the ear, preach on the housetops. And do not fear those who kill the body but cannot kill the soul. But rather fear Him who is able to destroy both soul and body in hell (Matt. 10:24–28).

When you open your mouth and begin to tell others about Jesus and about what He has done in your life, the worst thing that person can do to you is to kill you. And as Paul said, "To me, to live is Christ, and to die is gain" (Phil. 1:21). So if they do the worst thing to you, it's actually the best thing *for* you!

Jesus tells us to fear the One who can destroy both body and soul. This is the same One who has told us to go, . . . and as we go, teach all nations and baptize them in the name of the Father, and of the Son, and of the Holy Ghost.

Let me assure you that when you really get a holy fear of almighty God, you'll lose all fear of people.

When you come to the point at which you say, "I regard what You say, God, and I'm going to do this because You said to do it, You empowered me to do it, You've shown me that it's the purpose for my life, and You've shown me that it's the purpose of the Holy Spirit; therefore, I am going to open my mouth and speak," let me assure you that the fear of God will rise up in you—which is the beginning of all wisdom—and the fear of people will die in your life; and no matter what the Holy Spirit tells you to do, you'll do it. Guess what that will do? He will teach you how to prosper in every area of your life!

This calling to win souls is not part of the fivefold ministry of the church leadership (apostles, prophets, evangelists, pastors, teachers, as described in Eph. 4:11). The purpose of the church leadership is to EQUIP the people of God to do the job of soul winning!

Who wins the Super Bowl? The coach or the players? It's the

players! The same holds true for soul-winning. The laity wins the souls. The leaders equip the laity for the task.

That is the exact opposite of what many church people think. They believe that it's the pastor's responsibility to preach a sermon that will win souls. That's not what the Bible says. The Bible teaches that soul winning is the job of every believer in the Lord Jesus, and while the pastor is to be an example of soul winning because he is called to win souls just as every other believer is called to win souls, that is not the pastor's number one responsibility in the church. His or her responsibility is to equip the laymen and laywomen to do the job more effectively.

Can you imagine what would happen if every person in your church took soul winning seriously and made it a top priority to win at least one person a week to Jesus? Your local church would have a population explosion such as you have never seen! Imagine if every person sought diligently to win just one new person to Jesus each month . . . or even each year! You would truly be multiplying and subduing and replenishing the earth with the goodness of God.

Consider the story of the good Samaritan. We call him the good Samaritan because we look at him as someone special. Are you aware that the Bible doesn't call him the good Samaritan? He is called a "certain Samaritan" (see Luke 10:33).

That story in the Bible has three main characters or groups of characters. The first were the thieves. Their approach to life was this: *"What's yours is mine, and I'm going to get it if I can."*

Then there were the Levites, who characterize most people who fill up our churches on Sundays and Wednesday nights. Most churchgoing people consider going to church to *be* the manifestation of their salvation. The reason people go to church is really to be infused with a little revelation in order to go out on the streets and give it away! These Levites walked by and said, in essence, "We're on our way to church [in Jerusalem], and we don't have time to take responsibility for this guy." Their attitude was *"What's mine is mine, and you aren't going to get it."*

God did not say that He was going to bless Abraham—the father of all of us who have faith and live in faith—so that he could sit on that blessing until it rotted and he rotted along with it. No! God said that He was going to bless Abraham and MAKE HIM A BLESSING! That was God's opinion on the matter. The Levites had come a long way from the truth.

How many of us today are doing much better? We see people who are dying, confused, hurting, and struggling every day of our lives, and rather than take the time and effort to adjust our schedules and our agendas to open our mouths and tell them about Jesus, we simply walk on.

But there was a "certain Samaritan"—a regular guy—who had the attitude "What is mine is yours, and you can have it if you need it."

That's the attitude the Lord Jesus calls us to have today when it comes to our faith. What is mine—the relationship I have with Jesus Christ, which is the only truly valuable thing I have—is yours. I have received it freely. Freely I share it with you. What He's done for me, He'll do for you. Everything I know about God and about Jesus and about the Holy Spirit I give to you.

What must we do? We must open our mouths and speak the name of Jesus. Not as the world speaks it, mind you. Have you ever noticed that nobody says, "Oh, Buddha!" as a curse word? They never say, "Oh, Man-made!" Have you ever stopped to wonder why? Because the spirits of this world are doing everything in their power to desecrate the one name that is above all other names, that has the power whereby people can be saved. Because Jesus is the only name whereby people can be saved, the spirits of this age do everything they can to make the name of Jesus nothing more than a byword.

Everywhere you turn, you'll find people today who have a story to tell, and it's not a good story. They say, "Things are really bad at my house." You need to open your mouth and say, "Jesus can change that."

They say, "You have no idea what all is wrong with my marriage." And you open your mouth and say, "Jesus can change that."

They say, "You wouldn't believe the problems I'm having with my children." You say, "Jesus can change that."

That's all you need to say. And then watch the rivers of living water begin to flow from your life. They may ask you, "How can He change that?" Watch the rivers flow from your life. They may ask, "Do you really think Jesus can do anything about it?" Watch the rivers flow from you life. It's easy, once you have started. And to get started, all you need to say is "Jesus can change that" when something negative comes up in a conversation.

"But," you say, "what if they ask me a question for which I don't have the answer?"

Speak what you do know. You can always say, "I don't know the answer to your difficult question, but I do know this . . ." and share from your own experience. Tell them what you KNOW to be true in your own life. Jesus said, "We speak what We know" (John 3:11). He didn't say, "We speak what we think." And what did Paul say? By his own words Paul said that he spoke of the crucifixion, resurrection, and ascension of Jesus Christ (see 1 Cor. 15:3–4). Do you know today that Jesus Christ was crucified for your sins and for the sins of all humankind? Do you know that you can experience forgiveness of your sins when you ask Him to do so with true repentance? Do you know that Jesus Christ was resurrected from the dead? Do you know something of His resurrection power in lifting you from the "death" of your problems and circumstances? Then you know a lot, friend. It's enough to begin a truly good conversation about the presence and power of Jesus Christ! You have enough good information to turn people around everywhere you go—and turn them around for all eternity!

Notice one more thing. This certain Samaritan was not a paramedic. He didn't show up with penicillin and oxygen tanks. He offered what he had. He said, "Man, I've got a strip of cloth here I can tear off the edge of my garment. I've got a little oil and a little wine in my knapsack. Here, let me help you with what I've got until I can get you to a place where they can help you better."

You don't need five degrees after your name to be qualified to tell someone about Jesus. You don't need to strive to get more before you start giving from what you already have. Start giving what you DO know. Start giving what you DO have.

You may say, "I don't have enough!"

Then get some more. That's what church services are all about! That's what Christian books and tapes and most Christian television programs are all about! The primary role of the apostles, prophets, evangelists, pastors, and teachers is to equip the laymen and the laywomen of the church to do the primary work of the church, which is to win souls and to deliver those who are oppressed of the devil. God doesn't have a plan B. That's His plan. And we're either doing it, or we aren't.

You are commanded to win souls. You are empowered to do the job. You will find personal fulfillment only when you do win souls, and you'll find that your compassion will cease to flow when you don't. And there's one final and supreme reason you are to win souls. It's this. . . .

Reason 5: People Are Dying and Going to Hell

The fifth and foremost reason you are to win souls is because people are dying without Christ and going to hell. In your generation. In your city. On your block. In your family. Now. And the result is an eternal one.

When was the last time you went to a funeral and looked at the body of the deceased person and confronted the finality and the reality of death? I believe that it's good for us occasionally to stop and FACE the finality of death. What's done in life . . . is done. There's no recall program that gives a second chance. Death marks the END of life on this earth.

I've never had a vision of the fires of hell. I have heard testimonies of people who actually saw the fires of hell in a near-death experience or in an after-death experience. They describe a place of eternal punishment where the torment is a thousand times worse than a physical fire, because the fire torments but does not consume. It's eternal damnation. Eternal separation from God. Eternal separation from everything that we desire in our lives.

I often wonder why we don't hear more preaching about hell. Preachers seemed to stop preaching about hell some twenty years ago. A spirit of liberalism and pseudosophistication seemed to enter the church world about that time, and people began to stop preaching about the blood of Jesus and the fire of hell.

I declare to you today that there are a heaven and a hell. A fire burns without ceasing, and the worm does not die (see Mark 9:44). There is a place of continual, ongoing consumption and eternal death and an existence of damnation apart from God. It's a central truth of God's Word; and either all of God's Word is true, or none of it is. It's a central theme in the teaching of Jesus, and either all of Jesus' teaching is true or none of it is. Are you aware that Jesus taught more about hell and about how to avoid it than He did about heaven and how to enjoy it? Hell is a reality, and it's time we faced up to that as a fact of our daily existence.

Not only that, but there's a hell on this earth. Millions of people are living in it every day because they are living a life without Christ. They are, even now, experiencing pain and agony—a living death—because they are separated from God.

The result is that millions of people are living in hell right now, even as you read this book, and the majority of those people are going to die and spend eternity in hell, and the sum total of their lives will be zero. Nothing of this existence will have counted for anything.

I've noticed that I face a choice at some point during the day about which way my day is going to end up. I begin my day with prayer. I start out with victory, and my mornings are nearly always good mornings. But about midway through the day I always seem to encounter a decision point. I can decide if my day is going to go down the tubes or if I'm going to continue to walk in the Spirit and END my day with victory.

The other day that moment hit about three o'clock in the afternoon. I had been up since five o'clock that morning, and I had been working hard all day. By midafternoon my work was finished, and I was tired; so I went home. Sitting in my favorite chair, I asked, "God, what should I do with the rest of my day?"

I was impressed by the Holy Spirit to call my barber and see if I could get a haircut. The strange thing was that I didn't really need a haircut. I just felt impressed to call and make an appointment.

I said, "Sandy, if you have an opening this afternoon, I think I'll come down and get a trim."

She said, "Get down here right now." Her response wasn't her usual polite, mild-mannered, happy, polite, "Sure, I have a time. . . ." No! It was an order that she barked into the phone.

I asked, "What's going on?"

She said, "We have a witch in here, or someone like a witch. One of our new employees brought her in, and she's been over in the corner doing this séance deal, and we don't know what to do. Get down here!"

I said as I hung up the phone, "Well, glory to God, I know what to do." And then under my breath I added, "Lord, I guess I know what to do with the rest of my day!" and I jumped into my car and was on my way. By the time I got to the shop, the woman who was not of God was already gone, but the employee who had brought her into the shop was under intense conviction of the Holy Spirit, and she was sitting with Sandy in the back room. It was as if I had shown up just at the time the baby was about to be delivered.

I sometimes get amused when I hear people say, "I got so-and-so 'saved.'" Not really. The Holy Spirit has been whittling away on them for years. He's been sending this one and that one along to chop away at them so that they reach the point at which only one more chop will fell the tree. That final guy gets credit for chopping down the tree, but what he really did was give just the last chop necessary. And furthermore, he's not even the chopper. He's only the ax! The Holy Spirit is the One who's doing the chopping. He's just an instrument in the hands of God the Holy Spirit.

Well, that's the way it was this day. A number of people had been praying for this young woman for weeks and had been talking to her and witnessing to her about Jesus. I showed up just in time to lead her in a sinner's prayer. She was gloriously born again that afternoon, sitting in that back room of the barbershop. She didn't just gain a little more information about God. No! She was gloriously saved. And the next Sunday she walked down the aisle of the Church on the Rock with tears streaming down her face, and she has come into the fellowship of the church, has been baptized, and is growing in Christ!

Why am I sharing this with you?

Because I believe that every day of your life you come to a crossroads moment. The day can end on a down note or an up note, depending on what you decide in that moment. And generally speaking, if you'll really stop and be objective about those moments in your life, you'll realize that the best decision you can make to end your day on an up note for God is to do SOMETHING that will further the winning of souls. It may mean writing a note. It may mean making a phone call. It may mean going to visit someone or making arrangements to meet someone for dinner. It may mean stopping by the hospital on your way home from work. I guarantee you . . . if you will be faithful in that midday moment of decision and will follow through on what the Holy Spirit prompts you to do . . . souls will be saved because of your faithfulness.

You may not FEEL as if you are accomplishing anything. But you are! You may be just one more chop against a tree that the Holy Spirit is whittling down. But without that chop, that soul will be one step farther from salvation and heaven and one step closer to damnation and hell.

Watch for those moments to come at midday.

Make a decision to do something related to winning souls in that moment.

Follow through on that decision. And see what God will do!

Become a True Watchman

As a teenager I encountered a Scripture that changed my life forever. I want to close this chapter by sharing it with you.

Son of man, I have made you a watchman for the house of Israel; therefore hear a word from My mouth, and give them warning from Me: When I say to the wicked, "You shall surely die," and you give him no warning, nor speak to warn the wicked from his wicked way, to save his life, that same wicked man shall die in his iniquity; but his blood I will require at your hand. Yet, if you warn the wicked, and he does not turn from his wickedness, nor from his wicked way, he shall die in his iniquity; but you have delivered your soul (Ezek. 3:17–19).

When most people come up to me and say, "I'm a watchman," I usually shiver all over, because generally what they mean is that they believe they are called by God to watch over ME.

I don't believe any of us are called to watch or to judge other believers. We are called to encourage them, to pray for them, and to bless them. We aren't called to keep them in line or to run their lives. There IS One who IS called to keep me in line or to keep you in line. It's Jesus Christ.

That is equally true—and perhaps especially true—for pastors. John wrote in the Revelation that Jesus holds pastors as stars in His hands (see Rev. 1:20). He can hold them up or put them down, close His hand or open it. He can cast them away or hold them tight. That's His decision. That's His role. It's awesome to recognize that you are in the palm of Jesus' hand and to know that God alone is responsible for your life and that you are responsible only to Him. That's a fearful place to be in the sense of holy fear and holy awe.

To be a watchman in this verse is not to be a watchman over your pastor or to be a superior watching over other people in the church. It's to be a watchman over those who do not know the Lord Jesus Christ, those who do not have a personal relationship with God our Father, and those who are following a path of sin. It's the sinners over whom you are to be a watchman and for whom God will hold you responsible!

This verse plainly says that if you do *not* give the wicked man a warning, in an effort to bring him to a decision that will result in his eternal salvation, then you are responsible for his life. He will die in iniquity, and his blood will be on your hands.

On the other hand, if you do give the wicked man a warning—even if he doesn't heed it—you are no longer responsible for him.

The Scriptures continue:

> Again, when a righteous man turns from his righteousness and commits iniquity, and I lay a stumbling block before him, he shall die; because you did not give him warning, he shall die in his sin, and his righteousness which he has done shall not be remembered; but his blood I will require at your hand. Nevertheless if you warn the righteous man that the righteous should not sin, and he does not sin, he shall surely live because he took warning; also you will have delivered your soul (Ezek. 3:20–21).

If you see brothers or sisters in Christ who are sinning, you have a responsibility to warn them. Not to judge them. Not to blast them publicly. Not to point a finger. You have a responsibility to warn them privately. If you discern that brothers or sisters are sinning and you don't give that warning, you are responsible for them. But if you do give a warning—even if they don't heed it—you are free of all responsibility.

Furthermore, in giving a warning, you are warning the erring brothers or sisters—just as you warned the sinner—of what GOD will do if they don't change their ways. You aren't warning them about what you will do or threatening them in any way. You aren't warning them about what you will say to others or about what the church will do. You are warning them on the basis of Scripture about what God will do.

You must—and I repeat, MUST—have a scriptural basis for telling sinners or erring brothers or sisters in the Lord that what they are doing is wrong in the sight of God.

A lot of things you don't like may not be sins before God. We've got to recognize that. Not everybody is going to do things just the way you do them or the way I do them. It's OK to have differences in style or in expression. It only matters ultimately what God thinks about something. Is the act or the condition or the attitude a sin before God? Is it going to separate that person from God and thereby cause him to go to hell instead of to heaven? That's what you are warning the person about. And you must have a scriptural basis on which to make your warning.

In delivering your soul, you are delivering your soul TODAY from having the wellspring of wisdom in your life blocked. You are maintaining a position before God in which wisdom can be poured out into your life.

Also notice that God clearly points to the possibility that the heathen or the erring brother WILL heed your warning. In those instances not only YOU will be delivered but the other person as well.

James also said this in another way: "Brethren, if anyone among you wanders from the truth, and someone turns him back, let him know that he who turns a sinner from the error of his way will save a soul from death and cover a multitude of sins" (James 5:19–20).

The point is, Do you fear God more than you fear people? Or do you fear what people will think of you more than you fear what God will say to you someday?

The question we must really answer is this: Am I willing to give a word of warning to deliver my own soul and to do my part in saving the souls of others?

One of my favorite stories in all the Bible is in the second chapter of Mark.

Again He entered Capernaum after some days, and it was heard that He was in the house. Immediately many gathered together, so that there was no longer room to receive them, not even near the door. And He preached the word to them. Then they came to Him, bringing a paralytic who was carried by four men. And when they could not come near Him because of the crowd, they uncovered the roof where He was. And when they had broken through, they let down the bed on which the paralytic was lying (Mark 2:1–4).

There's a progression as this story unfolds. First there was *anticipation*. The people were excited, telling one another that Jesus was in the house.

The *proclamation* of Jesus in the midst brought forth *cooperation*. Those four men got together and did something for one of their friends.

Their cooperation resulted in *reconciliation*. This man's sins were reconciled before God. His healing was complete so that he could be fully reconciled to his community.

Reconciliation brought *confrontation* against those who spoke against the words of Jesus, which was ultimately a confrontation between God and the devil.

And in that type of confrontation we'll always see *manifestation*. God's power will be manifest to overcome the enemy.

The result of this story was that a man was healed and saved. Jesus concluded, "I did not come to call the righteous, but sinners, to repentance" (Mark 2:17).

Friend, that's our call today. If each one of us would bring just one more person to the house of God next Sunday to be healed and saved, we'd raise the roofs of our churches too! I bless the day that happens. We'd pack out the church buildings that are half-empty each Sunday from coast to coast. And I believe we'd start to hear healing and salvation stories in a way we've never heard them before.

Our call is to sinners, that they might come to repentance. And when we bring people to Jesus, we'll hear Him say again and again, "Your sins are forgiven you. . . . Arise, take up your bed, and go your way!" (Mark 2:5, 11).

The wise person is a soul winner. In fact, the wisest thing you can DO is win souls! God Himself said so!

_____Let's pray about it._____

Father, I pray that You will give me the courage to become a soul winner. I want to be a wise person. I want to have Your wisdom flowing through my life. I want to see souls won to You. Give me strength where I am weak. Give me boldness where I am timid. Give me courage where I am fearful. I pray this in the name of Jesus. Amen.

Part Two

Releasing the Wisdom of God into Your Life

*If you receive my words, and treasure my
commands within you, so that you
incline your ear to wisdom,
and apply your heart to understanding;
yes, if you cry out for discernment,
and lift up your voice for understanding,
if you seek her as silver,
and search for her as for hidden treasures;
then you will understand the fear of the Lord,
and find the knowledge of God.*

—Proverbs 2:1–5

Chapter 5

Sow to Your Life the Word of God

*He who received seed on the good
ground is he who hears the word and
understands it, who indeed bears
fruit and produces: some a
hundredfold, some sixty, some thirty.*

—Matthew 13:23

Do you CHOOSE to be wise?
Have you made a choice for wisdom?

Are you even aware that you have a choice about wisdom?

Friend, you can choose to be a wise person or a fool. That choice faces every person.

Many people approach wisdom as something that you are born with—a genetic or inborn trait. Therefore, they automatically accept that some people are wiser than others. They believe that some people are more blessed with wisdom than other people. As a result, they do not strive for wisdom. They do not choose to have it.

Wisdom is a choice. It's something you can have if you choose to have it and choose to do the things that God requires for you to get it. Wisdom comes from God. It is not something inbred into human nature as an innate ability. Wisdom is a gift or a grace that comes from God, and, like all gifts from God, you must choose to receive it. It's available to you. God not only permits you to have it but also desires you to have it. You must accept it, however, and in the accepting lies a choice.

However, we human beings pursue—or choose—only those things in life that we first "need." We make virtually all of our choices in life out of a sense of need. We need warmth; so we choose to wear a coat on a wintry day. We need love; so we choose to enter into relationships. We need approval; so we choose to give our best effort to a project at work.

Wisdom becomes a choice in your life only when you first feel it as a need.

And as we discussed in the first section of this book, the beginning of wisdom—or the beginning of feeling a need for wisdom—comes with having a fear of the Lord. Do you need God in your life? Do you deeply desire a relationship with the most holy God?

Solomon said, "The fear of the LORD is the beginning of knowledge, but fools despise wisdom and instruction" (Prov. 1:7). David said, "Blessed is the man who fears the LORD, who delights greatly in His commandments" (Ps. 112:1).

When you realize that you do not fear God in that manner, cry out to Him, "O God, baptize me with a fear of You. Let me see You as I have never seen You before. Cause me to hate the things You hate and to love the things You love."

God will always answer a prayer that you might have a holy and awesome fear of the Lord.

"How do you know God will always answer that prayer, Larry?"

Because God will always answer a prayer that is in accordance with His will, and we know repeatedly from His Word that it is His will that we have a fear of the Lord, that we hate evil, and that we love the commandments of God. Pray for a baptism in the fear of the Lord and pray it sincerely, . . . and He'll give it to you!

From that fear of the Lord will flow a heartfelt NEED for wisdom. Out of that need you will either CHOOSE to pursue wisdom, or you will suppress that need and choose to pursue something else with your time and energy.

Most people I know CHOOSE something other than wisdom as their number one priority in life, including their prayer life.

Psalm 112 lists a number of needs that people on this earth today feel so deeply that they kill one another and themselves to meet them. These things are listed as attributes of the righteous man, but they are also, in a larger sense, things that EVERY person wants or needs in life. For most people these needs become their priorities. Watch for these needs as you read Psalm 112.

Praise the LORD!
Blessed is the man who fears the LORD,
Who delights greatly in His commandments.
His descendants will be mighty on earth;
The generation of the upright will be blessed.
Wealth and riches will be in his house,
And his righteousness endures forever.
Unto the upright there arises light in the darkness;
He is gracious, and full of compassion, and righteous.
A good man deals graciously and lends;
He will guide his affairs with discretion.
Surely he will never be shaken;
The righteous will be in everlasting remembrance.
He will not be afraid of evil tidings;
His heart is steadfast, trusting in the LORD.
His heart is established;
He will not be afraid,
Until he sees his desire upon his enemies.
He has dispersed abroad,
He has given to the poor;
His righteousness endures forever;
His horn will be exalted with honor.
The wicked will see it and be grieved;
He will gnash his teeth and melt away;
The desire of the wicked shall perish.

Note especially these desires of men and women everywhere and in all generations:
- mighty descendants
- godly children
- wealth and riches
- a good reputation
- courage so that you are never afraid, no matter what hits you
- the destruction of your enemies

Now most people I know CHOOSE to have those things listed above. They feel a need for them. They desire them. They want them. They make a good effort to have them. They pursue them as priorities.

But Solomon said that the principal, most important thing you'll EVER need is not any one of these things. It's WISDOM. Why? Because WISDOM is the key—the prerequisite—to having everything else.

Do you sense a need for wisdom today? Is it a REQUIREMENT of your life?

The real need of your heart and mine must not be for mighty descendants but for WISDOM to raise up mighty descendants.

The real need of your heart and mine must not be for wealth but for wisdom about how to become good stewards of the resources God entrusts to us.

That same principle holds true for everything the psalmist identified as the desires of humans. The real NEED undergirding our lives must be for WISDOM—for when we have God's wisdom, we'll KNOW how to have the other desires of our heart met fully and in a way that is fulfilling.

Do you feel a deep *need* today for God's wisdom in how to raise your children?

Do you feel a deep *need* today for God's wisdom in how to conduct your business or personal finances?

Do you feel a deep *need* today for God's wisdom in how to take care of your body?

Do you really NEED wisdom?

Is God's WISDOM your number one prayer request? Is it the

number one choice of your life? Is it the supreme thing you NEED and desire with all your heart?

I'm not talking about something that's just nice to have. I'm not talking about having something that's optional. I'm not talking about something that's an extra you might tack onto your spiritual baggage. I'm talking about the single most important NEED that you have today. I'm talking about REQUIRING God's wisdom just as much as you require air to breathe and water to drink and food to eat.

Wisdom is our greatest NEED. We must get to the point at which we acknowledge that need and give place to it.

Then—and only then—we will CHOOSE to make God's wisdom our top priority every day.

Then we will make WISDOM the foremost prayer we pray.

Then we will seek the WISDOM God has for us. And specifically, we will find ourselves seeking the Wisdom Literature that God has put in the Bible.

As long as you don't care whether you have God's wisdom, you probably won't care much about the Wisdom Literature of the Bible. But, let me assure you, when you begin to feel a deep need for God's wisdom, and you make it THE priority in your life, you'll hardly be able to wait to get to the wisdom books of the Bible.

By Wisdom Literature I'm referring to Psalms, Proverbs, Ecclesiastes, and the Song of Solomon. If you let virtually any Bible fall open naturally in the middle, you'll find yourself in one of the wisdom books.

Psalms is the book of praise in the Bible.

Proverbs is the book of practical wisdom—and it is the heart of the Wisdom Literature.

Ecclesiastes is the explanation of a man who had an experience with learning wisdom.

The Song of Solomon tells how to stay committed in a love relationship with your spouse.

Imagine for a moment a parent saying to his or her child, "Look, I'm going to put something in your hand, and when I give it to you, if you'll take care of it, then it's going to be yours, and I'll be able to give you more. I trust you with this thing I put in your hand; and if you are faithful in keeping it, I'll give you more."

Do you believe that if you were that parent and made that commitment to your child, you would follow through and be faithful to give that child more if he kept his part of the agreement? Would you be good to your word?

But imagine that you put a gift in your child's hand and said, "Now you need to take care of this and use it properly, and if you do, you are going to get more; . . . but . . . if you don't take care of it, you aren't going to get any more." Then you came back to find that the child had neglected the thing you had given him. The gift had never been used. It had been neglected and perhaps even abused. What would you do? You probably wouldn't entrust more to your child.

God has put the book of Proverbs in your hand as just such a gift. This book is in the Bible so you might learn wisdom. And if you are faithful to the wisdom that you find in the book of Proverbs, God is going to impart more and more wisdom to you.

I do not believe that a person can come to God and say, "God, give me wisdom. Give me more and more wisdom" and receive wisdom IF he or she has neglected the wisdom that God has already provided in the book of Proverbs.

I believe that God will say to such a person, "No, I can't give you any more direct wisdom. You haven't used what I have already given you. I have put in your hand a wisdom book and in particular, the book of Proverbs. Go back and use what I've already given you and if that doesn't meet your need for wisdom, THEN you come back to me. But first you need to use what I have already given you."

Are you familiar with the book of Proverbs today?

Do you really KNOW what God's opinion is, as expressed in the book of Proverbs?

Are you living your life according to the wisdom that you find in Proverbs?

I believe the book of Proverbs is the key book in the Bible for conveying God's wisdom to us. It's up to us to read this book, to know what it says, to commit it to our spirits, and to live by it. Then, and only then, are we in a position to cry out, "O God, give me MORE wisdom."

God is saying to you today, "Are you going to CHOOSE wisdom? Are you going to CHOOSE to take the wisdom that I've already made available to you and to apply it to your life?"

I believe we can answer yes to that question by making a commitment to reading and applying the book of Proverbs to our lives on a daily basis.

I want to share with you four very practical ways of reading and applying this book to your life.

First, note that Proverbs has thirty-one chapters. That means that Proverbs has a chapter for every day of the month for most months of the year. In some months you need to read an extra chapter and in February three extra chapters. But for most months you'll find that one chapter of Proverbs corresponds to each day of the month.

For a number of years I have made it my practice to read the chapter of Proverbs that corresponds to the date of the month, day in and day out. I did it today. Today is the eleventh of the month, and I read the eleventh chapter of Proverbs this morning. On the eighth of the month you would have found me reading the entire eighth chapter of Proverbs. On the sixteenth of the month I'll read the entire sixteenth chapter of Proverbs.

Each chapter of Proverbs contains a world of instruction. It's as if God said, "Here, this is My operations manual for your life." Most of us are aware of operations manuals and instructional manuals. They come with virtually every appliance or kit or toy or vehicle we buy. Proverbs is your operations manual for daily living. And a wealth of instruction lies in each chapter.

In fact, so much instruction is in each chapter that you aren't going to be able to absorb it all at one sitting or at one reading. You're not going to be able to mine ALL the wisdom of the book of Proverbs at one digging or in one month. And so you make a commitment to read the book of Proverbs again and again and again and again, month after month and year after year for the rest of your life.

Next month when you read a chapter from Proverbs for a second time . . . or a third time . . . or a one hundred third time, . . . you are going to find something NEW in that chapter that you overlooked or forgot about or neglected to see or didn't understand the last time or the last one hundred two times you read it.

That's the wonder of the Word of God and particularly of the book of Proverbs. You never encompass the full breadth of it. You never get to the full depth of it.

Why?

Because YOU are changing along the way. You are becoming more and more conformed to the likeness of God. Events and situations and circumstances of your life are also changing. Relationships are growing and changing over time and with experience. And as you change and the world around you changes, the book of Proverbs has new meaning for you . . . new application to your life, . . . and you'll have a new and deeper understanding of it with every reading.

That's what makes it WISDOM Literature. It's wisdom for you at ALL times. You never get too sophisticated or too knowledgeable or too wise for the book of Proverbs!

Reading a chapter of Proverbs every day puts into practice what I call sowing to the things of the Spirit or sowing to the Lord.

We each must have a regular, consistent time each day of our lives when we sow to our spirit the things of His Spirit. When we sow to our minds and hearts the Word of God, when we spend time with God so that we can give our praise and thanksgiving to Him, present our petitions before His throne, and listen to Him for His direction in our lives, it's sowing to the spirit the things of the Spirit.

When you sow to the spirit, you break up the hard places in your heart. You repent more and more of things in your life that are displeasing to God. You prepare your life to be good soil into which you are planting the good seeds of His Word. You water your soul with tears of joy, even as you weed out the tares that spring up in your life.

The best seeds of wisdom I know to plant into your spirit daily are the seeds of wisdom that come from the book of Proverbs.

As you read the chapter that corresponds to the date of the month, I suggest that you do it this way.

1. Pray, "Holy Spirit, let one of these verses leap off the page to me today in a special way. Let this be a nugget of wisdom just for me today. Light it with neon in my mind and heart. Let me know that this is Your word to me today."

As you read, I believe you'll find that several verses leap off the page to you. You'll see them as if you've never seen them before.

2. As you read the chapter and verses begin to stand out, mark one or more of them with a pencil. You may even want to write them on a card or a slip of paper that you can carry with you all day in your pocket or purse.

3. Meditate on that verse (or those verses) throughout the day. If you have written them on a card or a slip of paper, consult it periodically through the day. Perhaps you'll want to put it someplace on your desk where you can read it several times during the day. Perhaps you'll want to put it on the visor of your car so you can read it as you are waiting for lights to change from red to green. Perhaps you'll want to put it in your appointment book so you see it every time you consult your appointment book.

Say it over and over to yourself. By the end of the day you'll probably have it memorized. Think about what the verse means. Think about how it applies to your life.

Let me share with you how this practice worked for me this morning. As I said, I am writing this on the eleventh of the month; so my chapter in Proverbs today was Proverbs 11. Read this chapter with me. You may even want to read it aloud. As you read, note the verses that stand out in a special way to you! But before you read, let's pray together that the Holy Spirit will quicken one or more verses to you.

Father, we come to You today crying out for wisdom. Cause the book of Proverbs to come alive in our spirits and to be applied to our lives. Reveal Your direction to us today, one by one, from this passage of Your Word. We ask this with faith, believing, in the name of Jesus. Amen.

Now let's read Proverbs 11.

A false balance is an abomination to the LORD,
But a just weight is His delight.
When pride comes, then comes shame;
But with the humble is wisdom.
The integrity of the upright will guide them,
But the perversity of the unfaithful will destroy them.
Riches do not profit in the day of wrath,
But righteousness delivers from death.
The righteousness of the blameless will direct his way aright,
But the wicked will fall by his own wickedness.
The righteousness of the upright will deliver them,
But the unfaithful will be taken by their own lust.
When a wicked man dies, his expectations will perish,
And the hope of the unjust perishes.
The righteous is delivered from trouble,
And it comes to the wicked instead.
The hypocrite with his mouth destroys his neighbor,
But through knowledge the righteous will be delivered.
When it goes well with the righteous, the city rejoices;
And when the wicked perish, there is shouting.
By the blessing of the upright the city is exalted,
But it is overthrown by the mouth of the wicked.
He who is devoid of wisdom despises his neighbor,
But a man of understanding holds his peace.
A talebearer reveals secrets,
But he who is of a faithful spirit conceals a matter.
Where there is no counsel, the people fall;
But in the multitude of counselors there is safety.
He who is surety for a stranger will suffer for it,
But one who hates being surety is secure.
A gracious woman retains honor,
But ruthless men retain riches.
The merciful man does good for his own soul,
But he who is cruel troubles his own flesh.
The wicked man does deceptive work,
But to him who sows righteousness will be a sure reward.
As righteousness leads to life,
So he who pursues evil pursues it to his own death.

Those who are of a perverse heart are an abomination to the LORD,
But such as are blameless in their ways are His delight.
Though they join forces, the wicked will not go unpunished;
But the posterity of the righteous will be delivered.
As a ring of gold in a swine's snout,
So is a lovely woman who lacks discretion.
The desire of the righteous is only good,
But the expectation of the wicked is wrath.
There is one who scatters, yet increases more;
And there is one who withholds more than is right,
But it leads to poverty.
The generous soul will be made rich,
And he who waters will also be watered himself.
The people will curse him who withholds grain,
But blessing will be on the head of him who sells it.
He who diligently seeks good finds favor,
But trouble will come to him who seeks evil.
He who trusts in his riches will fall,
But the righteous will flourish like foliage.
He who troubles his own house will inherit the wind,
And the fool will be servant to the wise of heart.
The fruit of the righteous is a tree of life,
And he who wins souls is wise.
If the righteous will be recompensed on the earth,
How much more the wicked and the sinner.

As you read that chapter, did one or more verses stand out to you? Did you mark them or note them in some way? If one or more didn't stand out to you, go back and read it again, perhaps a little more slowly.

Generally, in my life three or four verses stand out. I narrow that down to ONE VERSE that I carry with me daily. I CHOOSE a verse and CHOOSE to plant that one verse deep into my spirit by meditating on it throughout the day.

Meditate on the Word

What does it mean to meditate?

The word *meditate* is the Hebrew word for *mutter,* which means to "say something again and again." You repeat it over and over in your mind. The idea is that of a cow chewing its cud—chewing its food, regurgitating it, rechewing it, and so forth. That is not a particularly pleasant analogy but one that is really appropriate when applied to what happens to our minds—we rethink the verse of Proverbs again and again and again throughout a day, mentally pondering it and "chewing on it" in our minds.

Have you ever heard a song and then found that you just couldn't get it out of your mind? Your mind kept singing the song even when you tried to stop. That's similar to what it means to meditate on a verse of Proverbs throughout a day.

Do you ever find yourself talking to yourself as you go about your routine chores during the day or while you are driving along in your car? Meditating, from a biblical standpoint, involves talking to yourself. It's not something you do silently as in Eastern religions. It's something you vocalize. You are repeating . . . muttering . . . rehearsing the Word of God.

Let's read what the Bible has to say about the value, or end result, of meditating on the Scriptures. In Psalm 1 we read, "Blessed is the man who walks not in the counsel of the ungodly, nor stands in the path of sinners, nor sits in the seat of the scornful; but his delight is in the law of the LORD, and in His law he meditates day and night" (vv. 1–2).

This person has chosen wisdom. He has chosen not to seek the advice of the ungodly, nor to act the way the ungodly act, nor even to associate silently and unobtrusively with the ungodly. He is choosing God's way—the law of the Lord—and he is meditating on it.

Let me add just a word about "the seat of the scornful." If you choose to associate with those who are bad-mouthing or ridiculing fellow Christians, you are sitting in the seat of the scornful. Even if you don't do it yourself but simply enjoy being in the presence of those who are cynical or sarcastic about the things of God, you cannot be blessed.

Let me also point out to you that we are to meditate on the law of the Lord day and night. I'll be discussing that a little later, but notice it here—day and night.

Here is the promise for the life of one who has chosen the things of God and is meditating on them.

He shall be like a tree
Planted by the rivers of water,
That brings forth its fruit in its season,
Whose leaf also shall not wither;
And whatever he does shall prosper (Ps. 1:3).

Have you ever had plants in your house that withered? They began to wilt and eventually started turning yellow or brown. I've seen a lot of saints that look like "withering saints." They start to withdraw a little spiritually. They start looking tired. Their faith is more effort than joy.

This psalm says that if you will be faithful in meditating on the Word of God every day . . . every day . . . every day . . . then you will not wither. You will have a wellspring of joy in your life that bubbles up like an artesian well. It will be a river flowing from you like rivers of living water. You won't have to run to and fro seeking to prime the pump of your spiritual life. The life will be within you and flowing from you.

That can't happen if trash in your life is clogging up the works and polluting the flow of God's Spirit in you. You cannot be a person who does not wither in his or her spirit if you get your advice from the ungodly or take into your ears the garbage that comes from the scornful.

You must make a decision that you will not listen to certain advice or certain criticism. Choose instead to bless those who speak evil to you, to pray for them, to build them up, and to encourage them.

If you feel that you are called to kick, then recognize that you're

not a sheep but a goat. A goat always says, "But, but, but, but, but."
He's butting something all the time. You'll never correct others by
kicking at them.

Choose to Stay Planted
by the River of LIFE

Choose not to be a withering saint. Choose to be a tree planted
by the river of life.

Realize also that you are going to meditate on SOMETHING,
whether you like it or not. We don't have a mechanism for turning
off our brains. They think even when we are asleep. Choose to put
into your mind something that will nourish your brain and water it
properly.

Now I'm not saying that we should hide our heads in the sand
about what is going on in the world. Reading the newspapers and
magazines to be aware of what is happening in the world isn't the
same as feeding on them. Isn't it amazing that the scandals that hit
certain Christian ministries in recent years sold so many newspapers and magazines in this nation? Why? Because people love to
scoff. It gives them a sense of power, albeit a false sense of power. It
gives them a sense of righteousness, which is really self-
righteousness and not God's righteousness.

What should your response be when you read things in a newspaper that are contrary to God and a godly nature? Say, "Well, it's in
the newspaper, but I'm not going to be a part of it. I'm not going to
talk about it or promote it by bringing it up in conversations. I'm
not going to take this into my life or let it affect my faith and my
relationship with God in any way. I'm going to keep my eyes on
Jesus today and not on what the newspaper has said."

And then learn what your Bible has to say about the matter.
Most Christians I know spend a lot more time reading the secular
newspapers and magazines and listening to secular television programs than they do reading the Word of God. Spend time in the
Word. Get the Bible's opinion on the matter. That's why I believe
that it is so important to begin each day by reading the Word of
God, then specifically reading the chapter of Proverbs that corresponds to the date of the month.

Get the Word of God flowing into your life to nourish your mind and your spirit. Choose to be planted by the rivers of water.

Are you aware that you need more wisdom today than you've ever needed before? The pressures on you are greater than they have ever been. The responsibilities are more pressing. The challenges are bigger. The mountains are higher.

Some of us think that as we grow in the Lord and become more mature in the Lord, things will get easier. Have you discovered yet that life doesn't get less complicated?

Abraham was seventy-five years old when he got the word that he would be the father of a great nation. He was ninety-nine when Sarah actually conceived and one hundred when Isaac was born. Several years later God said, "Hey, Abraham, I want you to sacrifice your son to Me on an altar atop Mount Moriah." Things didn't get easier for Abraham! They got more complicated!

The good news is that with the increased complications comes more wisdom . . . IF you will sow to the Lord.

If you choose to depend only on others to spoon-feed you everything you have from God—and in so doing, you fail to feed on the Word of God for yourself—you are not going to become a TREE planted by the rivers of water. Your roots won't be deep. Your branches won't lift high. You won't be strong to withstand the evil winds that blow around you.

Meditating on the Word of God is the key to becoming a green tree in the midst of an otherwise dry and parched land.

Finally, this psalm says that you will fruitful. You will prosper. Galatians 6:7–9 promises us,

Do not be deceived, God is not mocked; for whatever a man sows, that he will also reap. For he who sows to his flesh will of the flesh reap corruption, but he who sows to the Spirit will of the Spirit reap everlasting life. And let us not grow weary while doing good, for in due season we shall reap if we do not lose heart.

Due season. Prosperity. Fruitfulness. They WILL come as you meditate in the Word of God day in . . . and day out, . . . day in . . . and day out.

Let us review briefly:

1. Read the chapter of Proverbs that corresponds to the date of the month.

2. Ask the Holy Spirit to cause one verse to stand out in a special way to you. Record it.

3. Meditate on that verse of Proverbs all day. Talk to yourself about it. Think about it. Dwell on it.

4. Repeat that verse of Proverbs to yourself and think about it as you prepare to sleep. Make it your last thought as you drift off to sleep.

I believe that this is what the psalmist meant when he said to meditate on the law of the Lord both day and night.

I believe that your last thought just before you begin to sleep goes straight into your spirit. It actually germinates through your thought processes as you sleep.

Now what happens if the last thing you think about is the dirty joke of a late-night talk-show host? What happens if the last thing you put into your mind is a novel or a magazine? What happens if the last thing you think about in the day is a violent television show in which you saw countless people blown away? Those things sink deep into your spirit and germinate in your subconscious as you sleep. Your mind attempts to accommodate those things and to make sense of them. They become a part of your mind-set for the next day.

Now it isn't easy to do this. Generally, you're exhausted at that point and at your weakest. You don't WANT to think about anything. That's precisely the point, however, when you need most to think about the Word of God. If you have been meditating on the Word all day, it isn't as difficult to say as you prepare to sleep, "Dear Lord, thank You for Your Word." Repeat the verse of Proverbs to yourself and say, "I want that to work in my life, Lord. I want to be a wise person."

As you sleep, then, that proverb will instruct you. It will wash your spirit. It will program your mind toward the things of God. And you'll awaken with a mind-set that is geared toward your having a godly nature. You'll find that proverb begins to happen in your life. Because it's part of the perspective that you have on the world, it influences the way you make decisions and the way you act.

Then you add another one the next day. And another one the next day. And another one the next day. And pretty soon you are meditating day and night ONLY on the things of God. Your behavior is changing from the inside out. Your mind is becoming renewed and more like the mind of Christ every day. Your spirit is becoming refreshed so that you no longer wither but are planted by streams of water. You are producing the fruit of the Holy Spirit in your life, and you are prospering in all that you do.

It all begins by taking the Word of God into your life on a daily basis, feeding on it, nourishing your mind with it, and dwelling in it day and night. Your life will begin to be rooted in the wisdom of God!

But what happens if you reject God's book of wisdom? What happens if you KNOW the value of the book of Proverbs but you don't appropriate it to, or take it into, your life? What happens if you decide to bypass Proverbs and seek God's wisdom from another source? I don't believe that you'll experience the wisdom of God.

I believe that it is your privilege, and your responsibility, to avail yourself FIRST of the wisdom God has already provided for you. It's your privilege, and your responsibility, to appropriate that to your life. And furthermore, I believe that you MUST do this first before God will ever entrust you with a great, supernatural impartation of wisdom about any particular issue or project or work or circumstance or problem.

You may say, "But, dear God, I want wisdom about how to cure cancer."

Or "God, I want wisdom about how to make sure that all of the hungry people in the world are fed."

Or "God, I long to know how to win entire nations for Your kingdom."

No matter what your ultimate desire, I believe the Lord would respond to you, "Begin with the book of Proverbs. Meditate on it day and night."

Be faithful to the wisdom God has already put in your hand. And as you grow in that, He will entrust you with greater and greater insight into more specific challenges.

_____*Let's pray about it.*_____

Father, I ask You to help me as I make a commitment to sow to my spirit the things of Your Spirit and especially the wisdom You have already given to me in the book of Proverbs. Help me to be faithful in reading this book each day. Cause Your Word to come alive in my life. Bring Your Word to my remembrance. I desire to grow in wisdom. Help me, O God. I believe that You will, as I pray this in the name of Jesus. Amen.

Chapter 6

Eight Steps for Releasing Wisdom into Your Life

*The weapons of our warfare
are not carnal but mighty in God for pulling
down strongholds, casting down
arguments and every high thing that
exalts itself against the knowledge
of God, bringing every thought into
captivity to the obedience of Christ.*
—2 Corinthians 10:4–5

God truly wants to impart wisdom to your life. If you ever get to the point at which you DECIDE that you want the supernatural wisdom of God instead of your own natural wisdom and that you will do whatever He prompts you to do, leaving the consequences of your life totally in His hands, I believe that He will impart to you His wisdom. He truly WANTS you to have His wisdom. He WANTS you to live according to His wisdom. He's waiting for you to ask.

Recently, I spent a full hour praying in the Spirit and seeking God. My heart's cry was for God's wisdom. I didn't allow any other thought to enter my mind. I CONCENTRATED on the greatest request of my heart—to have more of God's wisdom. The Bible tells us to take every thought captive, and that's what we need to do when we come to God DETERMINED to get an answer from Him. We need to take every stray thought captive and maintain our focus and concentration on the one thing we desire God to do. My one prayer that night was to seek God's wisdom.

At the end of that hour I found that my mind was flooded with ideas. It was as if a wellspring of revelation had burst forth in my soul. My mind was filled to overflowing with ideas and insights for my personal life, my family, my church, the prayer ministry.

I believe that can happen to every man, woman, boy, or girl who DECIDES to seek God in a singular fashion for wisdom. I believe that God will impart to you a supernatural wisdom that will be so rock-solid in your soul that you will know without a doubt that God has spoken to you and revealed to you His wisdom.

Do you believe that you can know the will of God?

That's a critical question to answer if you desire God's supernatural wisdom to govern your life. I have discovered that many people believe that God has a will for their lives. They believe that He has a divine purpose and plan and direction and desire for every human life. But . . . they are unsure about how to discover the will of God for their lives. They believe it's "out there," but they don't know how to tap into it or have it present on a daily basis in their lives.

Having God's wisdom in your life is knowing God's will for your life. It's knowing what God desires you to do about every situation or circumstance as it arises; and as you then ACT on what you know to be God's wisdom, the will of God—His plans and purposes and directions and desires for you—will unfold.

I have a slogan in my office that says:

IF YOU DON'T KNOW, DON'T GO.

Once you know, you must go. But until you know, you are better off to stay still before God, seeking God's wisdom, asking Him for wisdom, and waiting before God in prayer until you have it!

There are eight key steps for releasing wisdom into our lives. The first step is closely linked with the idea "If you don't know, don't go."

Step 1: Admit That You Don't Know

You must come to the point at which you are willing to say, "I don't know." Without fear. Without chagrin. Without paranoia. Without embarrassment.

Have you ever noticed that children aren't afraid to say, "I don't know"? In fact, it seems to be their theme song during a particular stage of life. You say, "What do you want to be when you grow up?" The child looks you right in the eye and says, "I dunno."

"What are you going to do when you get home tonight?"

"I dunno."

"What are your name and address?"

"I dunno."

I thought there was something wrong with my children because they responded to every question I asked with "I dunno."

And then comes that arrogant stage when they think they know it all! They say, "I'm seventeen years old now, and I know everything there is to know!"

The Bible says that we are to come to God as children. It's not a crime to come before Him and say, "I dunno." On the contrary! That's exactly the position He desires for us to take. James wrote that God gives wisdom to all who ask Him for it, and He gives it liberally and "without reproach" (James 1:5). That means that God will never say, "You dummy." God will never put you down for coming to Him and saying, "I dunno."

It's when we think we know it all that we are in big trouble.

In 2 Chronicles 20 we read about Jehoshaphat, the king of Judah, who awoke one morning in Jerusalem to find that he was completely surrounded by his enemies.

The people of Moab had joined with the people of Ammon and the people who lived on Mount Seir, and these three enemies had come up against Jehoshaphat.

And Jehoshaphat did four things. First, he set himself to seek the Lord. Second, he proclaimed a fast throughout all Judah. He called all the people together so they might stand as one person and with one voice cry out to God.

Third, Jehoshaphat entered the house of the Lord and began to pray, reminding God of all His blessings and promises to His people.

And fourth, Jehoshaphat concluded his prayer with this admission: "We have no power against this great multitude that is coming against us; nor do we know what to do, but our eyes are upon You" (2 Chron. 20:12).

"I dunno!" The king himself said this to God!

Now this was the king! Everyone in the land looked to him as the smartest and most powerful person in the land. This was the leader. And there he stood, as a big adult with a lot of big responsibilities, and he said before God and all the congregation, "We're weak, God. We don't know what to do. BUT OUR EYES ARE ON YOU."

When I first came to Rockwall, the posture I took before the Lord was "I don't know what to do here. I don't know how to build a church from nothing. I don't know how to put together a great army of spiritual warriors. I don't know, God!"

Through the last ten years of pastoring this church I've become convinced of two things. First, when a preacher thinks that he knows what to do, he is dead in the water. I believe that's one of the foremost problems with "professional ministry." Seminaries are training young men and women to think that they know what to do in every situation. And the truth of the matter is, MOST of us DON'T know what to do MOST of the time.

Second, the smartest position that any minister—or any Christian, for that matter—can ever be in is the position that Jehoshaphat chose to be in: "I dunno. But my eyes are on You, God."

Look around at our society. Our society—like all societies on earth—is made up mostly of underachievers. Not everybody can be a superstar all the time. That's just not human nature. But we're taught day in and day out through the media that we choose to watch, read, or hear that we all CAN be superstars, that we all SHOULD be superstars, and that we should be superstars ALL THE TIME. We're told how to put our best foot forward, say the right things, use positive thinking, and brush with the right toothpaste—all with the promise that we can be the sexiest, smartest, wealthiest, best-liked, and most powerful and influential person on the block. What happens when reality doesn't match the ideal? You get a whole lot of underachievers on Valium and other drugs, trying to avoid the pain of not measuring up.

On the other hand, the overachievers work hard in the flesh and try to do it all on their own. How do they end up? On Maalox because of the holes that have developed in their bellies. They're worried about losing what they've got and, at the same time, about getting more than they can use. And worry is literally eating them up.

So you have a whole society on either Valium or Maalox. And it comes down to both groups' unwillingness to look themselves, God, and one another in the eyes and say, "I dunno."

It isn't enough, however, only to say, "I dunno." You've got to take that second step to put yourself in the position in which God can impart His wisdom to you. You've got to say, "But . . . my eyes are on You, O God."

God isn't going to freak out when we say, "God, I don't know what to do in this situation." He's going to say, "Great. I've been trying to get you to say that for a long time!"

And then when we say, "But, God, my eyes are on You," He responds to us, "Great! Now let's do it My way."

I see this so often in Christians. They think that because they are Christians, they know how to solve every problem and answer every question. Let some of them loose on a situation and they'll be saying, "Boy, I know how to do this. I'll bind something over here. I'll loose something over there. I'll tell them to let it go. And then I'll tell them to hold on!" And pretty soon, they also end up on either Valium or Maalox.

The Christian—above ALL—should be standing in the presence of God and saying, "I dunno. But my eyes are on You."

Do you believe that if you learn to do things God's way that things will go better? That things will turn out right? It's when we say, "I don't know, but I know that YOU know, God" that we are in a position in which the wisdom of God can start moving in the situation.

When we first married, my wife, Melva, did not want me to

know that she didn't know how to cook. With a college degree and ten years of voice training and thirteen years of piano training, she was—and is—one of the most talented, intelligent women I've ever met. But she didn't know how to cook, and she didn't want me to know that she didn't know.

A few days after the wedding I said, "Boy, I'm hungry. Let's eat something." And she said, "OK. I'll get in the kitchen and make you something to eat."

And she proceeded to go into the kitchen and scramble some eggs—with a plastic spatula.

Think about it for a second. What do you suppose happened to that plastic spatula in a hot pan with those eggs? To put it bluntly, the spatula became the eggs, and the eggs became the spatula. And I ate it, saying all the time, "Boy, Melva, these are great eggs."

It would have been better for me had Melva admitted, "I don't know how to cook." It would have been better for both of us had I admitted, "I dunno what you did to these eggs, Melva."

But we had both been programmed to think, "I've got everything under control. I know exactly what to do." Friend, God is the only One who has everything under control. God is the only One who knows exactly what to do all the time, in every circumstance and every situation."

One of the most liberating realizations I've ever had was the realization that I didn't HAVE to know it all or HAVE it all. I didn't have to make it through this life on my own intellect, my own ability, my own wisdom, or my own strength. How freeing it is to be able to come to God and say, "I dunno. But . . . my eyes are on You!

Step 2: Choose to Pray It Before You Say It

I have found repeatedly that my first response to a situation is not a clear and accurate one. I believe that is true for all of us. Our first reaction is generally rooted in the flesh, not in the spirit; and thus, we simply are not seeing the situation from the proper perspective, which is God's perspective.

Pray in your spirit before you speak!

We often engage our mouths before we pray, and, generally speaking, we get ourselves into major trouble that way.

James wrote that we cannot tame our tongues in the natural sphere. But there is One, the Holy Spirit, who CAN tame the tongue. When we are faced with a troubling situation or incident in our lives, our first response must not be to speak but to pray. Ask the Holy Spirit to give you the words to speak that are of God.

I have found that if I "pray it before I say it," 95 percent of the time I don't need to say anything. God will usually tell me to hush up and watch and listen.

I remember a time when I was the youth pastor at Beverly Hills Baptist Church. During my six years there I worked under the associate pastor of the church, and he and I had conflicts from time to time. Have you ever had a conflict in your workplace? The Bible says that as long as we are in this world, we are going to have tribulation, and since many of us spend a significant portion of our lives at work, that is one of the prime places where we are going to experience tribulation. It's just as true in church settings as in non-church settings. People are different. They have different opinions and ways of doing things and ways of looking at things. And that fact can breed conflict and tribulation.

Now this associate pastor was basically an administrator. I am basically a minister. That represents a major difference in approach to most circumstances in life.

I also readily admit that in my ministry you can usually find two things: dynamite and debris. The two seem to go together. When you get dynamite at work, you get debris. When something explodes, there are usually pieces to pick up. Now the good side of that is that when dynamite clears an area—a stronghold in one's life or a negative stronghold of the enemy in a local church body—the Holy Spirit can begin to do a new work. The bad side of dynamite is that lots of people don't like the noise and confusion and unsettledness that come with that kind of explosion in the hearts of men and women. I'm better now than I used to be in that area of debris, and, praise God, I believe I'm going to be better ten years from now than I am presently. But eighteen years ago we had a dynamite youth group at Beverly Hills Baptist Church and, along with it, some debris.

Our youth group in that church went from fifty young people to fourteen. Have you ever experienced growth like that? From fifty to fourteen nearly overnight. I went to that group and said, "We aren't going to have any more haunted houses and wiener roasts and skating parties. We're going to "read the red"—the red-inked words of Jesus—"and pray for the power."

A girl came up to me and said, "Let me tell you something. If you don't do what we want you to do, we're going to run you off just like we ran off the last four youth directors."

I said, "Honey, you can't run me off because you didn't run me in. Jesus brought me here."

She said, "You'll see. My daddy is the chairman of the board of deacons, and you're in trouble."

Seven days later I cast seven demons out of that young woman. Today she's still serving God. And with that miracle God birthed a revival among those young people. With the remaining fourteen young people, we began to have Tuesday-night Bible study and Thursday-night Bible study, in addition to Wednesday-night church and Sunday services. From those fourteen young people that youth group exploded until we soon had 140 teenagers at prayer meetings and Bible study.

The church had about thirty-five hundred members at that time, and nearly one thousand of those were youth. Melva and I lived in a trailer house behind the church, and we were like the old woman who lived in the shoe. We had so many kids we didn't know what to do! Dynamite was at work. And as I said, there was debris.

Brother Howard Conatser's approach was, "Anything you can believe God for, you can do." Well, . . . I was believing God to reach every young person in the entire nation! We were believing for youth concerts to be aired weekly on national television.

I recall going to Brother Howard and saying, "I want a weekly, national television program to reach young people."

He said, "Larry, our church can barely afford a weekly, half-hour program to reach this local area! How are you going to afford that?"

I said, "I don't know where the money is going to come from, and I'm not asking you for the money; I'm just asking you to pray for me, and if God provides it, don't hold me back or hold it against me. We want to start by having youth concerts once a month."

He responded, "Anything you can believe God for, you can do!"

We began to believe God for this, and God began to provide the finances. A man who didn't even attend that church came to me one day and said, "Larry, I want to underwrite your first concert." He paid for it in full. And every month thereafter we just prayed in the finances needed. Those monthly concerts drew thousands of teens, and at each concert they heard the gospel! I took one offering during the concert, and it was supernatural how the money came in each time to meet the exact costs of the concert—which were about ten thousand dollars a concert for the performers, the use of the building, the advertising, and so forth. Now ten thousand dollars is a large offering from a bunch of teenagers. But God moved in their hearts month after month, and the financial needs were met.

Well, these concerts made my administrator very nervous. His foremost thought always seemed to be, "We've scheduled this concert. What if the money doesn't come in?" I remember his coming to me in December one year and saying, "What if it snows? What if the kids don't come? How are you expecting to raise the ten thousand dollars you need to cover your expenses?"

I said, "Well, I'm just trusting God. God can bring in the money in the beak of a raven if He wants to. He has put this vision for these youth concerts into our hearts, and He's going to provide the money for the expenses."

He just stared at me as if I had lost my mind.

One day I walked into our staff meeting to find about fifty or sixty people seated there. My supervisor stood and said, "Let me tell you, we're not going to have any flakes on this church staff."

Now to call someone a flake where I came from in east Texas was a serious charge.

I sat back in my chair and relaxed. "Praise God, he's not talking about me."

He went on a little more, and then he said, "Let me tell you what a flake is. A flake is somebody who walks a check at a birthday party."

I thought to myself, *Boy, I'm sure glad I never did anything like that.* And then, to my surprise, he said, "Stand up, Larry."

I stood. He said, "You know, Larry, the other night you were at this man's birthday party"—and he called his name—"and we received word that you walked your check."

What had really happened? I was scheduled to do a television taping and had to leave the party early; so I went over to my friend, Jim McDaniel, and I said, "I've got to leave now, Jim; so here's the money for my dinner." He said, "No, Larry, I'm paying for your meal. I invited you here, and you're my guest tonight." I said, "Thanks, Jim. That's just great. I appreciate it." And I left.

Well, someone saw me leave before the waitress passed out the checks, and she told my supervisor that I had walked on my meal that night. And there I stood, in front of the entire staff of that church, set up as the living definition of a flake.

A warm feeling was starting to rise on the inside of me. I felt as if my supervisor had waited for just that moment, just that opportunity to blast me in front of everyone else. I was angry at his not coming to me in private to question me if he felt my behavior was in need of questioning. I wanted to take him apart and rip his head off in the name of Jesus, and just as I was about to open my mouth to speak, I heard in my spirit the words that the Lord had given me some years before: "Pray it; don't say it."

In my spirit I said, "Lord, I want to say something so bad. What can I say to right this wrong once and for all?" And as clear as I've ever heard anything, I heard the Lord say, "Just keep your mouth shut. I'll take care of this."

I knew in a flash that if I said ANYTHING at that moment, I would come out the loser in the long run. Even if I won the argument in that hour, I was going to lose the war, no matter what I said. I did just what the Lord told me to say. I said nothing. I sat down, and the rest of the meeting continued.

It was noon when the meeting ended, and I went over to my trailer house and lay down on the floor to relax and unwind. I felt like a fool. I felt angry at myself for being angry. And as I lay there and prayed, the Lord spoke into my spirit, "You watch Me. I'm going to take care of this."

By the time I returned to my office after lunch, the Lord had already resolved the problem! Word had traveled quickly about what had happened at the meeting, and it had reached the ears of my friend, Jim McDaniel. Jim called my administrator and came over to the church, and as I entered my office that afternoon, they were both standing there waiting for me. They each gave me their personal apology, and my administrator and I became closer than we had ever been before.

We need to pray it before we say it—particularly when we are in tight situations!

Making that decision to pray FIRST leads us to the third step. . . .

Step 3: Wait upon the Lord

In 1 Corinthians 2:9 we read: "As it is written: 'Eye has not seen, nor ear heard, nor have entered into the heart of man the things which God has prepared for those who love Him.'"

The apostle Paul, writing here to the Corinthian church, quoted a passage from the prophet Isaiah, in which Isaiah wrote: "Men have not heard nor perceived by the ear, nor has the eye seen any God besides You, who acts for the one who waits for Him" (Isa. 64:4). The apostle Paul used the word *love* instead of *waits*. He interpreted the act of waiting as an act of loving.

When you wait on the Lord, then, for an answer, you are saying, in effect, "God, I'm here. I reverence You. I fear You with an awesome respect. I love You. And I'm waiting here in Your presence until I hear what You want me to do."

Jesus said, "If you love Me, keep My commandments" (John 14:15). How are you ever going to know the commandments in order to keep them if you never listen to the Lord to hear what He is commanding you to do?

The Bible says, "Those who wait on the LORD shall renew their strength" (Isa. 40:31). I love that verse. The word *renew* can also be translated as *exchanged*. In other words, Isaiah said, "Those who wait on the Lord shall exchange their strength for His strength." That's a great exchange, friend! I'd much rather have His strength than my strength any day, any hour, any minute, any second!

The word *wait* in that verse is a Hebrew word that means "to bind about by twisting." The idea is that of a vine as it wraps itself around a pole or a tree. Have you ever held a sprig of ivy in your hand? It's pliable. It's flexible. It's easily broken or bent. But let that ivy wrap itself around a tree several thousand times, and you'll hardly be able to separate it from the tree. It BINDS itself to the tree. It is capable of standing strong and tall because it is attached to the tree. That's the concept conveyed by the Hebrew word *wait*. It refers to a binding process as we wrap ourselves around God and become fused to God. His strength becomes our strength.

Earlier in his letter to the Corinthians the apostle Paul wrote these words.

> We speak wisdom among those who are mature, yet not the wisdom of this age, nor of the rulers of this age, who are coming to nothing. But we speak the wisdom of God in a mystery, the hidden wisdom which God ordained before the ages for our glory, which none of the rulers of this age knew; for had they known, they would not have crucified the Lord of glory" (1 Cor. 2:6–8).

Note that word *mystery*. This is not a mystery that is so obscure or far-out that you can't discover it. It's a concealed thing from the eyes of the natural world. It's not a mystery to the believer; it's a mystery only to those who are not in communication with God.

Then Paul went on to write:

> God has revealed them to us through His Spirit. For the Spirit searches all things, yes, the deep things of God. For what man knows the things of a man except the spirit of the man which is in him? Even so no one knows the things of God except the Spirit of God. Now we have received, not the spirit of the world, but the Spirit who is from God, that we might know the things that have been freely given to us by God (1 Cor. 2:10–12).

Doesn't this make faith explode in your heart? You can KNOW the deep things of God. He's made available His Spirit so that you might know all of the things—those vast riches of knowing what eye has not seen, what ear has not heard—and know them FREELY. The word *freely* means "liberally" or "in a measure of fullness."

In other words, everything you need to know or desire to know about God, GOD WANTS YOU TO KNOW!

Everything you need to know or desire to know about how to live as a man or a woman of God in this world, GOD WANTS YOU TO KNOW!

Everything you need to know or need to understand about how to have your needs met, GOD WANTS YOU TO KNOW! He makes that wisdom available freely—generously, in abundance, without constraint.

Paul continued:

> These things we also speak, not in words which man's wisdom teaches but which the Holy Spirit teaches, comparing spiritual things with spiritual. But the natural man does not receive the things of the Spirit of God, for they are foolishness to him; nor can he know them, because they are spiritually discerned. But he who is spiritual judges all things, yet he himself is rightly judged by no one (1 Cor. 2:13–15).

God defines the spiritual person as one who judges all things. This means that the truly spiritual person is capable of discerning between natural wisdom and spiritual wisdom. The truly spiritual person is able to discern what God is truly saying about a matter and then acts on it.

God has everything you need. He has the answer for every question you can possibly ask. He has the solution for any problem you might ever encounter. And He freely wants to impart it to you.

Our challenge is to come to the point at which we are willing to decide that it is God's answers and God's solutions that we truly want in our lives.

And then Paul wrote, "'Who has known the mind of the LORD

that he may instruct Him?" But we have the mind of Christ" (1 Cor. 2:16).

Paul was saying, "Who among men is smart enough to advise God? Who among men knows more than God knows?" The answer is implied: *nobody!* And yet Paul went on to give this monumental declaration: You have the mind of Christ. In other words—there's nothing YOU can impart to God that He doesn't already know. There's nothing you can tell Him that He doesn't comprehend or understand fully. But conversely, everything that God knows and understands, He wants to impart to you. He's made it available. You HAVE the mind of Christ, if only you are willing to seek it and receive it and act on it!

Nothing that God knows will be kept hidden from you . . . if you will only ask Him to reveal the mystery to you. Nothing that God understands about a situation will be kept a secret. He's willing to tell all.

This directly relates to something Paul had written earlier to the Corinthians: everything you need has been provided for you through your new birth in Jesus Christ. Every bit of health . . . every bit of sustenance . . . every bit of wisdom has been provided for you through the atonement of Jesus Christ and your acceptance of Him as personal Savior and Lord of your life.

Now this is a critically important concept for you to understand today. You aren't seeking to get something else from heaven that goes beyond your salvation from sin and new birth in Christ Jesus. How can you possibly get more than the EVERYTHING that God has already provided for you? If you have been born again and filled with the Spirit of God, how are you going to get MORE than that? If you indeed have the almighty, awesome Holy Spirit of God residing in your life, what more can you need or obtain?

As Colossians 3:11 says, "Christ is all and in all."

Can you say today that Jesus Christ lives within your heart? Then, friend, you already HAVE the wisdom of God within you.

The question is not "Do I have the wisdom of God?" Rather, it's "How do I release the wisdom of God that is already resident in me through the mind of Christ?"

Paul wrote to the Corinthians, "Of Him you are in Christ Jesus, who became for us wisdom from God—and righteousness and sanctification and redemption—that, as it is written, 'He who glories, let him glory in the LORD'" (1 Cor. 1:30–31).

God, by His Spirit, has already imparted to you the Source of all the wisdom you need.

Once you are saved, . . . you don't need to feel compelled to go out and find redemption or more salvation.

Once you are saved, . . . you don't need to feel compelled to go to some other source to find sanctification or righteousness.

And once you are saved, . . . you don't need to feel compelled to go out and find "wisdom" from some other source. Wisdom resides within you when you have Jesus Christ residing within you!

Say aloud to yourself today, "I HAVE the mind of Christ."

"But, Larry," you say, "if I have the mind of Christ, why am I so ignorant and struggling so?"

It's because you need to learn how to RELEASE that wisdom. You need to learn how to pray for wisdom to be released into your life!

The next five steps we are going to discuss in this chapter are the direct steps you need to take to release the wisdom of God resident in you so that it can flow outward into your life. Those four steps are found in the book of James. Follow with me as we discuss them.

James is the book of Wisdom Literature of the New Testament, as far as I am concerned. The apostle James was immersed in the Wisdom Literature of the Old Testament, which is evident because he quoted so frequently from it. He was also the senior pastor of the church in Jerusalem. He knew how to APPLY wisdom to daily life.

And in the first few verses of his epistle he came right to the point.

My brethren, count it all joy when you fall into various trials, knowing that the testing of your faith produces patience. But let patience have its perfect work, that you may be perfect and complete, lacking nothing. If any of you lacks wisdom, let him ask of God, who gives to all liberally and without reproach, and it will be given to him. But let him ask in faith, with no doubting, for he who doubts is like a wave of the sea driven and tossed by the wind" (James 1:2–6).

What do we DO as we wait before the Lord?

Step 4: Rejoice!

I spoke recently with a woman who began telling me about a major struggle in her family that had arisen because of a major illness. She said that when the family went to their physician, the first question he asked them was, "Have you been rejoicing?"

Dear God, let all physicians find the wisdom for health that this man had found!

The fact of the matter is that rejoicing even in the midst of various trials is a key to your receiving EVERYTHING God has for you—your health, wealth, righteousness, wisdom. Yes, wisdom!

Do you have at least one circumstance or situation in your life about which you can say today, "I don't know what's going on"? I mean, you don't have a clue. We all have that, don't we? There's at least one area—and sometimes many areas—in which we don't have any idea what to do or what will happen or what to think or say.

God is saying through James that when we come to those points of trial, we are to REJOICE. God is not going to release wisdom to you until you first rejoice.

Now what is the fountainhead of your rejoicing? It's your faith. It's saying, "God, I believe You. And because I believe in You, even if I don't have the answers I need or the wisdom I desire, I know that YOU have it, and I trust in You. I'm going to praise You!" That attitude of praise, even in the midst of terrible difficulties, is the first key to opening up the wisdom of God to you!

When Jesus said to His disciples, "Let us go over to the other side" and proceeded to enter the boat to cross the Sea of Galilee, He KNEW what was going to happen. The disciples didn't know.

But Jesus did. And still, He went to an area of the boat where He could spread out, get comfortable, and go to sleep! He knew that there would be a storm, and He also knew that they would come through that storm! He had full confidence that they were going to get to the other side.

I've never seen anyone go in life from one place to the next in obedience to God without a struggle—a storm, a wilderness, a test—some type of struggle. There's always a struggle!

Now in a storm the raging forces against you can sometimes become so loud and make you so off balance that you can't seem to hear God. In a wilderness the fear of the wild animals crying out in the darkness or the constant adjustments to the natural elements of heat in the daytime and cold at night may keep you from hearing God.

In a testing time very often you KNOW what God has said, but you are facing a question as to whether you believe it; or you may be hoping that God will change His mind and give you different marching orders. Shadrach, Meshach, and Abed-Nego faced such a struggle. They didn't KNOW whether they would come through the fiery furnace that Nebuchadnezzar said they'd face if they refused to bow down to his golden image. They didn't KNOW with certainty what the outcome would be. But they did know one thing, and it was the right thing to know. They knew that they needed to REJOICE in the midst of their circumstance.

They began to praise God, crying out, "Our God whom we serve is able to deliver us from the burning fiery furnace, and He will deliver us from your hand, O king" (Dan. 3:17). They knew that one way or another, God was going to be with them, and they were going to be with God.

What happens when you choose NOT to rejoice?

You negate the power of faith in your life. You declare the activity of your faith to be null and void.

The apostle Peter said, "Do not think it strange concerning the fiery trial which is to try you, as though some strange thing happened to you" (1 Pet. 4:12–13).

What happens, though, when a trial hits you? Your first reaction is usually, "Boy, this is the strangest thing." You can't see beyond your self. You start to think that you are the only person in the history of the world who has ever encountered your particular problem.

Peter said, "It's not so strange at all." Don't let the strangeness of your situation keep you from praise.

For what happens when you don't praise?

A lack of praise says, "God, You don't have everything under control. God, You're not really in charge. God, I can't trust You." And then you begin to move into doubt, which is the place where fear can overtake you and completely quench any effectiveness of your faith.

The just shall live by faith (see Hab. 2:4; Rom. 1:17). And the condemned will live by unbelief.

In the midst of your circumstance today make a declaration before God:

1. God, You know where I am. You know all about this situation. You see the ending and the beginning. God, You KNOW.

2. God, You have my best interests in mind. You are working all things together for my good. I am going to be conformed to the image of Christ through this struggle. And I'm going to REJOICE and count it all joy!

Often I have people come to me in counseling sessions and begin, "Oh, pastor, I'm so confused. I don't know what to do next. I . . ." And I interrupt them: "Well, let's rejoice together!"

They stare at me blankly. "Do what?"

"Rejoice!"

"Rejoice?"

"Yes, rejoice!

They say, "But this is a terrible situation. What is there to rejoice about?"

My response is this: "Your situation may be terrible, but you have a great God. Rejoice in HIM. Not in your situation. Rejoice in GOD! Count this experience as joy before the Lord."

What happens when you begin to rejoice?

You draw waters from the well of salvation. In Isaiah 12:3 we read, "Therefore with joy you will draw water from the wells of salvation." You need to pump the pump of praise!

Your praise will release the full force of your faith. It brings it to the fore of your awareness.

And that's the first key to releasing wisdom in your life!

Step 5: Ask Boldly—Cry Out to God for Wisdom

In 1 Kings 3 we read about Solomon's encounter with the Lord through a dream.

> At Gibeon the Lord appeared to Solomon in a dream by night; and God said, "Ask! What shall I give you?" And Solomon said: "You have shown great mercy to your servant David my father, because he walked before You in truth, in righteousness, and in uprightness of heart with You; You have continued this great kindness for him, and You have given him a son to sit on his throne, as it is this day. Now, O Lord my God, You have made Your servant king instead of my father David, but I am a little child; I do not know how to go out or come in. And Your servant is in the midst of Your people whom You have chosen, a great people, too numerous to be numbered or counted. Therefore give to Your servant an understanding heart to judge Your people, that I may discern between good and evil. For who is able to judge this great people of Yours?" (1 Kings 3:5–9).

Right after his inauguration as king of the united nation of Israel, Solomon is told by the Lord, "I will give you anything you ask."

Consider that for a moment. How would you feel today if God came to you and said, "I'll give you anything you want. Just ask Me for it. You ask for it. You get it."

God wants us to ask Him for things and to ask Him specifically. Well, Solomon had an answer! He said, "I want wisdom."

But look at the way he began his request before God. He started with an admission born of humility: "God, I don't know what to do."

Solomon readily admitted before God that he didn't know how

to be king. He didn't know how to wage war. He didn't know how to make judgments. He didn't know how to govern.

One of the largest privately held companies in America today is Cardone Industries—an automotive parts remanufacturing firm in Philadelphia, Pennsylvania. It will do more than 110 million dollars in business this year and normally grows at a rate of from 10 percent to 15 percent annually. Cardone Industries was founded less than twenty years ago by Michael Cardone, Sr.—a great man of faith—and it's run today by Michael Cardone, Jr., a graduate of Oral Roberts University and a dynamic young businessman. I was sitting with Michael and some of his vice-presidents recently in a dinner meeting and one of Michael's executive vice-presidents and his right-hand man, Mark Spuler, turned to me and said, "Do you want to know the secret of our success?"

"I sure do," I replied.

He said, "The secret to our success is this, first and foremost: we don't know what's going on. But also, we know who DOES know what's going on. And we're walking one step at a time in His footprints!"

Solomon said, "I am as a little child who doesn't know his way around" (1 Kings 3:7 TLB).

And then Solomon said, "Give me an understanding mind" (v. 9 TLB).

He was specific. He knew exactly what he wanted from God.

Consider for a moment all of the things Solomon COULD have asked for. On a very practical level Solomon could have asked for long life—to be healthy and to live to an old age. He could have asked for all of his enemies to be defeated. He could have asked for riches. He could have asked for great power. He could have asked for fame. He could have asked for popularity. He could have asked for . . . you name it! He chose wisdom.

In this passage the words used for *wisdom* are "an understanding heart." They can also be translated as a "hearing ear." The implication is that you have an ability to hear God and to know God in your inner person. You HAVE that ability. And Solomon said, "I want to be able to discern between good and evil."

Now how did the Lord respond to Solomon's reply?

He was delighted. Solomon had asked for exactly the right thing from God's perspective. Read how God responded.

> The speech pleased the Lord, that Solomon had asked this thing. Then God said to him, "Because you have asked this thing, and have not asked long life for yourself, nor have asked riches for yourself, nor have asked the life of your enemies, but have asked for yourself understanding to discern justice, behold, I have done according to your words; see, I have given you a wise and understanding heart, so that there has not been anyone like you before you, nor shall any like you arise after you. And I have also given you what you have not asked: both riches and honor, so that there shall not be anyone like you among the kings all your days. So if you walk in My ways, to keep My statutes and My commandments, as your father David walked, then I will lengthen your days" (1 Kings 3:10–14).

Solomon asked for wisdom, and God promised Him *abundant* wisdom, saying that He would make him the wisest person who ever lived. But God also said that because Solomon made the best choice in asking for wisdom, He would also give to him the things he did not ask for: riches and honor.

Are you convinced today that it's all right for God's people to have riches and honor that are rooted in the wisdom of God? This passage says that God was PLEASED by Solomon's request and that He rewarded him with an abundance of the thing he requested, PLUS MORE. His asking for wisdom was a key to his receiving riches and honor.

James 1:5 says, "If any of you lacks wisdom, let him ask of God, who gives to all liberally and without reproach."

That means that we must come to God as Solomon did and say, "God, I really don't understand this. I don't know the answer. I don't have the solution. I need Your wisdom. I ASK You for it."

And James said that God will give it to you generously and without reproach. "Without reproach" means without criticism. When we come to God asking for wisdom, God never says, "Don't come to me with that question." He never says, "You should know the answer." God never makes fun of you for not knowing. He hears your cry for wisdom and ANSWERS IT.

We must come to God in humility and admit that we don't know but that we are trusting God to give us the wisdom we need. And then we must ask boldly for it.

And by boldly I mean BOLDLY.

Proverbs 2:3–5 says,

> Yes, if you cry out for discernment, and lift up your voice for understanding, if you seek her as silver, and search for her as for hidden treasures; then you will understand the fear of the Lord, and find the knowledge of God.

How fervently are we to seek wisdom? As most people are searching for money—for silver and gold and hidden treasures!

Look around. Most people in our society are seeking primarily money. In a recent survey of teenagers most responded that they wanted to have a job someday in which they would make a lot of money. They didn't really care what the job was, or how fulfilled they might be in it, or whether it was the right job for them. They cared only that the job had a big salary attached to it. Friend, they're in trouble—and so are you if your number one motivation in life is to get money.

And yet the Bible recognizes that men and women are, in their natural states, greedy. The writer of the book of Proverbs said, "Be greedy for wisdom." Turn that same fervor, that same spirit of striving, that same insatiable hunger toward gaining God's WISDOM. For when you do, certain things will come your way, and they will all be good things. The chapter goes on to say that you are going to be shielded, guarded, and preserved on all sides. You are going to be delivered from the way of evil and from your enemies.

You've got to want WISDOM, however, as much as most people want silver and gold. You've got to CRY OUT for wisdom. To go after it with all your might and energy. To want it more than you want anything else in this life.

Step 6: Persevere Until
You Get God's Wisdom

Don't let go of God until you get an answer from Him!

You must have an attitude that says, "God, I'm going to ask You for wisdom in this matter, and I'm not going to move or take any further action until I receive direction from You. I'm not going to turn You loose until I get Your wisdom. I'm digging in my heels before You right now, and I refuse to go forward without hearing from You."

James 1:2–3 says, "My brethren, count it all joy when you fall into various trials, knowing that the testing of your faith produces patience." Another word for *patience* in this context is *perseverance*. Yet another word is *endurance*.

Do you remember Jacob?

I refer to him as the grabber. He grabbed his brother's ankle as he came from his mother's womb. He grabbed his brother's blessing. He grabbed his brother's birthright. But then Jacob got grabbed by Laban. The tables were turned. And God began to plant perseverance in Jacob's life. The years passed, and Jacob became a wealthy man in Laban's household. Finally, the time came for him to depart with his family and his flocks and herds and to return to the land of his fathers.

Now Jacob was heading back to the land where his brother Esau lived. He was afraid of Esau because he had grabbed from Esau the things that rightfully belonged to Esau. He had sent presents ahead to Esau in hopes of assuaging his anger. And now it was the night before Jacob himself was to cross over into the land, and he was scared. He had sent his family across the brook after dark, along with all their servants. Jacob remained behind . . . alone. He didn't know what to do, and he KNEW he didn't know what to do.

I've encountered many people in precisely Jacob's position. They've made bad choices in their family relationships, and they're about to face the family member they've wronged, and they're scared to death. They don't know what to do.

And it was precisely at that moment that Jacob made the best decision of his life. Instead of reaching out to grab for the things of this world that were going to pass away, Jacob reached out and grabbed hold of the angel of the Lord. Jacob grabbed for the things of God. In Genesis 32:24–26 we read:

> Then Jacob was left alone; and a Man wrestled with him until the breaking of day. Now when He saw that He did not prevail against him, He touched the socket of his hip; and the socket of Jacob's hip was out of joint as He wrestled with him. And He said, "Let Me go, for the day breaks." But he said, "I will not let You go unless You bless me!"

Jacob persevered. He didn't let go, . . . no matter how many minutes and hours passed, . . . no matter how cold it got out in the desert night air, . . . no matter how much it hurt to hang on. He didn't let go . . . even when his hip was pulled from its socket!

(When you seek God for His wisdom, you may not walk away the same way you came. You may lose some of your cockiness and be unable to do your own "jive walk" out of His presence.)

Jacob didn't even let go when the angel commanded him to let go. He hung on! And he said, "I WILL NOT LET YOU GO UNLESS YOU BLESS ME!" Jacob wasn't going to let him go *until* he had the answer he needed. *Until* he had the blessing he wanted. *Until* he had the wisdom he required. Jacob grabbed hold and REFUSED to let go.

Friend, you cannot be a casual inquirer if you truly want the wisdom of God in your life.

The Bible says, "Without faith it is impossible to please Him, for He who comes to God must believe that He is, and that He is a rewarder of those who diligently seek Him" (Heb. 11:6). Note the word *diligently*. If you are to receive God's rewards, you must be a diligent seeker. You must persevere with God.

You must say, "God, I want Your wisdom. And I'm not going to let go until I have it!"

And what happened to Jacob? "He said to him, 'What is your

name?' And he said, 'Jacob.' And He said, 'Your name shall no longer be called Jacob, but Israel; for you have struggled with God and with men, and have prevailed'" (Gen. 32:28).

God changed Jacob's name from the one who grabs to prince with God. What a change that is! God rewarded Jacob's perseverance! He wasn't annoyed by it. He wasn't repelled by it. He didn't ignore it. He REWARDED it!

"Then Jacob asked Him, saying, 'Tell me Your name, I pray.' And He said, 'Why is it that you ask about My name?' And He blessed him there. And Jacob called the name of the place Peniel: 'For I have seen God face to face, and my life is preserved'" (Gen. 32:29–30).

Peniel literally means "face of God." Jacob saw God's face. He had a face-to-face encounter with God almighty. And let me assure you of one thing. You will never have a deep walk with God until you have a Peniel experience. You've got to come to the point in your life in which you seek God as a requirement for your life, . . . in which you say, "God, I've got to have Your wisdom in my life, and I won't move until I have it," . . . in which you say, "God, I don't know what to do, but You know what to do, and I won't move until You give me Your answer."

That's persistence!

Remember the widow who came to the unjust judge and said, "Give me what belongs to me." He said, "No." She came again the next day. The answer was still no. She came again and again and again and again . . . day after day after day after day . . . until the judge finally said, "This woman is driving me crazy. I'm going to give her what she wants just so she'll leave me alone." And listen to what Jesus said about this: "Hear what the unjust judge says. And will not your Father who is in heaven give you everything you need if you have real faith?" (see Luke 18:6–8).

This woman is often called the importunate widow. *Importunity* means "shameless persistence." She wasn't too embarrassed. She wasn't too timid. She wasn't too reluctant. She wasn't too scared. She had an attitude of "I won't give up until I get what's mine, no matter what you do or what you say."

Let me tell you, importunity and real faith are almost synonymous in the Bible!

You have the mind of Christ already in you. God is looking for the person who will be relentless in his desire to have that mind of Christ released into action and the wisdom of God come pouring into his life.

Jesus also told a story about a man who went to his friend's house at midnight.

Have you ever had a friend show up at midnight? That's probably when your patience is just about at its weakest point, right?

Well, this man came and said, "I need something." And the friend said, in essence, "Call me tomorrow. Call the office. Call my associates. See you down the road."

The man said, "No. I'm going to stand out here making a ruckus until you give me what I need" (see Luke 11:5–8).

He got what he wanted!

And Jesus said, "Hey, that's real faith."

The Bible says, "Ask, and it will be given to you" (Luke 11:9). One translation of the word *ask* in the Bible is "to require." You aren't just asking idly as you go down the road of life. Ask as if your life depended on it. Ask as if it's a basic requirement for your life. When you ask in that manner, it SHALL be given to you.

Now you must ask ordinantly. People ask for many things that are inordinant. I had a man come to me recently and say, "I'm asking God for my wife to file for divorce." I said, "I don't think God is going to give you what you are asking for. It's contrary to His commandments. It's an inordinant request."

Another man came to me one time and said, "I'm asking God to destroy my competitor across the street."

"Destroy?" I asked.

He said, "Yes. Wipe him out. I wouldn't care if God killed him."

I said, "I don't think God is going to answer you. You are asking inordinantly."

God has no obligation to answer your requests that are contrary to His Word or His commandments.

But when you stand and say, "God, You said I have all the wisdom that I need freely in Christ Jesus, and I'm going to stand here until I get it," you are making an ordinant request. It's within the commandments and the Word of God. You are within your God-given rights to grab hold of the horns of the altar and cry out, "God, I don't know how to do this. But You know, and I'm going to trust You for wisdom. I'll walk in Your footsteps as You lead. And if I get out of Your footsteps, I'm going to repent and get back into them! But I'm not getting up from here until I have Your wisdom TODAY!

Step 7: Declare by Faith,
"I Have the Wisdom of God"

Your seventh key to releasing the wisdom of God into your life is to declare that you HAVE the wisdom of God.

"But, Larry," you may say, "what if I still don't know what to do at that point?"

The Bible tells us to ASK God for the things we need . . . and to ask in faith, nothing wavering, . . . and the Bible promise is that when we ask in that fashion, God WILL give us the things we need. That includes wisdom.

Let me describe how this works for me. When I ask God for His wisdom in a matter . . .

and ask with praise that acknowledges that God alone is the Source of wisdom . . .

and ask with humility that is rooted in the fact that I know I cannot operate in my own wisdom . . .

and ask with an attitude of perseverance—that I won't let go until I receive God's wisdom . . .

then a moment comes when I feel a release in my heart and an answer in my mind. In that moment I KNOW that I have God's wisdom on the matter. I often say, "I have a knowing in my knower." That's the best way I can describe this feeling.

Jacob did not KNOW what was going to happen to him when he met Esau. God didn't spell out for him in advance what Esau's reaction would be. But Jacob knew in his own being that he had touched the Lord, that he had received God's blessing, and that the deal was a "done deal."

Recently, the Lord asked me to spend an hour with Him, just

sitting with Him in prayer. I had a dozen reasons why that wasn't the best use of my time, but I knew that God was calling me to an hour of prayer. So I sat in my big easy chair and just prayed for an hour.

I had been talking to God previously about a certain situation in my ministry, but that wasn't the sole purpose or the focus for this time of prayer. I was simply spending time with God that evening.

At the end of that hour God released a revelation in my spirit about what to do in that situation, and I had a witness in my spirit that I did, indeed, have God's wisdom in this matter.

I have found that these times of revelation usually come after a period of wrestling with a problem, when you "let go of it" for a moment and seek God. It's as if you put your spirit in neutral for a while. You put the clutch in, spiritually speaking, and you spend time with God. Then God reengages you in the proper gear and reveals to you His answer, and along with it comes the assurance that it is HIS answer.

You may not know all the details. But that's where faith comes into the process.

The Bible says that faith is the substance of things hoped for and the evidence of things unseen (Heb. 11:1). That witness in your spirit is something you can count on as evidence as you await the arrival of the very thing you need.

The Bible also says that without faith it is impossible to please God. You aren't going to get the full release of God's wisdom in your life unless you move forward with faith.

You aren't going to get God's full wisdom on any matter in a flash. It doesn't arrive as a giant ticker tape in front of your eyes. It doesn't come in a neat formula or with a sign that says, "Just add water."

Wisdom comes when you count it all joy that you are in a position in which God can work in you and through you to perfect you and to establish His kingdom on this earth. You look around and say, "Here I am, God. I'm surrounded by the gossip-ites, the unhappy-ites, the threatening-ites, and I declare to You that I am going to rejoice in the midst of this situation. You are greatly to be praised, O God. You never change. You are the Most High God. You are the Savior and Deliverer. You are the Healer. You are the Restorer. You are the Rewarder. You alone are worthy to be praised."

Wisdom comes when you admit that you simply do not know what to do. You say, "God, I don't know where to turn. I don't know what to say. I don't know how to think. I don't even know what to believe for. I need Your wisdom in my life. My own wisdom is so limited and so weak. I need YOU, O God." Wisdom comes when you cry out to God with an attitude that says, "God, I'm not going to let go of You until You release Your wisdom into my life. I'm not letting go . . . I'm not letting go . . . I'm not letting go."

Wisdom comes when you come to that point when you KNOW that it is settled in your soul. When you KNOW that God is going to act on your behalf. When you KNOW that God is going to give you the right words to say at the right time. When you KNOW that God is releasing His wisdom. And you declare, "God, I don't see all the details, but I believe that I've got Your wisdom. I believe that I've got Your answer."

When you reach the point of knowing that you have God's wisdom, then you must declare to yourself that you HAVE God's wisdom and move forward.

James said, "Let him ask in faith, with no doubting, for he who doubts is like a wave of the sea driven and tossed by the wind. For let not that man suppose that he will receive anything from the Lord; he is a double-minded man, unstable in all his ways" (James 1:6–8).

If you are ever going to see God's wisdom released into your life, you are going to have to come to that point of surety, of certainty, of knowing and declaring that God's wisdom HAS been released to you. You cannot waver on that point. You cannot hem and haw about it. You must declare with the full force of your faith, "I HAVE the wisdom of God in this matter."

Someone may say to you, "So what are you going to do?"

You may not have an answer to that question. You may say, "I don't know the details yet." But you CAN say, SHOULD say, MUST say, "I know that I have the wisdom of God in my life. I

have the mind of Christ. The details are going to unfold as I follow
God step-by-step with my faith."

"But, Larry," you say, "first you said that I was to admit that I
didn't have wisdom, and now you're saying that I must declare that
I have it."

First you are declaring that you don't have the answer and that
you don't possess in your natural mind the wisdom to get the answer. With your carnal knowledge you don't have the solution. You
are admitting your limitations and your lack of ability to generate
wisdom. But now . . . in declaring that you HAVE wisdom . . . you
are making a faith declaration that you are hooked up with God,
who is the Source of all wisdom; that you are operating with the
mind of Christ, which you have received by your faith; and that you
therefore HAVE the wisdom of God working on your case. You are
acknowledging God's unlimited wisdom and His ability to give you
the answers you need!

Abraham—like other giants in the faith—had experiences in
which he called that which was not as though it were (see Heb.
11). The same principle is at work here as you declare that you
HAVE the wisdom of God. You are accepting it by your faith. You
are declaring it by your faith. You are expecting it to materialize in
front of you as you move forward by faith.

Everything in the kingdom realm of God works by faith. You are
saved by faith. Everything else that you expect to receive as a part
of your inheritance as God's child will come to you BY FAITH,
including wisdom.

Now how do you get this faith?

Well, you already have it. The Bible says that every person has a
MEASURE of faith. It's inborn. You've always had faith.

How do you tap into that faith and begin to release it to do its
work in your life?

By hearing the Word of God. By letting it sink deep into your
spirit. By molding your life to it. By letting your mind conform to
its standards. By allowing the commandments of God to permeate
your mind and spirit so that you think them, breathe them, feel
them, live them.

That's what happened when you were saved, or born again. It happened by your hearing the Word of God. You heard what the Word had to say about sin . . . and about forgiveness . . . and about the shed blood of Jesus that bought your forgiveness . . . and about repenting and being born again.

But then you needed to ACT on what you heard. The final step of faith is not HEARING the Word of God but ACTING on it. The Bible says that we are to be doers of the Word and not hearers only. In 1 John 1:9 we read that if we confess our sins, God is faithful to forgive us of them. In Romans 10:9 we read that he who believes in his heart and confesses with his mouth SHALL be saved. There's believing the Word of God and confessing the Word of God. There's hearing and DOING.

And the same holds true for wisdom. You gain wisdom by hearing the Word of God . . .

by knowing God's promises . . .

by knowing God's commandments . . .

by immersing yourself in the Word of God.

You RELEASE wisdom in your life by ACTING on the Word of God with your faith and by confessing that you do not have wisdom in your natural self (just as you can't save yourself by your own ability) but that in Christ Jesus you HAVE God's wisdom (just as you have God's salvation through Christ Jesus).

Wisdom breaks forth from inside your soul into your life through this act of confessing that you HAVE the wisdom of God. You declare it so. And in so doing, the wisdom of God can begin to be manifest in the situation you are facing, the questions you are asking, the problems with which you are struggling.

Rejoice today in your circumstance! Praise God! Take a position of prayer: "Pray it before you say it."

Humble yourself before God and admit that you can't operate in your own natural, carnal wisdom. Say, "I don't know what to do, God."

Ask God for His wisdom.

Persevere with God until you get the answer in your spirit. Hang on to God and don't let go until you have that release in your inner being that you HAVE God's wisdom. Don't let go until you have it! And then declare that you have it!

Step 8: Obey Wisdom

Putting yourself into a position to receive God's wisdom and actually receiving it matter very little unless you actually ACT on the wisdom God has imparted to you.

When God says, "Do this," nothing will happen unless you DO IT.

When God says, "Say this," nothing will happen unless you SAY IT.

When God says, "Move now," nothing will happen unless you MOVE.

Indeed, much of God's wisdom will continue to be unfolded to you AS you move.

This is part of the PROCESS of growing in wisdom. Virtually everything that happens to us happens by PROCESS.

Healing is a process. Financial prosperity is a process. And so is your full salvation. All of these things may begin in an instant. There may be a turnaround moment. But the ongoing growth is a PROCESS.

Your salvation BEGINS in an instant—with your believing and declaring it by your faith. But from that moment you are in a growing process in your salvation. The Bible says that we GROW in grace and in the knowledge of our Lord and Savior Jesus Christ (see 2 Pet. 3:18). The Bible teaches that we grow up into full perfection, or into the full stature of Christ Jesus (Eph. 4:13).

I've watched my children in awe as they have grown. One day they were tiny babies, and it seemed that the next time I turned around, they were children; and now they are entering their teenage years, moving toward adulthood. It's awesome to watch children grow up and to watch them look more and more like you and your spouse. And yet, I realize that everything in John Aaron that makes him the handsome young teenager he is today was IN him when he was born. As he lay in that crib, he didn't look at all as he looks today. But he had all the makings for the man he is becoming. He had all of the genetic code that he was ever going to have. The same is true for Joanna and Joy. They were born with their individual genetic codes already in place.

Now as John, Joanna, and Joy were nurtured and cared for—with good food and the proper amount of rest and so forth—that genetic code within them was allowed to work to the FULLNESS of its potential. Melva and I provided the most healthful environment we could for them—spiritually, mentally, emotionally, and physically. But nothing that we fed our children or gave to them or provided for them caused a change to take place in their genetic codes.

On the other hand, we could have impeded the process of growth in their lives by failing to provide the right kinds of nourishment and the right environment for them. We could have stunted their growth. We could have inhibited their progress and caused them to come to LESS than their potential. Still, nothing we would have done from a negative standpoint could have caused their eye color to change or their physical traits to be altered. Those things were a part of the genetic codes with which they were born.

The same holds true for us in our spiritual growth. When you are born again, a definitive change occurs in your spirit. You no longer have your old "spiritual genetic code." You now have within you the spiritual genetic code of the Lord Jesus Christ Himself. You are His brother, a joint heir with Him of God the Father, and you have the mind and genetic code of Jesus Christ to determine your future spiritual growth.

It is up to you to nurture that growing process—to give yourself the right kinds of spiritual food and to put yourself into the right spiritual environment to release the full potential of that spiritual genetic code that causes you to GROW in Christ. It is up to you to exercise your spiritual body to become strong. It is up to you to study the Word of God under the tutelage of the Holy Spirit to release fully the mind of Christ working within you. But all of the "spiritual genetic code" you'll ever need—including all of the gifts of the Holy Spirit—are planted within your spirit when you accept Jesus Christ into your life and declare Him to be Lord of your life.

Physical healing works according to the same principle. Healing is part of the spiritual genetic code released into your life. The same holds true for financial stewardship and family well-being. It's up to you and me to NURTURE the maturing process in each area of our lives and to put ourselves into the right environment so our full potential might be reached. The provision, however, for our "perfection"—our completeness, our wholeness—is there in Christ Jesus, and it BEGINS to be released the moment we accept His provision for us and declare it by our faith to become active in the reality of our lives.

That's what we are doing when we declare by our faith that we HAVE the wisdom of God. We are declaring that we have, as part of our spiritual genetic code, the WISDOM of God. We believe with our hearts and in our minds that it is part of our inheritance from the Lord Jesus Christ. We know in our spirits that it is so. And the moment we declare it, that wisdom can then begin to be manifested in our lives in its fullness—with all the details, directives, and outcomes we need WHEN WE NEED THEM and AS WE NEED THEM.

Put very simply . . .

Wisdom will grow within you as you walk within it.

_____*Let's pray about it.*_____

Father, I ask You in the name of Jesus of Nazareth that the Holy Spirit will work in my life today, . . . that You will pour out a supernatural revelation of Your wisdom as I repent of the confidence that I've placed in my own wisdom . . . that You will give me a heart of shameless persistence to have the things from You that You desire for me to have. Give me courage to act in my faith. I praise You for Your presence. I praise You for Your wisdom. I desire more than anything for Your wisdom to break forth in my life. I thank You for it right now. And I declare that I SHALL have it. In Jesus' name. Amen.

Chapter 7

The Courage to Obey Wisdom

Therefore whoever hears these sayings of Mine,
and does them, I will liken him to a wise man
who built his house on the rock.
—Matthew 7:24

Will you act on God's gift of wisdom in your life? Will you choose to use it? Do you have the courage to obey wisdom?

With the choice to have wisdom must also come the courage to implement that choice in your life. All of your choosing to have wisdom—including your sowing to the things of God and your releasing God's wisdom into your life—will come to naught if you fail to ACT on God's wisdom, if you fail to implement it in your life on a daily basis.

Wisdom isn't just for "thinking about" or "talking about." Wisdom is for WALKING OUT. Recently, one of our church members, Lorne Liechty, shared an experience with me. Lorne, an attorney, was faithful in attending a Wednesday-night series that I taught on wisdom at the Church on the Rock. This is what he told me. . . .

"I was in a conference last week with my colleagues at the law firm where I work, and we were having a high-level discussion about a particular case, which was a very difficult one. We had discussed the case from a variety of angles for some time and had come to a point at which none of us knew what to do. Finally, I thought to myself, *I'm just going to do what the pastor said*. So I got up and excused myself from the room.

"I went into an adjacent room and prayed, 'God, I don't know what to do in this situation. I admit to You that I don't have the answer. My eyes are on You. I trust You to give me Your wisdom, and I ask You now to give me Your wisdom in this matter.' I stayed there until I felt an assurance in my heart that God, indeed, was imparting His wisdom to me, and then I declared, just as you had taught us, 'I have the wisdom of God in this matter.' I still didn't know exactly what to do but I believed that I had God's wisdom.

"As I walked back into the conference room, it was as if my mind was suddenly flooded with an idea. I shared it with the senior attorneys, and they looked at one another and said, 'Why didn't we think about that?' Pastor, it was the precise course of direction to take!"

God's wisdom had become a living, active thing in that moment. It wasn't a theory. It wasn't a truism. It wasn't something waiting to be made manifest. Wisdom had become a real SOLUTION to a real problem. It was a WAY that could be followed with certainty, a path to take, a direction to follow.

We must come to a new awareness that God's ways are not our ways. The paths He puts before us to walk are not necessarily the ones we would choose or imagine. From my observation our minds operate totally contrary to the mind of God most of the time. Look around. The evidence is everywhere. People are not doing a very good job of managing themselves, their families, their work, their environment, their entire state of being! Human wisdom doesn't work. I guarantee you that the wisdom of demons doesn't work for our good. Only God's wisdom works for our good in every situation and every circumstance all the time! It's GOD's wisdom we must seek . . . and have . . . and require . . . as Lorne did.

Also realize that it took courage for Lorne to walk back into that room and tell a room filled with his peers and superiors, "This is what I think we should do."

God's wisdom is not just for our knowing. It's for our doing. It's for application to our lives. Jesus taught,

> Whoever hears these sayings of Mine, and does them, I will liken him to a wise man who built his house on the rock: and the rain descended, the floods came, and the winds blew and beat on that house; and it did not fall, for it was founded on the rock. Now everyone who hears these sayings of Mine, and does not do them, will be like a foolish man who built his house on the sand: and the rain descended, the floods came, and the winds blew and beat on that house; and it fell. And great was its fall (Matt. 7:24–27).

First, you hear the sayings of Jesus. Then you are required to DO them. Hearing isn't enough to earn you the respect of Jesus as a wise person. DOING what you know to do makes someone truly wise.

Let me assure you that the rain is descending and that the floods are coming. In fact, they are here. We're being deluged in this nation today with an unholy downpour of drugs, crime, immorality, abuse, and treachery on all fronts. The national debt continues to rise, the morality and the morale of our young people continue to sink, and more and more of our nation is being bought by those who make no profession whatsoever that Jesus is Lord. Houses—homes that aren't built on the wisdom of God—are falling right and left into devastation and divorce. The lives of innocent children are being swept away in the debris of hatred between parents. Jesus nailed the truth to the wall when He said, "And great was its fall."

On the other hand, Jesus promised that the man who hears and DOES what He says to do will build a house that WILL NOT FALL. It will withstand every onslaught. It will withstand every deluge and flood. I can't think of a better reason to seek God's wisdom and to DO it!

The Lord said to Solomon,

Behold, I have done according to your words; see, I have given you a wise and understanding heart, so that there has not been anyone like you before you, nor shall any like you arise after you. And I have also given you what you have not asked: both riches and honor, so that there shall not be anyone like you among the kings all your days (1 Kings 3:12–13).

But notice that the Lord went on to say to Solomon, "So if you walk in My ways, to keep My statutes and My commandments, as your father David walked, then I will lengthen your days" (1 Kings 3:14).

Note that important word *so*. There was more to God's promise and provision to Solomon than God's pouring out wisdom into his heart. Solomon had the responsibility to walk in God's ways, to keep God's statutes, and to keep God's commandments. DOING was the sole purpose for and the desired output of HAVING wisdom.

Let's consider for a moment what happened when Solomon DID as the Lord had said.

Judah and Israel were as numerous as the sand by the sea in multitude, eating and drinking and rejoicing. So Solomon reigned over all kingdoms from the River to the land of the Philistines, as far as the border of Egypt. They brought tribute and served Solomon all the days of his life. . . . There was no lack in their supply. . . . And God gave Solomon wisdom and exceedingly great understanding, and largeness of heart like the sand on the seashore. Thus Solomon's wisdom excelled the wisdom of all the men of the East and all the wisdom of Egypt. For he was wiser than all men. . . . He spoke three thousand proverbs, and his songs were one thousand and five. . . . And men of all nations, from all the kings of the earth who had heard of his wisdom, came to hear the wisdom of Solomon (1 Kings 4:20–34, selected).

Solomon had wisdom about politics and government. He had wisdom about botany, astronomy, zoology, and agriculture. He had wisdom about interpersonal relationships and military maneuvers. Where did he get wisdom about these practical matters of life? From God!

I believe that Solomon lived much of his life, day by day, just as he lived that first day of his reign. I believe that he came before God and said, "God, I don't know how to lead Your people. I'm just like a little child; but if You'll teach me, O Lord, I will have a hearing ear."

Because Solomon came before God in that manner, he was given everything . . . and I mean EVERYTHING . . . that his heart, mind, and soul desired. The queen of Sheba, who was massively wealthy and influential in her day, came by camel several thousand miles, and the only thing she could say in summation of all she saw in Solomon's house was that what she had been told wasn't even half of all there was to tell. She was breathless.

How I long for the day when the people of this world come to Christians and say, "I'm breathless at all God has given to you. I'm breathless at the wisdom you have and the treasures God has given to you. I'm breathless at your stature, favor, and blessing. We've been told a lot about you, but now that we've seen God's blessing on you, we realize that what has been told isn't even half of all there is to tell!" What a day that would be in the life of the church!

What wisdom Solomon had! What favor and blessing he received from God! And yet . . . I don't believe any sadder words exist than these: *and yet*. In his latter days Solomon lacked one thing—the courage to obey what he knew to be right. The pivotal words are these in the Scriptures: "But King Solomon loved many foreign women" (1 Kings 11:1).

The Lord had said explicitly to the children of Israel, "You shall not intermarry with them [the daughters of Egypt, Moab, Ammon, Edom, Sidon, and the Hittites], nor they with you. For surely they will turn away your hearts after their gods" (1 Kings 11:2).

AND YET the Scripture says,

Solomon clung to these in love. And he had seven hundred wives, princesses, and three hundred concubines; and his wives turned away his heart. For it was so, when Solomon was old, that his wives turned his heart after other gods; and his heart was not loyal to the LORD his God, as was the heart of his father David (1 Kings 11:2–4).

In those days it was common for kings to have large harems with women from many nations. There were two reasons for this. One was a need for status, which was rooted in lust and a need to show power. A man was regarded as powerful according to his ability to provide for and to keep satisfied a number of women. The larger the number of women in the harem, the greater that man's ability to provide and, thus, the greater his power.

The second reason was rooted in politics. Again, the need for power was at the root. A king would marry to put himself into a position for political favor and political alliances. In one passage about Solomon we read that Solomon married the Pharaoh's daughter to make a treaty with the land of Egypt.

Stop to consider what happens today. Although men might not marry hundreds of wives or take hundreds of concubines, men *and women* are still turning away from the wisdom of God to satisfy their own needs, which are rooted in a desire for fame, power, and insatiable sexual fulfillment, that is, lust. Those things still entice men and women away from DOING what they know to be the wisdom of God!

This is the same Solomon who wrote the words in Proverbs 2, 5, 6, and 7—chapters that all deal with the same theme: how to be faithful to one wife! His favorite analogy for faithfulness to God is faithfulness to one wife! This man KNEW what to do. He just didn't DO what he knew to do.

This man had it all. He was known for his great victories, blessings, and provisions. But he also didn't know how to keep his heart and how to DO what he knew to do. It wasn't a lack of wisdom that led to his downfall. It was a lack of COURAGE to obey that wisdom. Solomon didn't have the courage of his convictions to walk out and to live out the wisdom that God had put in his mind and heart.

If it happened to Solomon, how much more can it happen to us today. The Scriptures say that God came to Solomon and warned him about it.

The LORD became angry with Solomon, because his heart had turned from the LORD God of Israel, who had appeared to him twice, and had commanded him concerning this thing, that he should not go after other gods; but he did not keep what the LORD had commanded (1 Kings 11:9–10).

God had come to Solomon not once, but TWICE, to warn him about his willful disregard for the commandments of God. Solomon refused to hear God. He turned his heart away from God. And the result was the anger of God.

Oh, friend, let us never be in a position to experience the wrath of God! What happened to Solomon? God said,

Because you have done this, and have not kept My covenant and My statutes, which I have commanded you, I will surely tear the kingdom away from you and give it to your servant. Nevertheless I will not do it in your days, for the sake of your father David; but I will tear it out of the hand of your son (1 Kings 11:11–12).

An awesome truth lies in that passage of Scripture. What you do in your life will influence not only your own life but also generations to come. We've lost sight of that in our society today. But the truth of God remains sure. What we do NOW affects not only us but also our children and their children.

Solomon's sons, Jeroboam and Rehoboam, got into a civil war because of their father's disobedience to the wisdom he had received from God. The kingdom was rent asunder and has never been put back together!

Read these sobering words from Solomon in Proverbs 7.

Do not let your heart turn aside to her ways, do not stray into her paths; for she has cast down many wounded, and all who were slain by her were strong men. Her house is the way to hell, descending to the chambers of death (vv. 25–27).

Those are the words of a man who knows what he is talking about! Solomon was describing the harlot of false wisdom, but he also used an analogy that described his own situation.

Notice that Solomon said that the harlot of false wisdom—which entices men away from the wisdom of God and is characterized as loud, rebellious, crafty, impudent, enticing, and flattering—strikes at STRONG men. The enemy is not afraid to go after those who are the strongest in the wisdom of God.

"Dear me," you may say. "What hope do I have?" The point I want to make to you is that you are NEVER too wise to be a target of the enemy. You are never too wise to slip up, mess up, or stray from the wisdom of God. You must ALWAYS keep your heart with all diligence and must ALWAYS be about the task of renewing your mind.

You will *never* get to the point that you no longer need to come to God and say humbly, "God, I don't know what to do."

You will *never* get to the point that you no longer need ask God for wisdom.

You are *never* going to get to the point where you no longer need to sow to the things of the Lord. You will *never* get to the point that you automatically choose wisdom and follow through on that wisdom in your life.

Wisdom will ALWAYS be a choice you need to make. Wisdom will ALWAYS take courage. Wisdom will ALWAYS be a matter of *doing* as much as a matter of *knowing*.

Once you begin to receive God's wisdom—and receive more and more and more of His wisdom—the greater the need to have the courage to obey that wisdom.

How do you get the courage to obey wisdom? I believe that we can receive God's answer as we consider important questions.

Question 1: When Should Wisdom Be Obeyed?

The first key question about wisdom is this: When should wisdom be obeyed?

In Proverbs 3:27–28 we read these powerful words, "Do not withhold good from those to whom it is due, when it is in the power of your hand to do so. Do not say to your neighbor, 'Go, and come back, and tomorrow I will give it,' when you have it with you."

In other words, do what you know to do IMMEDIATELY upon knowing! Obey wisdom RIGHT AWAY.

If you know it's wrong, take action RIGHT NOW to set it right.

If you know it's right, take action on it RIGHT NOW!

Don't put it off. Don't ignore it. Don't wait for "the right time"—which generally will never come again, because the right time is NOW.

When you know to do something, . . . when you know you have the wisdom of God on a matter, . . . ACT on that knowledge immediately.

Jesus taught,

> If your right eye causes you to sin, pluck it out and cast it from you; for it is more profitable for you that one of your members perish, than for your whole body to be cast into hell. And if your right hand causes you to sin, cut it off and cast it from you; for it is more profitable for you that one of your members perish, than for your whole body to be cast into hell (Matt. 5:29–30).

Jesus wasn't talking about physical emasculation. He was talking about taking action on what you know to be right and wrong. He was saying if there's something in your life causing you to sin, GET RID OF IT. There's an urgency to His command.

You don't have to convene a conference about it.

You don't have to ponder long and hard about it.

You don't have to get into an internal debate over it.

Cut it off. And cast it away.

In other words, *stop it!* When the Lord reveals to you—as you are seeking His wisdom—that there is something in your life that you need to stop doing, STOP DOING IT! Right now. Immediately. Don't wait. Quit it and be done with it.

Furthermore, stop doing it *definitively*. That's what casting it away means. It means that you don't go back to it. You cut it off forever. Consider the statements of Jesus. Once you pluck out an eye, you can't stitch it back into place. Once you cut off a hand, it's gone. That's the way we are to be about sin in our lives as the Lord reveals it to us. We are to CUT IT OFF in a way that it never reattaches itself to us again.

If you know that you need to be doing something, . . . DO IT NOW.

If you know that you need to fix something, . . . FIX IT NOW

If you know that you've got to get rid of something, . . . GET RID OF IT NOW

Are you aware that the number one reason so many people die of cancer is because they WAIT before they take action on the knowledge they have? They observe the warning signs in their bodies. They know something is wrong. But they don't DO anything about it. They wait and hope it will go away. And because they WAIT, so many die unnecessarily.

That is true for many illnesses and ailments.

Most people I know who smoke *know* that it's not good for them to smoke. They *know* that they'd be healthier if they didn't smoke.

Most people I know who are seriously overweight *know* that it's not good for them to be overweight. They *know* that they'd be healthier and have more energy if they didn't weigh so much.

Most people I know who overuse their credit cards and get into debt *know* that they should be paying cash and getting into a position of living debt free.

People generally KNOW. They just don't DO.

And one of the key ingredients of DOING is to do it *NOW*.

Today.

Not tomorrow.

I believe that one of the worst spirits that dominates most Christians is the spirit of procrastination. That spirit keeps them from living in the full blessing of God. They experience only what I call a "subpar blessing." In golf terms I call it "bogey living." They are just one stroke beyond par. One stroke beyond the ideal game. One stroke from good.

Some months ago a brother in our church told me this story. He is a faithful member of our church, and during a special season of giving he felt strongly impressed to give his diamond dinner ring to help meet a particular need in God's kingdom. This ring had been a gift to him. It was a truly beautiful ring.

He said, "Pastor, I knew I was supposed to give that ring. I had no doubt about it. But I thought, *Well, this was a gift, so I had better go and think about it and pray about it for a while.* And so I did that. I started to pray about it, and immediately I knew with assurance again that I was supposed to give it. So I went back and prayed a little more about it. I suppose I was hoping that God would change His mind on the matter. Again, I knew I was to give it. But I procrastinated. I began to make excuses. I didn't take action."

"What happened?" I asked.

"About six weeks after that experience I was staying in a hotel in another city, and I left that ring behind in my hotel room one evening. When I came back to the room, it had been stolen."

That wasn't the glad ending to the story that I had hoped to hear.

He went on: "The next Sunday I found myself sitting in church in the same seat I had been sitting in when the Lord first impressed me to give that ring to His work. Pastor, I woke up at that moment to the fact that I had really allowed the devil to rip me off."

"To rip you off?"

"Yes," he said, "I had allowed the devil to rip me off and to rip me off doubly. He got the ring, which meant that the kingdom of God didn't get the blessing that the ring would have brought to it. But he also ripped off the blessing that I was going to receive by sowing that ring into the kingdom. The church got ripped off. I got ripped off. That's a double rip-off!"

I have great assurance today that if I lost everything I have in this natural world . . . right now, tonight . . . and I got up tomorrow morning and said, "God, give me wisdom," God would give me the wisdom that would result in my regaining everything I had lost and more! God says that His mercies are new every morning. There's always more wisdom. There's ALWAYS more wisdom.

If you have made a mistake that has resulted in loss, you can still come to God and say, "I made a mistake. I don't know how to remedy it. I don't know what to do. But my eyes are on You, Lord!"

Friend, that's good news!

There isn't a mistake you can make that God can't remedy. There isn't a situation in your life that God can't resolve. The key is to come to God asking for His wisdom, then to have the courage to OBEY that wisdom and to obey it immediately.

I have found that one of the biggest differences between winners and losers in life is this. A loser looks at the mess he has made and says, "Why did I get in this mess?" Then he starts looking for excuses and, generally speaking, for someone else to blame. Winners, on the other hand, say, "What am I going to do as a result of this mess?" Then he starts looking for answers. That's true for Christians and non-Christians alike, but I believe that it's especially sad when Christians take the wrong attitude.

When you are faced with a mess, don't try to blame it on someone else. That won't resolve the situation. Start looking to God with these words on your lips: "This is a mess, God. What shall I do? I don't know what to do, but I believe that You know what to do and that You will impart to me Your wisdom!"

Question 2: In What Matters Should You Obey the Wisdom of God?

In all matters.

Nothing is too big or too small to be touched by God's wisdom.

No issue of life or subject is off-limits for God's wisdom.

No decision you are facing today is unworthy or too trivial for you to seek God's wisdom about it.

Shortly after Melva and I married, we bought our first new car. Ricardo Montalban had just come on the television scene, and he was the spokesman for Chrysler Cordobas. Do you remember the commercials he did? He could really sell those cars. At least he sold me on them. I said to Melva one day, "Let's get ourselves a Cordoba."

I went down to the car lot and began to talk to the salesman, who showed me a whole line of beautiful Cordobas—a blue one, a black one, a red one, a white one. I looked at all these cars, and then I said, "God, which one?" I prayed about it. You might think that is a little fanatical, but the Bible says to pray about everything, and I believe that it means EVERYTHING. So I choose to pray about EVERYTHING, including the car I drive.

The Holy Spirit impressed me to buy the blue one.

That wasn't the answer I wanted. My favorite color has always been red, and as I was looking at this line of cars, I *wanted* the red one.

I prayed, "Are you sure you don't mean the red one, God?"

The Holy Spirit impressed me yet again, "Don't buy that red one. Buy the blue one."

Now the blue one was really ugly to me. I didn't want it. And do you know what I did? That's right. . . . I built my house on the sand. I bought the red one.

That car wasn't red as much as it was yellow—a bright lemon yellow. It wouldn't start. It wouldn't run. The power steering broke. The starter went out. It was a sorry piece of equipment. That car was parked in the Chrysler garage more than in my garage. Every time I got in it and it fouled up, I would remember that moment when I received the wisdom of God but didn't have the courage to obey it.

Now I'm not saying anything about Cordobas or Chryslers in general. I have a great feeling that the blue Cordoba is probably out there somewhere on the streets of Dallas, still running just fine. It was probably the best car its owner has ever had. I'm saying that God gave me the wisdom about what to do, and I didn't do it.

Friend, if God tells you to buy the blue one, buy the blue one, and buy it now.

Question 3: How Should We Obey God?

How do we obey the wisdom of God when that wisdom seemingly goes directly opposite what we want to do in our flesh or goes directly against the norms of society?

The answer is a simple one but not a simplistic or an easy one. We look to Jesus.

The Bible says that Jesus is the Author and the Finisher of our faith, "who for the joy that was set before Him endured the cross, despising the shame, and has sat down at the right hand of the throne of God" (Heb. 12:2).

The Lord Jesus today is in great delight because one day He knelt in the Garden of Gethsemane and cried out to God, "Give me Your wisdom. Show me what to do, . . . and I WILL DO IT." He said, "Not My will, but Yours, be done" (Luke 22:42, paraphrase).

Jesus prayed, "Father, remove this cup from Me." He wasn't eager to go to the cross. It wasn't His number one choice of things to do the next day. BUT He prayed, "Nevertheless, if that's Your will, I WILL DO IT" (paraphrase).

Jesus didn't just receive the revelation of God's will in that moment. He made a declaration of His commitment to DO that will. And the Scriptures say that Jesus endured the Cross.

That word *endure* says a lot. The Cross wasn't a pleasant experience. Far, far, far, far from it. Jesus didn't enjoy dying on the cross. He didn't like having the nails driven through His hands and feet. He ENDURED it.

Sometimes you'll receive the wisdom of God, and God will direct you to do something you don't really delight in doing. Sometimes the wisdom of God will be a bitter herb to you. It will be contrary to the way you want to do things or the way you want to experience life. But if you will swallow that bitter pill—or, in other words, go ahead and DO what you know to do, no matter how hard it is and no matter how much you have to ENDURE—then you'll find yourself in a position to be resurrected by God with great victory!

The discipline of obeying wisdom always comes before the delight of receiving God's promise!

In our world today most folks won't do anything that brings them any sense of discomfort. They won't do anything that brings them any pain. They won't do anything that brings them suffering.

I'm telling you today that God's wisdom doesn't always result in what you want or in a sense of pleasure, comfort, and ease.

At times God's wisdom says no, and everything within you wants a yes.

At times God's wisdom says to go, and everything within you wants to stay.

At times God's wisdom says to be silent, and everything in you wants to cry out.

At times God's wisdom says to buy something and you don't want to do it; and times when God's wisdom says not to buy that, and you feel as if the money is going to burn a hole in your pocket.

Many times the wisdom of God compels you to step forward, and your flesh says not to budge.

In fact . . .

You may very well find that MOST OF THE TIME God's wisdom cuts across the grain of what you want to do in life. The flesh and the spirit are in conflict. The Scripture says that there's a war between your flesh and your spirit. It's tough to obey the wisdom of God. But always *always*, ALWAYS, *ALWAYS* we have the promise of victory, resurrection, and reward when we obey the wisdom of God.

What did Jesus endure on the cross?

He endured the *shame* of it. Death by crucifixion was a despicable death. It was the most humiliating, publicly embarrassing, blatantly dehumanizing death a person could experience—to die along a public highway, half-naked, and labeled as a public enemy.

He endured the *pain* of it. Death by crucifixion was agonizing to His physical body. Jesus didn't have some type of supernatural body that didn't experience pain or suffering. He felt those nails. He felt that crown of thorns piercing His skull. He felt the raw, open wound that had been His back.

He endured the *loneliness* of it. Jesus felt as if even God had forsaken Him.

What are you unwilling to endure today in light of what He endured for you?

Are you afraid of a little ridicule from your neighbors? Are you afraid to give up a creature comfort? Are you afraid that you may be isolated from some of your friends?

If you are . . . and you are to the point of failing to ACT on the wisdom God gives you, . . . then God is under no obligation to give you the reward and victory associated with His resurrection power.

If you receive God's wisdom and refuse to act on it, then God is not obligated to give you further wisdom.

You do not have the option of saying, "God, I have your wisdom on this, and I don't like it. Give me a plan B." That isn't your prerogative! You have only one choice when you receive God's wisdom on a matter: to move forward and ACT on it or to disobey it.

When you obey, you put yourself into a position of reward, benefit, resurrection, victory. When you DISobey, you disobey. There's no plan B. God has no more responsibility to give you wisdom on that matter until and unless you obey what He has already told you to do.

You may be saying, "That's a hard teaching, Larry."

Yes, it is hard. It's tough. I've never said and, more importantly, the Bible has never said that following Jesus and walking in the wisdom of God are easy.

The writer of Hebrews said, however, that Jesus endured the cross "for the joy that was set before Him" (Heb. 12:2).

He had a purpose for going to the cross, and He had a goal; but above all, He had the promise of victory.

You aren't always going to know the precise outcome of your actions. You aren't always going to be able to see the big picture or know the long-range impact of what you do and say. But you CAN experience the joy that is set before you. You CAN know that God has something good in mind for you and that victory, resurrection, and blessing are coming your way as a result of your obedience and your endurance.

Your walk of faith is a walk. It's going from faith to faith. And at each level of faith . . . at each step up that faith ladder . . . you are going to find obedience, endurance, death, burial, and resurrection. Jesus' experience on the cross was the culmination of an entire life of obedience, endurance, death to self, and resurrection in

God. The Cross was the climax of a long walk marked by the same steps of faith. You won't encounter obedience just once. You'll encounter it again and again as your faith grows and as your wisdom increases.

Let's get very practical for a moment.

The Lord says to you, dear husband or dear wife, "Be faithful to your spouse." The flesh says to you, "Be unfaithful." The world says to you, "Be unfaithful." The forces of hell say to you, "Be unfaithful."

The wisdom of God is enduring. It doesn't change. It stands as a fixed standard. The temptations of the flesh, the world, and the devil are equally enduring. They are constant. You aren't going to be tempted just once at this point. You aren't going to be tempted just early in your marriage, or midway in your life, or later in life. That temptation is likely to be there just about every day, every month, every year of your entire married life! The key question is: is your ENDURANCE going to be as enduring as God's wisdom? Will you have the courage to obey wisdom and *continue* to have the courage to obey wisdom again and again and again?

What is your reward for faithful endurance in God's wisdom? I believe that it is the blessing of a love for your wife that is ecstatic. I'm not talking about an ordinary love. I'm talking about an extraordinary love. God will reward you with the kind of love that He designed for you to have in the first place.

Let's consider the issue of soul winning.

All the members of your church, including *you*, are called to be soul winners to every person they meet all the time. That's the wisdom of God for your life. He will give you no higher calling or more noble job on this earth.

Soul winning takes endurance. It sometimes requires enduring shame, pain, and loneliness.

The wisdom of the world, the flesh, and the devil about spiritual matters, including soul winning, is the exact opposite of God's wisdom. God's wisdom says, "Give away everything God gives to you. As He gives you love, give it away. As He gives you money, give it away. As He gives you joy, give it away!" The world's wisdom says,

"Get all you can and can all you get." The wisdom of the flesh says, "You can never get enough. If it's good, get more of it." The devil says, "God doesn't have anything better to give you than what you can get on your own."

What happens, however, when you obey God's wisdom? Let me assure you, there's no greater high in this life than in leading someone to Jesus. There's no greater sense of purpose, satisfaction, and joy than in telling someone about Jesus and having him make a decision to live in heaven instead of in hell.

God's promise is that when you give something of Him away, you're going to receive a multiplied amount of that same thing in your life. You were never called to be a reservoir of anything God gives you—not a reservoir of finances, nor a reservoir of revelation, nor a reservoir of God's light. You were called to be a blessing. That's the initial promise to Abraham: "I will bless you, and you will be a blessing."

I've noticed something about rivers. They get bigger and bigger (generally speaking, both wider and deeper) as they flow from tiny rivulets toward the oceans. They don't begin big and diminish. They begin small and grow. That's the promise of God to you in every area of your life. As you give your God-given blessings to others, you'll get even more blessing to give, which will result in even more blessings to give, and so on until you'll have so much blessing that you won't even know what to do with it all. (Both Malachi 3:10 and Luke 6:38 promise this!)

The greatest moments you can experience in life aren't going to be spent sitting curled up in front of your fireplace on a rainy night, watching television. The greatest moments in your life aren't going to be spent alone in an isolated place singing, "Make the world go away." The greatest moments in your life aren't going to be the ones you spend in the loving arms of your spouse. The greatest moments of your life are going to be the ones you spend telling someone about Jesus and praying the sinner's prayer with them. And if you don't know that to be true, then you haven't experienced soul winning.

The height of selfishness is having something that the world is dying for—literally—and sitting on it and not sharing it.

And the key to soul winning is to do it all the time. To everyone you meet. In every place. I truly believe that any conversation you have in which more than three sentences are spoken ought to include the name of Jesus. That's enduring as a soul winner. That's DOING what we know to be the wisdom of God and doing it with the joy that is set before us and with enduring power.

How are we to obey the wisdom God gives us? With endurance! We're to be consistent in the way we obey.

How are we to obey the wisdom God gives us? With an eye toward the joy that God has set before us! We're to have a holy expectation as we obey God's wisdom.

The wisdom of God says, "Obey."

The wisdom of the unholy trinity—the flesh, the world, and the devil—says, "Don't do it."

What will you do today? Do you have the courage to obey?

_____Let's pray about it._____

Father, I ask You today for ENDURING power to DO what You have called me to do and be. I ask for Your courage, Your strength, Your perseverance, Your ability to flow through my life so that I WILL go where You lead me, SAY what You compel me to say, and DO what You want me to do. Forgive me, dear Lord, for failing You. Forgive me for turning aside from doing what You have shown me to do. Give me the courage to begin setting things right TODAY, beginning now. I pray this in the name of Jesus. Amen.

Part Three

Applying Wisdom

Wisdom is justified by her children.
　　　　　　—Matthew 11:19

Either make the tree good and its fruit good,
or else make the tree bad and its fruit bad;
for a tree is known by its fruit.
　　　　　　—Matthew 12:33

Chapter 8

Wisdom and the Family

*By this all will know that you are
My disciples, if you have love
for one another.*
—John 13:35

Why have wisdom?

So it can impact your LIFE.

Wisdom isn't for heaven. It's for NOW, on this earth.

Wisdom isn't just for the knowing. It's for the doing.

Wisdom isn't for your mind. It's for your hands and feet to implement.

God imparts wisdom to you so you can make a difference in this world, . . . so you can extend His kingdom, . . . so you can enter into the fullness of His blessings for you.

Perhaps in no other arena is wisdom more practical or necessary than in family relationships.

Jesus had some astonishing words to say to His disciples about family relationships. We find His teaching in Luke 14:26: "If anyone comes to Me and does not hate his father and mother, wife and children, brothers and sisters, yes, and his own life also, he cannot be My disciple."

That may seem like a strange place to start in a chapter about wisdom and the family. But I believe that it reflects the issue that is at the crux of all family relationships—both the relationship between a husband and a wife, and that between a parent and a child.

Now *hate* is a very strong word. But Jesus was not saying that we must literally hate our family members. He was saying that *in comparison* to our love for Him our feelings for our family members will seem like hatred.

To begin to love your family, you must first love Jesus Christ. The wisest thing you can do for your family is to make Jesus Christ the Lord of your life and your home. You must be willing to lay your family on the altar of sacrifice in your spirit before God and to trust Him completely with their lives.

I do not mean in any way to engender an attitude of carelessness about our families—or about the relationship we have with our spouses or our children, our parents, our grandparents, or our other family members.

The overarching wisdom on this matter of your family is that you are willing to commit your family into the hands of God.

I came to this point in my teenage years in a prayerful agreement I made with my mother. My father at that time seemed to be a hopeless alcoholic. Nothing my mother, sister, and I did or said seemed to have any effect on my father, unless it was to make matters worse. Our family life suffered as a result of his addiction.

One day I said to my mother, "Mother, we are going to have to commit Daddy to the Lord. We can't carry him anymore."

We joined in a prayer turning over the full care, worry, and responsibility for my daddy's life to Jesus Christ. We entrusted my father fully to His care.

I believe that our act of committing my father to the love of Jesus actually opened the door for the Lord to have full sway and influence in Daddy's life. No longer were we standing in God's way, . . . no longer were we influencing his relationship with the Lord, . . . no longer were we holding back God's hands by our trying to be an earthly "savior" or "deliverer" or "healer" for Daddy in the Lord's place.

My father DID come to know the Lord Jesus as his personal

Savior and Lord. He was delivered from alcohol. Our family life DID improve. But it happened only when we were willing to entrust Daddy totally and completely to the Lord.

This same thing happened in a slightly different way with my son.

In 1977 I had a recurring nightmare that my three-year-old son, John Aaron, died. The first time the dream came, I rebuked the devil. The next time the dream came, I rebuked him stronger, but I was beginning to feel afraid about it. I was really too afraid to pray about it. The third time I had the dream, I awoke at about four o'clock in the morning, went in to my place of prayer, knelt there, and had an encounter with God. The Lord spoke in my spirit, "Are you willing to give him to Me?"

I knew that I had dedicated John Aaron to the Lord as a baby, but I also knew in my heart that I had not totally released John to the will of God. I came face-to-face with the fact that I was guilty of idolizing my son and my family.

Are you shocked by the idea that a parent can idolize his children or his family? You can! You can put your family concerns before your concerns about the Lord. You can put your family love ahead of your love for Jesus. You can be unwilling to trust God totally and completely with your family and hold on to them in your spirit, which becomes an act of disobedience and a lack of faith before God. Your love for your family member at that point becomes an inordinant love before God.

I said, "Lord, I dedicated John Aaron to You when he was born in 1974, and tonight I am declaring to You that I am not going to take him back. He's Yours." I spoke those words with a great sense of fear. The dream was still vivid in my mind, and I knew that the Lord might be using that dream to prepare me for John Aaron's death.

At the minute those words were fully released from my mouth, however, I had one of the clearest visions of my entire life. I saw John Aaron running into the presence of Jesus Christ in heaven. He leaped up into Jesus' arms, and as Jesus scooped him up and held him close, I saw the expression on John Aaron's face. It was one of total bliss, . . . total joy, . . . and total relaxation. At that moment all the pain and fear I had been experiencing about losing my son left me. I felt a complete release in my spirit, and the joy and relaxation I had seen on John Aaron's face entered my heart also.

By the time the vision ended and I came to myself, it was about 4:30 in the morning. I heard a knock at the door of the room in which I was praying, and I opened the door to find John Aaron standing there. He said, "Daddy, I just had a dream."

I asked, "John Aaron, what did you dream?"

He said, "I dreamed that I ran and jumped into the arms of Jesus."

When he said that, I had a benefit. If you are going to have a "fit," then you might as well have a benefit. You might as well turn it into a time of rejoicing. We went immediately into my bedroom, and I awoke Melva Jo. We stayed up the rest of the night and had a time of rejoicing. We prayed with John Aaron, and, as we prayed, the Lord spoke in my spirit: "Because you were willing to give him to Me, you are going to have many years to serve with him in ministry. Your relationship will not be an inordinant relationship. It will be a pure and loving relationship that is holy to Me."

That night I fully committed my family to the watch care of the Holy Spirit of God.

I believe that each of us must come to that point that we say, "God, my marriage is in Your hands. My children are in Your hand. Our family is in Your hand. I release them from my hand to Your hand. They are ultimately Your responsibility."

At that point—and only at that point—does the Lord have totally free rein to work in your family circumstances and family situations and family relationships.

Now this is not only something that a father and husband does. It is also something that a child needs to do with his or her parents. It is something that a wife and mother needs to do with regard to her husband and children. It's something that grandparents need to do regarding their grandchildren. As long as you are holding on to any other person and are unwilling to commit the person COMPLETELY to the watch care of God, you are impeding the work that God can do in that person's life.

Furthermore, as long as you are trying to be "God" for your family members—to be their source of supply, to be their source of love, to have all of their trust wrapped up in you, and so forth— then God's work in YOUR life is also impeded. You are limiting God. You are roping off areas of trust in which you won't allow God to work. And when you do that, you cannot truly be a disciple who is willing to go wherever God wants you to go or to do anything God asks you to do. You'll always have strings attached to your willingness to serve God—and, specifically, the "strings" of family members and your inordinate relationships with them.

I believe that your willingness to make an absolute declaration that "Jesus is Lord over my family members" is what Jesus Himself was alluding in Luke 14:26. He was saying that if you are not willing to cast your family members to the care of God and trust God with them, you cannot truly be His disciple. Something in your relationship with God will impede your discipleship and the discipleship of your family members.

Before you can move fully into God's wisdom for your family, you MUST be willing to commit them to God.

If you haven't made that commitment today, let's begin by praying together:

Father, we stand before You today to declare that Jesus bought my family with His shed blood on the cross of Calvary. He owns my family. And I love Him supremely. Therefore, I commit my family members into the hands of God today . . . and forever!

Once you have made that full and complete commitment in your heart, I believe that the Word of God has seven specific points of wisdom for your family members. I have summarized these wisdom statements into specific words. Let's explore them together. . . .

Word of Wisdom 1: Covenant

The word *covenant* relates to husbands and wives. It is not a popular word today. A more common word in our society today, even in Christian circles, is the word *contract*. But I declare to you today that a contract is not a covenant.

A contract made between two persons can be broken. A covenant cannot be broken.

Now let me speak a word right here to those of you who may be reading this who have been through a divorce and who have remarried. My word to you is this: you can do nothing about your past at this point except to repent of it, ask for God's mercy on your life, and move forward in forgiveness with a determination that you will not make the same mistake again.

At the same time, we must realize that divorce is not God's will for His children. It is not His permissible will. It is not His prescribed will. It is not in any way His will. His desire is for the marriage covenant to be just that—a covenant, an unbroken relationship.

Three concepts are involved in the creation of a biblical marriage covenant.

First, leave your father and mother.

That means more than just moving out of their house. It means that you leave behind the "baggage" of emotional ties and problems. You no longer expect your parents to support you financially. You leave behind the patterns of your previous life; you no longer expect to live your life according to previous routines. You also are no longer responsible for your parents' behavior. You make a clean break.

I cannot begin to tell you how many people I have counseled in my role as a pastor who have come to me with problems in their marriage that could be resolved by taking one simple step: "Leave Mom and Dad." Adult children of alcoholics and drug addicts often continue to feel emotionally responsible for their parents. So do the adult children of divorced parents. Many people are still tied to their parents financially. Others continue to be in codependent relationships with one or both parents in which they draw all of their sense of praise and reward—and conversely, punishment and criticism—from their parents.

The marriage covenant begins with the understanding that you will LEAVE mother and father.

Second, cleave only to your spouse.

To cleave means "to bond." It's the idea of bonding something with glue. You bond to your spouse both physically and emotionally.

Have you ever glued something together with a very strong glue? The bond is so tight that no amount of pulling or leverage can separate the two pieces. Nothing can be wedged in between. Well, that's the same concept as the cleaving aspect of a biblical covenant relationship with your spouse. You allow nothing to pull you apart. You allow nothing to get wedged between you!

Third, you become one flesh.

One plus one in marriage doesn't equal two. It equals one—before the Lord.

Once you are married, God no longer deals with you as an individual. He deals with you as a married person. In other words, He deals with you always in reference to your spouse. The Bible says, "You are no longer twain. You are one flesh."

In a practical way God's dealing in your life is like looking in a mirror and seeing your spouse reflected there. Any way that God begins to deal with you must be directly related to God's dealing in your spouse's life. There simply isn't a case in which God calls one spouse to do something and calls the other spouse to resist it or go the opposite direction. Now one spouse might be willing to follow God's call, and the other might be UNWILLING to follow God's call, and that results in conflict. But GOD doesn't call one spouse to do something that will cause friction or separation from the other person. From the moment your marriage vows are spoken, God deals with you as a couple, not as two unlinked individuals.

God's dealing in my life is always in direct correlation with His dealing in Melva Jo's life, and vice versa.

Now if spouses fall out of sorts with each other and do not strive for a harmony in their spirits, in their thinking, or in their relationship, then the Bible clearly says that their prayers will be hindered! The Bible teaches, "You husbands, dwell with them with understanding, giving honor to the wife, as to the weaker vessel, and as being heirs together of the grace of life, that your prayers may not be hindered" (1 Pet. 3:7).

If you are married, you are never going to be all you can be in this life for the Lord, apart from your spouse's being all he or she can be in the Lord. God no longer deals with you as two but as one.

That is a radical concept. I believe that's why the Bible says, "Let each one of you in particular so love his own wife as himself, and let the wife see that she respects her husband" (Eph. 5:33). Do you really understand, husband, that if you don't take care of your wife, you aren't really taking care of yourself? God no longer sees you as separate, but as one.

These, then, are the three covenant concepts: *leave, cleave, and be one.*

I'm sad that the ministry in many instances has been remiss in teaching people these three covenant concepts. These covenant concepts are the foundation for a Christian marriage from God's perspective.

Now I don't believe that marriage is something you are always supposed to be working at or putting up with. One man said to me one day, "I feel as if I'm in jail."

That isn't the way God designed it to work. Marriage is intended to be the most freeing institution on earth. I don't believe in a concept of marriage that is just a convention so the couple can go to church together in the same car or share the same house. I believe that the Bible is true when it says that God wants a husband to be "enraptured with her love" (Prov. 5:19). That Hebrew word for *enraptured* literally means "ravished" or "intoxicated." The idea is that one is reeling with love.

Have you ever asked a newly married young man, "Do you love her?"

"Boy, do I!"

And then six months later you see him, and you ask, "Do you love her?"

"Yeah, I love her."

And then a year or so later you see him again, and you ask, "Do you love her?"

"I'm still with her."

Somewhere along the way he has lost that loving feeling. That's not the way God intended it. And I'm convinced that if you meet the conditions of the marriage covenant—leave, cleave, and be one—that you will find a deep, abiding love that is spiritual, emotional, physical, and committed. When you meet the conditions of the covenant, you are in a position to ask God to baptize you with a baptism of love for your spouse, and He will do it! He commanded you to do it, and He will give you the grace and ability to do it—just as He gives you the grace and ability to do anything else He commands you to do . . . IF you will meet the basic conditions of the covenant. In the case of marriage the basic conditions are *leave, cleave, and be one.*

I pray this every day as a part of my prayer time. I encourage you to do the same. When I come to the part of the Lord's Prayer in which we say, "Your kingdom come, Your will be done," I pray, "Lord, Your kingdom come in my family," and then I add, . . . "I choose to leave father and mother and to cleave only to my wife and to be one with her."

I choose to lay any emotional ties or anything inordinant before God for a proper relationship with my wife. I break that tie in prayer when I say, "I *choose* to leave father and mother. I *choose* to cleave to my wife. I *choose* to be one with her." It is an act of my will.

And then I pray, "I ask You this day, God, to infuse me with a love for my wife that will flow through me and flow through her, through us to our children, and through them to their children, for as long as the Lord tarries."

Word of Wisdom 2: Communicate

We have lost so much of our ability to communicate in this day and age because so many of us spend so much time at home in front of the television. We have become professional couch potatoes.

Let me share with you some practical illustrations about communication, drawn from my own marriage.

First, MAKE the time for communication with your spouse and children.

Melva and I schedule time every week for several hours just to be together and to communicate. Last Saturday we left the house together about two o'clock in the afternoon and just drove around in the car and rolled the windows down and played the radio loud and had a big ol' time laughing and talking. (Now a man pulled me over and cursed at me about my driving. . . . Well, we certainly had something to communicate about after that!)

I hear again and again as I provide pastoral counseling a line such as "We just don't have any time together" or "We just don't seem to be communicating."

Those two problems go together. It takes time to communicate. It takes a willingness to communicate before you'll set aside the time to do so! Make the time. Take the time. Schedule the time.

My dad and I had an interesting relationship during my growing-up years. My dad wasn't a Christian until I was twenty-one years old. He was an alcoholic and sometimes left us for several days, even weeks, leaving us in hurt and turmoil. Yet I never was angry at him or bitter against him. Why? Because as an eight-year-old boy, I started going out with my dad on a fairly regular basis to play golf with him. Dad talked to me. We were friends. He was my hero. He took time to teach me how to play golf. And all through my teenage years I spent time with my dad, and we talked together about all sorts of things in life.

That paid off for him later, when he had a terrible time in life. Because I never got bitter, I was in a position for God to use me to lead my own daddy to the Lord.

Now my son hates to play golf. I can't understand it. I thought a love for golf would be in his genes. I put a club in his hand one day, and we went out to the course, and I said, "Now, John, you're going to love this," . . . and he came home saying, "This is the stupidest game I've ever played." I thought maybe he'd like it a little better when he was older; but even now when he plays a hole or two, he says, "Dad, this is a drag. Why do you *like* this?"

I've got to admit that I was a little offended at first. I had automatically assumed that my son would like the game I like. But when I realized he didn't, I made a decision to FIND something he liked that we could do together. It took some time before we could find something that we both enjoyed, but we finally did. Dirt bikes. We will get on our four-wheelers and go tearing around the back-forty lot near the church and have a great time together. That was a breakthrough for us.

I take my little girls out for a SOFT DRINK . . . one at a time, just the two of us together to talk and laugh.

Communication takes time.

Second, make laughter a part of your life and your communication.

Some people are so serious ALL THE TIME that I'm amazed their faces don't crack when they smile. If you are that serious, something's wrong!

Proverbs 17:22 says, "A merry heart does good, like medicine."

Are you aware that medical researchers in just the past few years have confirmed that proverb as a scientific fact? Laughter—as well as exercise—releases a chemical reaction in the brain, called the endorphin effect, that aids in de-stressing your entire physical system. (Tim Hansel has written a book about this called, *You Gotta Keep Dancin'*, which I recommend.)

Some of us need to laugh more.

You don't have to go too far to find humor. Just look in the mirror.

Read some jokes aloud to yourself. I found these statements recently. They were released by an insurance company as actual statements people made in filling out accident reports.

Coming home, I drove into the wrong house and collided with a tree I didn't have.

The guy was all over the road. I had to swerve a number of times before I finally hit him.

I pulled away from the side of the road, glanced at my mother-in-law, and headed over the embankment.

In an attempt to kill a fly, I drove into a telephone pole.

I had been driving my car for forty years when I fell asleep at the wheel and had an accident.

The pedestrian had no idea which way to go; so I ran over him.

The telephone pole was approaching fast. I was attempting to swerve out of its path when I struck it with the front end of my car.

Now here are some jokes from Tim Hansel's *You Gotta Keep Dancin'* that actually appeared in church bulletins.

This afternoon there will be a meeting in the north and south ends of the church, and children will be christened at both ends.

Tuesday at 7:00 P.M. there will be an ice-cream social. All ladies giving milk, please come early.

Wednesday the ladies' literary society and Mrs. Lacy will sing "Put Me in My Little Bed," accompanied by the reverend.

This Sunday being Easter, we will ask Mrs. Daily to come forward and lay an egg on the altar.

Recently, I read these aloud to my church congregation, and we had a great time laughing. Does that sound sacrilegious to you? It wasn't. It was the most relaxed, healing time that some of the people in that congregation had experienced all week!

I hope you at least SMILED as you read some of these!

Melva remembers coming home from school when she was a child to find her father, Mr. Bryant, sitting in his chair, reading the jokes from *Reader's Digest,* and laughing out loud, even though no one else was around. There's something to be said for finding things that cause you to laugh out loud—to have a good chuckle or a good giggle until the tears start to roll. There's something healthy about a family that laughs together.

Communicate to the point that you laugh!

Word of Wisdom 3: Correct

Melva and I have a goal in our family that we will attempt to adjust attitudes BEFORE problems arise.

A lot of people let their children have terrible attitudes as long as "they don't do anything wrong." We feel, however, that having a bad attitude is just as wrong before God as doing a bad deed. We have dealt with attitudes just as strongly as with deeds.

We refuse to sweep a problem under the rug and pretend that it isn't there. We've chosen instead to confront the real issues of life, not in a picky way but in a constructive way—with a view toward correcting the problem fairly, consistently, and without a spirit of punishing just for punishment's sake. Whenever punishment is necessary—and it is from time to time—we have always executed that with a view toward redemption. That means that we talk with the child, saying, "The punishment you are going to receive results from this attitude or this deed, but we believe that it will result in this NEW attitude or NEW behavior."

Joanna, our middle child, is a beautiful young woman. But she was a whiner when she was a little girl. She could tune up and cry at the least provocation. If something didn't go right, she'd react by crying.

And Melva would say to her, "I am not going to let you grow up to be a miserable person. I love you too much to let you grow up to be miserable. Now you use your self-control and when something doesn't go just the way you want it to go, you get hold of yourself and don't break down into tears."

Melva said that so many times to her that one day, when something went wrong and Joanna—in her usual pattern—started to cry, she turned her face to the wall instead, mustered up all of the self-control she had, and turned back and smiled instead. That was a great turning point in her life. From that day on, Joanna has been smiling. She has had victory in her life. She hasn't been overly emotional. She is a joy to be with, and she knows how to experience real pleasure in her life.

I contend that when Joanna was given the right correction and she made a decision to receive it, a change happened in her life that will make her an adult who can truly enjoy life and be a very happy adult.

I believe that is the way God corrects us. He punishes, when He must punish, in a way that the fruits of righteousness can grow in our lives. He prunes. He doesn't destroy or uproot.

Word of Wisdom 4: Confess

In James 5:16 we read, "Confess your trespasses [faults] to one another, and pray for one another, that you may be healed."

Are you willing to admit today that you are not a perfect person yet?

Sometimes God allows a fault to become massively glaring in your life so that you will be willing to confess your fault and to say, "I made a mistake. I was wrong. I'm sorry." Those are the hardest two sentences for many people to utter.

Parent, have you ever told your child, "I made a mistake. I was wrong. I'm sorry"? It's important to be able to say those words to your children and then to say, "Will you please forgive me?" If our children don't hear us say those words, they'll think that adults don't make mistakes. If you aren't willing to say to your child, "I blew it; will you forgive me?" your child will begin to think that you don't do anything wrong and that you never need forgiveness from other people. Then when they grow up and find that they DO make mistakes as an adult, they won't have a role model or an example to follow in correcting them.

For a number of months I traveled a great deal, going back and forth to Tulsa to help with the seminary at Oral Roberts University, while still pastoring the Church on the Rock and flying to other cities in the prayer ministry. One day on a plane I began to think about my children, and I began to cry. Now that was unusual for me. I don't cry easily. But I began to see them in my spirit, and I began to feel their hurt, their loneliness, their needs. I went to each one of them and said—one by one—"I'm sorry that I haven't been the kind of daddy I should have been in the last few months. I'm sorry. Will you forgive me?" I believe that did more to restore my relationship with my children than anything I could have done.

Some parents respond to a feeling that they have done something wrong by buying their children presents or by taking them someplace special. That doesn't truly resolve the problem but only compounds it. Then the child begins to think that the way to resolve problems is to throw money at them! What is really needed is a confession of faults to one another so the relationship can be HEALED.

The second part of James 5:16 is equally important: "pray for one another, that you may be healed." Once you've confessed a problem—and have it out in the open where it can be discussed and aired—then you need to pray about it. You need to find common ground in the Lord Jesus Christ to stand on. In that is great healing . . . for relationships between husbands and wives, . . .

for relationships between parents and children, . . .

for relationships between brothers and sisters.

If I had to boil down family relationships to one formula for success, it would be the one in that verse: *confess and pray.*

Now all of us are in the process of being healed of one thing or another. We all have faults in our lives that need to be confessed. It's time we recognized that healing process and nurtured it in our families.

Word of Wisdom 5: Care

The one thing that seems to be a common characteristic to all teenage suicides is this statement: "Nobody cares." That is a sad commentary on the age in which we live. But what is true for teenagers is also true for many adults. Too many truly believe, "Nobody cares."

One day in utter desperation, as David was sitting in a cave and hiding from King Saul, who was seeking him so that he could kill him, David admitted that his spirit was "overwhelmed within me," and he cried out to God, "There is no one who acknowledges me; refuge has failed me; no one cares for my soul" (Ps. 142:4). In other words, David was saying, "Nobody cares." What a sad statement that is.

We must learn to communicate that we care.

My wife says it this way: "A parent must communicate to each child, 'You are the most important person in the world to me.'"

Everybody needs to feel that he or she is the most important person in the world to somebody! Sadly, most people don't have that feeling. They don't believe that they are the most important person in the world to anybody! That hopelessness, compounded by satanic influences that attempt to convince a child that he is important only to Satan, has resulted in a rash of teenage suicides and crimes across the land.

Parent, communicate today that your child is the most important person in the world to you!

As a teenager I had a nervous breakdown. What pulled me through? My mother had instilled into my mind that I was the most important person in her life. When she came to the hospital to see me, she said, "You are going to make it."

I said, "I don't know if I am."

She said, "Yes, you are, Larry, because you are the most important person on the earth to me, and I'm going to pray for you until you make it."

You may not approve of your child's bad actions, but that's far different from approving or not approving of who they ARE as a beloved child of yours on this earth.

Some parents withhold approval of who a child IS because of what a child DOES. Don't do it! A child must, *must*, MUST, *MUST* know that he or she has the approval and love of a parent, even as he or she knows that the parent doesn't approve of certain actions. It is critical today for you to be able to make that separation as you deal with your children. You can say to your child, "I don't approve of what you are doing right now, but I love you no matter WHAT you do. No matter what happens, I will love you."

Are you aware that is the way God loves you? You could put down this book right now and go out and become a reprobate, and you would reap what you sow; but, nonetheless, the love of God WILL NOT change toward you.

God is not a probationist or a conditionalist who says, "I will love you IF you perform a certain way." God says, "I love you." Period.

He will hate your sin—oh, yes—he will HATE your sinful actions; but He says to you without condition, "I love you."

It is that grace of God that brings us to a position in which we can truly repent. It is not what we DO or what we PERFORM that causes God to love us and forgive us. He loves us already. He forgives us when we come to Him and say, "God, I'm sorry for my sins. I repent of them. Please forgive me and help me to sin no more." He will do it. Every time. The truth of the matter is that we can't EVER perform well enough to earn God's love. It isn't possible because that's not the basis on which we receive God's love. We receive it as a free gift, freely given.

That's care of the highest order!

Word of Wisdom 6: Caress

The word *caress* carries with it the idea of touching or hugging.

Are you aware that the largest sensory organ of your body is your skin? Through it you have the capacity to receive the most information about your outside world, including the world of other people.

Scientific researchers have found that a child—and, especially, an infant—who is not hugged or caressed will eventually withdraw emotionally and die. Another person in the area of child development wrote that for a child to develop normally, a child needs twelve hugs a day.

I believe that what is true for a child is also true for an adult! We all need someone to put his arms around us each day and give us a hug.

Melva and I have decided that we are going to give each other a minimum of twelve hugs a day. Now that may seem simple—even silly—to you; but, let me assure you, I like it! And if you and your spouse adopt that policy, I think you'll like it, too!

I saw a bumper sticker recently that said, "Hugs, not drugs." There's great truth in that statement! People are dying for the lack of a caress, and many are turning to substitutes for that good feeling that only love can truly supply. I mean that they are literally *dying*—

turning to drugs and alcohol and letting those chemicals destroy their lives—for the lack of a hug.

We hear a lot of talk these days about the drug war and about the dependency and addiction issues that underlie the use of drugs in this country. But, let me tell you, something underlies even the nature of addiction and the nature of dependency—and that's the lack of genuine affection and care that we give to one another, including hugs and caresses.

God's people are called to show genuine affection for one another. The Bible says, "Greet all the brethren with a holy kiss" (1 Thess. 5:26). At the Church on the Rock we often invite those in our congregation to join hands and pray for one another. We invite those in the congregation to greet one another with a holy hug. Now I want to emphasize the word *holy* there. Don't hug another man's wife or another woman's husband like you would your own spouse! Give him or her a good shoulder hug, not a bosom hug.

In your family make hugs a natural and regular event. Put your arms around your children, look them in the eye, and say, "I love you. I care about you. You are the most important person in the world to me."

One man said to me, "If I tell my wife that, I'll be lying."

I said to him, "Well, repent!"

Obey the covenant. And God, the covenant maker, will produce love in you that can readily express itself in that genuine statement of care, commitment, and affection.

"But," you say, "I'm just not the touching type."

I say to you, "BECOME the touching type." Learn to break down those barriers and reach out to the people you care most about in this world. Learn to show your affection. It's not something that's built into you. It's something you learned. And you can RElearn it, God's way.

Actually, I believe that most of us were born with a desire for touching and affection. That inborn desire was "taught out of us" by parents or other adults around us who were unable or afraid to show affection. If you don't like to touch or to be touched today, it's probably a result of something you LEARNED, incorrectly, as a child. Make a decision today that you will UNLEARN that bad habit and RELEARN how to be affectionate and to show that you love someone by touching.

In this day and age a lot appears in the news media about inordinant family touching. And I want to say a word about that here. Incest is an abomination to God. There's no other way to put it. Leviticus 18 spells it out clearly. Read the entire chapter. It begins, "I am the LORD your God. According to the doings of the land of Egypt, where you dwelt, you shall not do; and according to the doings of the land of Canaan, where I am bringing you, you shall not do; nor shall you walk in their ordinances" (vv. 2–3). Incest and all manner of carnality were common to Egypt and Canaan and the Lord said, "I'll have none of that among My people."

Instead, God said, "You shall observe My judgments and keep My ordinances, to walk in them: I am the LORD your God" (Lev. 18:4). And Leviticus 18 goes on to say, "None of you shall approach anyone who is near of kin to him, to uncover his nakedness: I am the LORD" (v. 6). All of the rules of God regarding incest and sexual impropriety are spelled out, including adultery, homosexuality, and bestiality. These are called defilements and abominations before God in the Bible, which are ways of saying one giant NO.

That's *not* what I'm referring to when I use the word *caress*. I'm talking about good old-fashioned, clean, pure-in-motive hugs and touching among family members that are signs of genuine affection.

I believe that it's critical for children to experience this affection from their parents and for children to witness their parents touching and hugging. Otherwise, the entire area of affection becomes confused in their minds. The media—television, music on the radio, movies—will warp the distinctions between love and sex and among affection and friendship and sex. Let your children see that you can touch your spouse without its being a sexual act. Let them see you showing affection with touching involved. That's the best form of sex education I know—to teach your children the difference between affectionate caressing and sexual desire.

Word of Wisdom 7: Conceive a Spiritual Vision for Your Family

This is perhaps the most important word I can share with you. Conceive. Most of us think of that in terms of physical conception—you conceived a baby. Some think of it as a mental thought or dream—you conceived of a new program or product or procedure or plan. I encourage you today to think of conception as a spiritual thing. Conceive a spiritual vision for your family!

My wife once had a vision in which she and I were walking up to the throne of God together. We were battle weary, but we were bringing our battle trophies—souls won to the Lord Jesus—to God to exchange them for His eternal reward. The most important people we were bringing with us were our three children. Melva has a spiritual vision for our marriage and for our family. She has an eternal perspective for the way we live our lives and for the REASON we do things a certain way in our family.

I believe that is critically important for each person to have.

Stop to consider for a moment WHY you are married and have children. Don't you think God KNEW that you would be married? Don't you think God KNEW that you would have the children you have? Ask yourself today WHY He ordained these in your life.

Most of us, however, never allow the Holy Spirit to give us a vision for the SPIRITUAL—the eternal—purpose for our marriages and families. And the Bible teaches that without a vision the people perish (see Prov. 29:18). Without a spiritual vision for the purpose for your marriage it will languish. It will lack direction and focus. It will not have an anchor when storms rage. Without a spiritual vision for your family, your family will lack hope and purpose. Your children will feel that lack of direction and, as a result, will lack the responsibility for seeing a vision come to pass.

Indeed, without a vision, the people do perish!

What is your vision today for your marriage and your family?

I have a vision that my children will live for Jesus all the days of their lives. I have a vision that my family will serve the Lord. I have a vision that someday we will stand in heaven together before the

Lord and that I will present my entire family to Jesus as my primary discipleship group. I believe that if I am faithful in my spiritual relationship with Melva, John, Joanna, and Joy, then I will be faithful in my spiritual relationship with all other people in my life.

Do you have a vision for the souls you and your spouse might win together for the Lord Jesus? Do you have a vision for the souls you and your children might win together for the Lord Jesus? Do you talk about that vision in your home? Do you express that vision to your spouse and your children?

Do you have a vision for the role of your family in the local church? Do you have a vision for the ways your family might be involved in your city for the Lord Jesus?

Make a decision today that you WILL have a spiritual vision for your marriage and your family. Ask the Holy Spirit to give you one!

Conceiving a spiritual vision for your family is the most critical concept I believe I can share with you as we seek God's wisdom for your family. Why? Because the central purpose of your life is to win the lost of this world to Jesus Christ.

The banner for your family—and for every family of believers—is this: *JESUS CHRIST IS LORD.*

Under that banner covenant relationships are forged.

Under that banner communication has a focus and a purpose.

Under that banner correction can best be conducted in love.

Under that banner you have the courage and responsibility to confess your faults to one another.

Under that banner care flows freely and genuinely.

Under that banner we can openly caress one another and show godly affection.

The key to it all is to have a spiritual vision for who you are in Jesus Christ . . . who you and your spouse are before the throne of heaven . . . and who you and your family are in the context of God's kingdom now and forever.

There's an eternal reason for your marriage. There's an eternal reason for your family on this earth. Discover it. Learn to live with it as an omnipresent idea and goal in your family.

Let me say a word to those of you who are living with a spouse who does not confess the Lord Jesus as Savior or is not committed to a godly life. Let that difficult situation work within you the character of God. A true believer—someone who is truly born again spiritually—has one goal in life: to become conformed to the image of Jesus Christ and to serve Him in every way possible every day.

I have no desire to be a "rich preacher." I have no desire to be famous. I have only one true desire: to be conformed to the image of Jesus Christ and to have the "product" of my life be the love and grace and purpose of Jesus. When I encounter a tough situation— or when Melva and I encounter a tough situation in our marriage or in our family—we resolve to allow that tough situation to form us MORE into the image Jesus Christ.

That's a decision of your will. You can make that choice. You MUST make that choice for wisdom to invade and pervade your family.

If your spouse does not desire to serve God in the way you desire it, let that tough situation FORM you more into the likeness of Christ. Don't let that situation be the undoing of your marriage or your faith. Let it be the birthing ground for the growth of your character to become more and more like Jesus.

If you and your spouse are facing a tough time in your marriage, don't let this time become the start of your undoing. Let it be the start of something constructive—in which you both determine that you will make this tough time a time to be conformed more to the likeness of Jesus.

It is through the fire of a struggle that we are refined. But it won't happen if we try to escape the fire or ignore the struggle or give up. Determine that you WILL work through this time. You WILL withstand. You WILL endure. You WILL emerge victorious and more like Jesus than ever before.

Every genuine relationship I know goes through times of confrontation and contortion (a time of twisting things as they presently are into a new configuration that is more like Jesus).

Many people I know face life as if they are living in a pressure cooker. Their teeth are clenched, and their eyes are blurred by the pressure of the struggle. And Jesus is standing there saying, "It doesn't matter to Me how much money you make. It doesn't matter to Me how successful you appear in the eyes of other human beings. Just love each other. Love those children. That's what matters to Me."

Jesus said, "By this all will know that you are My disciples, if you have love for one another" (John 13:35). When we make that our supreme goal, then—and only then—are we in a position to create families that not only endure but also overcome life's circumstances. I invite you to join me in a prayer that I pray every day. . . .

Let's pray about it.

Father, give me the wisdom to be the kind of family member You want me to be.

Show me how to be the right kind of child to my parents. Show me how to be the right kind of spouse to my spouse. Show me how to be the right kind of parent to my children. In Jesus' name I pray. Amen.

Chapter 9

Wisdom and Finances

I will bless you
And make your name great;
And you shall be a blessing.
—Genesis 12:2

Change.

It's an interesting word to begin a discussion of finances because so many of us think of change as the coins in our pocket or the money we get back from a cashier.

That's not the way I'm using the word, here, however.

I'm talking about making a change in the way we look at money—which is something I believe that most Christians need to do.

Change is always a key word in our searching, finding, and having the wisdom of God in our lives. God always asks us to change—to grow from where we are toward greater and greater perfection in Christ Jesus. The very process of growth requires change. A baby doesn't look or act like an adult. A baby changes as he or she becomes an adult. A sapling of a tree doesn't look or produce fruit like a full-grown tree. A sapling changes as it becomes a mature tree.

Change is inevitable, but change toward perfection is not automatic. That's a crucial difference for you to understand. You WILL change whether or not you want to change. But to change TOWARD THE GOOD requires effort and a willingness to change.

Perhaps nowhere is that more evident than in the way we as Christians deal with our money. Most of us need to change in order to grow into the full stature of the wisdom God desires for us. And we need to be WILLING to change.

For virtually all of us God's approach to our money and to our use of money is vastly different from our way.

Isaiah 55: 6–8 says,

Seek the LORD while He may be found, call upon Him while He is near. Let the wicked forsake his way, and the unrighteous man his thoughts; let him return to the LORD. . . . "For My thoughts are not your thoughts, nor are your ways My ways," says the LORD.

In The Living Bible verse 8 reads this way: "This plan of mine is not what you would work out, neither are my thoughts the same as yours!"

In Deuteronomy 8 we find a great warning and a great promise of God related to our finances. This chapter says, in summary, that if we obey the laws of the Lord our God, walk in His ways, and fear Him with a reverent awe, then great blessings will be ours. But, on the other hand, if we start to trust in our own ability and start to claim that the blessings we have are results of our own accomplishments, then we should look out. If we forget God and worship other gods and follow evil ways, the Word of God in this chapter says, "you shall certainly perish" (Deut. 8:19 TLB).

Toward the end of Deuteronomy 8 we find this verse: "Always remember that it is the Lord your God who gives you power to become rich, and he does it to fulfill his promise to your ancestors" (Deut. 8:18 TLB).

Are you aware today that you have a promise of God made to your ancestors in the faith that God is going to meet *all* of YOUR NEEDS according to His riches in glory (see Phil. 4:19)? Note that word *ALL*. Note the phrase *YOUR NEEDS*. That is the promise of God's Word through the ages to those who will love God, serve God, seek the things of God, obey God, and fear God with a reverential awe. That's His promise to YOU today.

Now many in the church have fallen under what I call a "spirit of piety." They believe that to be a devout person, you must be really poor. The poorer you are, the better Christian you are. That's been the overriding philosophy of one large segment of the church for the past fifty years. And while Christians have become poorer and poorer, as a whole, we have seen various cults owning more and more of our nation. Are you aware that Buddhists and Mormons today own more real estate and control more money in the United States of America than any other group? And what is their number one purpose? It's evangelism for their cause! They expect to use their wealth and power to promote their own beliefs and to convert others to their religious convictions.

A few years ago a member of our church sent us to Hawaii for a few days of vacation, and while we were there, Melva Jo and I went to the Polynesian Cultural Arts Center, which is owned and operated by Mormons. That center is actually a ten-billion-dollar tool for evangelism! Its primary purpose is to make money to support Mormon students to complete their education and to return to their island homes to convert their people to Mormonism.

(I came home to my church in Rockwall, which was building a new facility at that time, to find two of my church members almost at blows in their disagreement over whether we should pave our new parking lot with asphalt or concrete. I can't tell you how frustrated I was in light of where I had just been!)

I stood in amazement, and I stand in amazement today. Millions of Christians believe that they SHOULD be poor to be humble and pious before God. I declare to you today that Christians should be GREAT MONEY PRODUCERS to evangelize this world for Jesus Christ! We should shake off that false spirit of piety and get busy and capture the wealth of this world in order to use it to win souls for Jesus Christ and to deliver those who are living and dying every day in spiritual bondage!

Read Deuteronomy 8:18 again: "Always remember that it is the

Lord your God who gives you power to become rich, and he does it to fulfill his promise to your ancestors" (TLB).

Now God doesn't want to put you in the gravy so you can drown in it. No, He wants to bless you because He promised Abraham—and all of his descendants, who are people that will walk by faith—that He would bless Abraham and make him a blessing. (Read Gen. 12:2 again.) With Abraham God set up a cycle of blessing.

That cycle of blessing is this: God will bless you so that you might be a blessing, and out of that you will be further blessed so you can be a greater blessing, and out of that you will be blessed even further so you can be an even greater blessing . . . and so forth . . . until you arrive at the point of Malachi 3:10: you have received a blessing so great that you can't even contain it!

God wants to bless you NOT so you can get caught up in greed, selfishness, and pride . . . but so you can BE a blessing to others.

The devil has fought God's people on this teaching in a fierce way. This message has been so maligned and mistaught that it's a wonder that Christianity hasn't died of hunger and exposure to the elements. Why has the devil fought it so hard? Because he doesn't WANT all of that money going toward Christian evangelism. He doesn't WANT to see money used for saving souls and delivering the very ones he holds captive. That's so obvious that it's glaring.

It's time we read what the Bible has to say about blessing and riches. God wants you to have abundance—not just scratching by for the rest of your life but to have more than is sufficient. He doesn't even want you to be CONCERNED about money but rather to be concerned about using money to spread the gospel to all nations. He wants to bless you so you can bless others!

Have you ever received an inheritance of money? Did you have any problems receiving it or spending it? Probably not. Did you say to the person telling you about the inheritance, "No thank you, I don't need it. You keep it." Probably not! You probably saw that inherited money as the easiest money you'd ever come by. And you probably didn't have any problems accepting it and using it to buy something you wanted. More than likely, that money was extra money . . . beyond your level of need, . . . and it was used for something extra in your life.

Well, the Bible calls God's blessing to us an inheritance. We shouldn't have any problems receiving it and spending it. It's part of the inheritance promised to us by God through Abraham. And we are in Abraham through Jesus Christ. We today are the seed of Abraham. We are the heirs of all the promises made to Abraham AND joint heirs with Jesus Christ of all the blessings of God. You cannot become a greater heir than that!

Let's be honest with ourselves today about what God wants in way of our finances. Let's get God's wisdom for our finances.

To help us do that, let's explore together seven key questions about our finances.

Financial Question 1: Is Jesus Really the Lord of Your Life?

Now that might not seem to be a question that has anything to do with your finances, but, friend, let me assure you that it is THE most important question you can ask in relationship to your money.

Matthew 6:21 is a verse of Scripture that most of us know well: "Where your treasure is, there your heart will be also."

I challenge you today. Can you stand and declare without wavering that Jesus is the Lord of your life?

If you can do that, then you are also declaring that Jesus is the Lord over your finances. In fact, we are incorrect when we say, "our finances," "my finances," or "your finances." They are truly not OUR finances at all. None of us have anything that wasn't given to us by God. Including you. YOU don't have one thing today that you didn't get from God.

"But, Larry," you may say, "I am a medical doctor today because I had the intelligence to become a doctor and made the effort to go to medical school."

I ask you, "Who gave you your mental ability? Who gave you your brain? Who gave you the health and stamina and who provided the finances for you to go to medical school?"

"But, Larry," you say, "I'm a professional athlete, and I was just born with a natural ability and great strength."

I ask you, "Who gave you your physical strength and innate coordination?"

The physical body you live in. The family you were born into. The opportunities that have crossed your path. The faith you have. All are ultimately from God. Even the breath you breathe every minute is a gift from God.

And in reality, the money you have and the things you have are not your own. They are gifts to you *from* God—and entrusted to you *by* God.

God has given you these gifts to see what you will do with them. He is watching to see if you are greedy. He is watching to see if you are going to trust money more than you trust Him.

The Bible says that the greedy, lecherous clutching of money is the root of all evil (see 1 Tim. 6:10).

It's time we realized anew that a demonic spiritual power is behind every evil manifestation we see in the world today. Drugs are a real manifestation of evil. But a demonic spirit of addiction lies behind the drug problem. Adultery is a real manifestation. But a demonic spirit of lust drives that problem. The same principle holds true for money. There is nothing wrong with a one-hundred-dollar bill. That's a spiritually neutral piece of paper with printing on it. But a demonic spirit of greed and avarice works in relationship to money that can erupt in all other forms of evil.

God allows for our resources—our money—to become the testing ground to determine exactly where our hearts are in relationship to Him. Will we allow that demonic spirit of greed—of loving money—to take hold of us and so control us that we trust in our money and not in God? Or will we resist that demonic spirit?

You can say, "Jesus is the Lord of my life" all day and night and mean it. But the PROOF of whether Jesus is the Lord of your life is likely going to manifest itself in the ways you deal with the money and resources God has entrusted to you.

Where are you investing the stewardship of your life?

You may ask, "Are you talking about tithes, Larry?"

What is the true role of the tithe? The tithe is nothing more than the MONITOR of our heart's commitment. God doesn't NEED your money. He has all the wealth of this world, and should He ever run out, He can create more! No. That's not the point of your giving 10 percent of your income to God's work. The tithe is a manifestation, a gauge, a monitor of whether you trust God with your finances, . . .

of whether you put the work of God first, . . .

of whether you will follow God's commandments as they relate to finances, and thus . . .

of whether you honor God's commandments in your life.

Let's read what God said to Abraham: "Get out of your country, from your kindred, and from your father's house, to a land that I will show you. I will make you a great nation" (Gen. 12:1–2).

Now at that time Abraham was about seventy-five years old. He had spent his entire life in his clan. In those days your family, with all of its extensions, was really your city. It's where you dwelled. It's where you were known. It's where you had your identity. For God to say to Abraham, "Get up. Get out. And go to a place you haven't been told about yet" was a tremendous challenge. For Abraham to have been willing to do that was a true indication that Jehovah God was his Lord and that he had placed the fate of his entire life in Him. Abraham's security was not in his city, his family, his wealth, his background—it was in God.

Where is YOUR security today? Is it in the things around you, or is it in the Lord? Is Jesus REALLY the Lord of your life?

God gave this promise to Abraham: "I will bless you and make your name great; and you shall be a blessing. I will bless those who bless you, and I will curse him who curses you; and in you all the families of the earth shall be blessed" (Gen. 12:2–3).

God told Abraham that he was going to be famous. God was going to make a man's name great. Now most of us have been taught to react negatively against that. We are taught in our Sunday schools and churches that we should debase ourselves and make God's name great. But look closely at the process here. God was saying, "I'm going to make your name great, Abraham. And when everybody knows who you are, THEN when you point to me and say, 'Great is the Lord God' even more people are going to pay attention. You are going to be famous, Abraham, so that you can bring even greater glory to Me."

God wants to make you a person of renown today. He wants you to be known, to have a good reputation, to be honored by others in your city, state, and nation. Why? So you can turn around and say, "To God be the glory" and have a witness that is far greater than what you might have as a nobody with nothing.

You may not realize it, but Abraham was not a perfect man. He made some grave mistakes. He even sold his wife into another man's harem . . . twice!

As a Christian, you may make some mistakes. You aren't going to be a perfect person every day, every hour of your life. But let me assure you of this. God's promise is on your life because of your relationship to Jesus Christ and to Abraham. God's promise is to bless YOU and to make YOU a blessing.

Furthermore, God says that He will curse those who curse you. God promises to take care of your enemies. You don't have to. He will.

How do you get in position for such a great blessing? By putting your trust in the Lord. One hundred percent of it. All of it. You choose to trust Jesus Christ as your Lord and Him alone, and you choose to trust Him no matter what happens. That is the commitment that places you in the great covenant of blessing that God wants to have with you.

Is Jesus the Lord of your life today?

Is Jesus *REALLY* the Lord of your life?

If you cannot answer that question with a loud yea and amen, then I encourage you to face up to that right now. Acknowledge it. Repent of it. Get God's forgiveness. And move forward with a determination that Jesus WILL BE the Lord of your life every day of your life from this moment onward.

In Mark 10:17–22 we read an account of Jesus' encounter with a young man whom we have come to call the rich young ruler. This man came running out to Jesus, fell to his knees in front of Jesus in an act of obeisance, and asked Him, "Good Teacher, what shall I do that I may inherit eternal life?"

This young man had found the right person, and he asked the

right question, and he was even manifesting the right diligence and the right humility as he ran and knelt.

Jesus replied, "Why do you call Me good? No one is good but One, that is, God. You know the commandments: 'Do not commit adultery,' 'Do not murder,' 'Do not steal,' 'Do not bear false witness,' 'Do not defraud,' 'Honor your father and your mother.'"

The young man answered by saying, "Teacher, all these I have observed from my youth."

And Jesus looked at him and said, "One thing you lack: Go your way, sell whatever you have and give to the poor, and you will have treasure in heaven; and come, take up the cross, and follow Me."

The Bible says that this young man was saddened by what Jesus said and went away with grief in his heart. The reason? He had great possessions.

Now the great possessions weren't the ROOT of his problem. The root of his problem was that this young man put his money in front of his master. His money was more important to him than the lordship of Jesus. It wasn't the fact that he HAD money. It was the fact that he HAD MONEY WITH WHICH HE WOULDN'T PART FOR JESUS' SAKE.

Now as that young man walked away, Jesus turned to His disciples and said, "How hard it is for those who have riches to enter the kingdom of God!" (Mark 10:23). And they looked at him in astonishment. Why? You see, a number of very rich people had already come into relationship with Jesus. Are you aware that Nicodemus was what my son would call "heavy-duty rich"? So were many of the women who gave to Jesus of their substance. So was Zacchaeus. In fact, the first-century historian Josephus tells about a man named Zacchaeus who lived in Jericho who was worth several million dollars in that day. Now that was a GREAT fortune for the first century! That level of wealth makes today's multimillionaires look like paupers by comparison. Joseph of Arimathea, who gave his tomb for the burial of Jesus' body after the crucifixion, was also a very wealthy man. And the list goes on.

Jesus responded to their astonishment by saying, "Children, how hard it is for those who trust in riches to enter the kingdom of God!" (Mark 10:24).

Note those words *TRUST IN RICHES*. That's the heart of the matter. Jesus was pointing out that, to this young man, Jesus was not Lord. . . . Money was! This rich young ruler trusted in his riches. He was holding on to the very thing he couldn't keep, and it kept him from receiving the very thing he could never lose.

Jesus went on to say, "It is easier for a camel to go through the eye of a needle than for a rich man to enter the kingdom of God" (Mark 10:25).

The disciples asked, "Who then can be saved?" (v. 26).

Jesus said, "With men it is impossible, but not with God; for with God all things are possible" (v. 27).

You see, God alone can CHANGE a heart so that a person trusts in the right things. You can't do that by yourself. Your natural carnal tendency is always going to be to trust in your material possessions, your money, your wealth. It's just human nature. And you can't change it by yourself. But GOD can.

You can turn to God and say, "God, I'm not trusting in You with my whole heart. I realize that. I am trusting in my own riches. I know that's a sin, and I repent of it today. Please forgive me and give me the spiritual strength and courage I need to love and serve You with my WHOLE heart and to trust You and You alone with my life."

Now Peter went on to ask Jesus, in essence, "Well, we did leave everything to follow You. We DID put our trust solely in You." The implication is: "What are we going to get out of it, Lord?"

Jesus replied to him,

Assuredly, I say to you, there is no one who has left house or brothers or sisters or father or mother or wife or children or lands, for My sake and the gospel's, who shall not receive a hundredfold now in this time—houses and brothers and sisters and mothers and children and lands, with persecutions—and in the age to come, eternal life (Mark 10:29–30).

In this statement Jesus differentiated between spiritual riches and material-physical riches. He promised those who will TRUST HIM that they will have BOTH.

Some people say, "Well, God just wants us to have spiritual wealth. That's what He was really talking about when He said 'riches.'"

That's not what Jesus said.

Jesus said that you are going to have great physical and material riches NOW, in this time—in other words, in your lifetime here on earth. He even said that it will be a "hundredfold" increase over what you previously had BEFORE you began trusting God as your Source of supply, and Jesus as your Lord. Furthermore, Jesus says this blessing will come with persecutions. There are going to be those who don't WANT you to have that much—primarily the devil and his demons. They are going to try to keep you from having the level of prosperity God desires for you. You'll be "hit" for prospering, but that won't keep you from prospering if you persevere in your trust of Jesus as your Lord.

And *then* Jesus said, "You will also have spiritual blessing. You'll have eternal life in the age to come" (Mark 10:30, paraphrase).

In sum, you are going to have BOTH kinds of blessing. The kind you can see and touch and hug and enjoy and spend. And the kind that is intangible but everlasting.

Why will you experience this blessing?

We have to go all the way back to Abraham. You are going to get this blessing—this ABUNDANT level of hundredfold blessing—so you can BE a blessing to others.

The key to it all, however, is that JESUS MUST BE LORD OF YOUR LIFE. He must be LORD over everything you are and everything you have.

You cannot manipulate God. You cannot think of Him as some kind of slot machine. You cannot try to use God. It just won't work. And furthermore, that's not the point. The point is that when Jesus is LORD of your life, these other blessings will come to you. But they aren't your FIRST concern. Your FIRST concern is with Jesus. That's where your heart is. That's where your trust lies.

Now you don't need to be wealthy to trust in your things. You can trust in things even when you have only a few things to trust in.

I'm continually amazed at how many people get so wrapped up

in their stuff when they really don't have that much stuff to get wrapped up in! They are clinging to something—hanging on for dear life to it—yet when you look at it objectively from a distance, it doesn't really amount to much at all!

A number of years ago Melva Jo and I had nothing of financial means. I'm not talking about having just a little bit—which is what a lot of people mean when they say, "Oh, I don't have anything." I'm talking about zero. Nothing.

In 1974 God spoke to my heart to give everything we had to missions. We didn't have that much—a broken-down old Pontiac, a pile of secondhand furniture, our worn-out used clothing. We were living in a low-class apartment complex next door to seven illegal aliens. My salary was four hundred dollars a month take-home pay, which is what a youth pastor got in those days coming straight out of school in the Southern Baptist denomination. In sum, . . . we were poor people. And God said to give up everything we had.

Let me tell you, we started clutching that stuff. It was worth hardly anything, but we were clutching. And for six months I was sick—spiritually and physically. Finally, we decided to obey God.

I thought about that time a few months ago as I also remembered how we felt at the time we started receiving the first royalties from *Could You Not Tarry One Hour?*—my first book to hit the national marketplace. I decided to keep those royalty payments in the church until we needed them to buy a larger home. I knew the day was coming when we would need a bigger home because Melva Jo's parents were starting to make plans to come live with us. We had three kids, a cat, and two dogs. My nephew was living with us, too. And I knew we'd need a large home in the not-too-near future. So I kept those funds on the church books in anticipation of that day.

As the months passed, however, we became involved in our building program for the church facility we presently have in Rockwall, and all of that money was spent on the new building. When the time came for me to draw it out to purchase a home, . . . it was gone.

I asked the Lord, "What am I to do? I don't have wisdom in this matter. I need Your wisdom. I've got to have it!" In my heart I was hoping that God would give me a great idea for recouping those funds in some way.

The Lord said, "I want you to consider that money as seed you have planted in Me. It's gone. Consider it planted. Don't ever expect it back."

I said, "Well, what are we going to do, Lord? How are You going to provide this house that You know we need."

He said, "One other thing. I want you to sow your salary to the church too."

I gulped. That was not the answer I had expected. And yet I knew it was God giving me His wisdom in the matter. I did just what He said to do. And I did it with joy. I mean, I had *radical, liberating* joy in my heart as I went to the elders and told them that I was giving my entire salary back to the church.

Now that was in 1987, and do you realize what was happening at that time? The preacher bashing had just started in America. And it had started over the matter of finances. Many of the big names in Christianity at that time were hit, and hit hard. That same mindset of preacher bashing was starting to seep into the local church, including our own fellowship.

That radical measure was GOD'S WISDOM. It kept us free from the spirit and the judgment of that entire onslaught against God's leaders. And for the past two years we've gone from month to month, trusting God to provide materially and financially for us through the national prayer ministry that God has led us into. Praise God—we've not missed a meal. We were able to get the home we needed. Our needs have been met in full and beyond. And what a joy it has been, month after month, to serve the Church on the Rock without taking any money from the church.

I think it's interesting that our money in the United States reminds us of our true priority: "In GOD we trust." If you can't say with all honesty today, "Jesus is the Lord of my bank account. My trust is in Him," then face up to that, get your priorities right, and begin to seek the Lord FIRST. You'll never have God's wisdom on finances without taking that step.

Financial Question 2: Will You Make a Good Plan for Your Future?

For some people that question sounds almost sacrilegious. When I say, "Do you have a good plan for your financial future?" they look at me as if to say, "I'm spiritual. I don't need a plan. I walk by faith, not by plans."

Look at Proverbs 24:3–4: "Any enterprise is built by wise planning, becomes strong through common sense, and profits wonderfully by keeping abreast of the facts" (TLB).

Earlier in Proverbs, we read: "We should make plans—counting on God to direct us" (Prov. 16:9 TLB).

Many people I meet seem to feel that God is just going to rain down on them what they need without any effort or thought on their part. It's as if they expect to go outside and look at trees in their backyards and find one-hundred-dollar bills growing on them.

You will never get ahead with that kind of thinking. Not now. Not five years from now. Not ever. Because it's not the wisdom of God.

You must make a plan for your future.

Let me share a plan I instituted as we began the Church on the Rock in 1980. We kept that plan in place until we embarked on a massive building project, and last year we reinstituted it. Apart from the time when we were involved in building our ten-million-dollar facility, we operated that plan when we had a little bit—in terms of financial resources—and when we had a lot.

This is also the plan that Melva Jo and I have lived by since we were married in 1974. I heartily recommend it to you for your own family and personal finances, and I recommend it from personal experience.

I call the plan the 8-1-1 plan. What are the basics of this plan?

The first premise is that you will be faithful in giving to God. The second premise is that you will save regularly. And the third premise is that you will live on only 80 percent of what you earn.

The plan is based on the idea that your total income is represented by the number 10. Here's how it breaks down.

• *Give one-tenth of your income to God's work.*

That's the tithe. It's the biblical standard for giving. It's a commandment of God. You need to do that for "heart" reasons before God—to show God that your heart is in the right place with regard to your finances.

• *Save one-tenth.*

Be faithful in doing this. Make the first check you write—from every amount of money you receive—a check for one-tenth to God's work. But make the second check you write a deposit into your own savings account.

• *Live on the rest—80 percent.*

Now this is contrary to the way most people in the United States of America live today. Most people I encounter are making ten apples and trying to live off fourteen! They have overextended themselves on credit to live a life-style that they wished they had but that in reality they will never have because of their overspending. Living beyond your means or even living to the level of your means—making ten apples and spending all ten—is a surefire way *never* to get ahead.

Make this a starting point. Soon you may be able to live on 70 percent, give 20 percent to God's work and save 10 percent. You may be able to reduce your living even more and raise your giving even higher as time passes. In fact, I believe that you WILL be able to do that, because that is what God's cycle of blessing describes. The Hebrew approach to prosperity was more and more resources so you can be a greater and greater blessing; only the Christian church has interpreted God's Word to mean that you should have less and less (which means you are forced to give less and less)!

Now why should you save?

A number of people say to me, "Isn't saving money contrary to believing that Jesus is coming soon?"

We don't know when Jesus is coming. But we do know that He told us to occupy until He does come. He told us that the rain falls on the just and the unjust—in other words, calamities and hard times come to everyone. At times all of us need extra money for one reason or another, and that's where a savings account comes in.

"Well," you say, "show me a verse of Scripture that talks about saving."

I'll show you two of them.

"The wise man saves for the future, but the foolish man spends whatever he gets" (Prov. 21:20 TLB).

"Houses and riches are an inheritance from fathers" (Prov. 19:14).

Now you can't leave an inheritance of houses and riches to your children unless you have a good investment plan for your life. If you are spending the full amount you earn on consumable living items, then you will never be able to accumulate an estate to pass along to your children.

"Well," you say, "I'm leaving my children a godly inheritance. I'm leaving them an inheritance of faith in God."

There's nothing more important that you can do. But the Bible also encourages you to leave your children something of tangible means in this world.

Let me also share this insight with you, based on my experience in pastoring. There's a link between saving and tithing. I've found that those who tithe faithfully—those who consistently and regularly plant 10 percent of their earnings back into God's work—are the people who are most consistent in saving. They have a discipline where money is concerned. They aren't robbing God (see Mal. 3:8). And they aren't robbing themselves. They know how to USE money. Their priorities are straight.

Now this 8-1-1 plan will work IF you will work it. You CAN live on 80 percent of what you earn.

When I was making only $480 a month, this is how Melva Jo and I spent that money.

• We gave a tithe of $48 a month to the church.
• We put $48 a month into our savings account.
• We spent $70 a month on food. We paid $150 rent on our mobile home (which was actually a small trailer house that we called a mobile home.) We paid our utilities, which ran about $50 a month. Our gasoline was about $60.

And the total of that was $426 a month. We had $54 a month

left over! In other words, we had more left over for fun stuff than we had given either to God's work OR to our savings account!

This 8-1-1 plan is the plan that we instituted at the church. From the tithes and offerings we received, we set aside at least 10 percent every month as a savings account. At the time we began our building project, we had one million dollars in cash reserves. I praise God that we had it. It was fully spent within a matter of months, and I praise God for that too. We never intended—then or now—to become a bank. We want to be a funnel for God's resources! But the money was there when we needed it. We had one million dollars to put down on our building project, which was one million dollars we didn't need to borrow or pay interest on. And I believe with all my heart that God was pleased that we had that one million dollars as a seed to put into our new church facility.

"But, Larry," you say, "I can't live on only 80 percent of my income."

Then I ask you, "Are you willing to change?"

Are you willing to change your life-style? Are you willing to humble yourself and live in full accordance with God's financial wisdom?

I know some people who never seem to be able to get ahead, no matter HOW much money they earn. Why? Because they are living with a mind-set that what they have—no matter the level, ten dollars, ten thousand dollars, or ten million dollars—it's never enough. And with that mind-set it never will be enough.

We live in a yuppie-fied generation that believes that if a person doesn't look a certain way, own certain things, and go certain places, that person just hasn't arrived. Let me assure you, the only way to arrive is to reject that way of thinking and to live not only within your means but also within God's wisdom for your finances.

Melva Jo and I lived as poor people lived when we were first married. That's because we WERE poor people! We could have said, "Hey, we're both college graduates. We should uphold a certain image so that people will perceive us in a better way." But we didn't. We didn't care HOW people perceived us. We determined to operate within God's principles.

I've met parents today who won't tithe because they feel they just must have designer jeans for their four-year-old son. Melva Jo went to Goodwill to buy baby clothes for our little boy! "That's terrible," you say. Not really. She always found good, clean garments that had been worn only a few times. Babies grow quickly. Very few babies ever truly wear out a garment of clothing. We didn't think it at all terrible. What is terrible, in my opinion, are parents who are so shackled by what society thinks they SHOULD do that they rob God of His tithes and offerings to achieve temporary applause from their peers!

Let's recognize that yuppie mind-set for what it is: pride at work. God has made some promises to the proud, and unfortunately, they aren't good ones. Proverbs 18:12 sums them up: "Pride ends in destruction; humility ends in honor" (TLB).

You've got to be humble enough to change your ways if you can't live within your means today and to build a savings account. You've got to be humble enough to change if you aren't giving 10 percent of your earnings to God's work. If you aren't humble enough to change, you won't ever be out of financial trouble.

God cannot bless foolishness or impropriety. He cannot bless fiscal irresponsibility. He cannot bless the person who will not seek HIS financial wisdom. Even if you tithe one of your apples, and you choose to live on twelve apples instead of the nine apples you have left, God is not obligated to bless that behavior!

Financial Question 3: Do You Have Balanced, Disciplined Work Habits?

Proverbs 10:4–5 gives us the key to answering this question: "Lazy men are soon poor; hard workers get rich. A wise youth makes hay while the sun shines, but what a shame to see a lad who sleeps away his hour of opportunity" (TLB).

God expects you to work.

God also expects you to live a balanced life.

I've met a number of young people today who buy into the first of those expectations but not the second. They get out of college, get married, and say, "We've got to have certain things." Both husband and wife set out to work at such a pace that they forget God, have little time for each other, and build up so much stress that their health suffers, not to mention their marriage.

I'd rather live on $480 a month and give my tithe and put some money away and sit around and stare at Melva Jo than live a lifestyle in which I was too busy to give to God my time and money and too busy to enjoy my family and so stressed that I couldn't even shave in the mornings without nearly cutting my head off.

I have a little secret to help people get promotions in their workplaces. It's this: WORK.

One woman said to me recently about those she is asked to supervise at work, "I've tried for a year, and I can't find ONE person to whom I can say, 'Do these five things' and come back several hours later and find that they are done. Everybody has excuses but no work to show for the hours."

I have an insider tip to you if you are looking for a promotion. It applies no matter where you work or what kind of work you do. If your boss gives you five things to do, then DO those five things to the best of your ability and then look for one more thing to do to help that person or that company.

If you will do that, you'll run that company someday—or start one like it and run it! The successful person in any corporation is always the person who says, "I can do those things I'm required to do, but even beyond that I'm going to seek something EXTRA to do."

(Now if your boss won't "allow" you to do extra, then I believe you should consider working outside that company. Find some way you can do MORE than is required of you. You may find that your part-time effort outside your company becomes as lucrative or more so than your full-time job! I've seen it happen dozens of times. If your company doesn't reward your extra effort, God will!)

Now I'm not advocating that all wives work. I've seen a mind-set at work in church circles that believes that the wife of every pastor should do something to help the pastor earn HIS salary. When I was first interviewed for a job, several men asked me what Melva Jo was going to do in the church. They knew that she had abundant musical talent, and they were hoping, really, that they could get two employees for the price of one. I said straight away, "You are hiring me, not my wife."

However, after I got involved in that ministry as a youth pastor, we both realized that the church greatly needed a youth choir. Now I was already doing my job. We had a Tuesday-night meeting, a Wednesday-night meeting, a Thursday-night meeting, a Saturday-morning prayer breakfast, two services on Sunday, and a youth retreat once a month. We saw ourselves coming and going. But that was the way I chose to do youth ministry, and the youth group grew to one thousand members. We were doing everything that was required and then some. But we saw a need—for a youth choir.

We didn't go back and say, "Well, Melva Jo is getting involved. What more can you give us in the way of money?" No. We just took on something extra to do. We started with twenty young people, and over the months Melva Jo built a youth choir with more than 140 teenagers!

We did everything that was required of us . . . and then took on one more thing.

That one more thing was what Brother Howard Conaster took before the church. He said, "We want the youth choir to sing one Sunday evening a month, and you, Larry, are to preach that Sunday-evening service."

Do you know what that did for me?

It prepared me for a public ministry. By the time I was twenty-two years old, I was preaching to between three thousand and five thousand people once a month. That's what qualified me to preach to a congregation of thousands every Sunday at the Church on the Rock and to preach regularly to congregations of thousands of people across this nation in our national prayer ministry.

That one extra thing we took on prepared me physically and mentally to preach to the groups God has put before me without any sense of paranoia, fear, or intimidation. A lot of people say to me, "Well, Larry, you are just gifted in public speaking." No, I'm EXPERIENCED in public speaking. And it came about because of an extra effort of hard work that I put in more than fifteen years ago!

I've often wondered what would have happened had I not done that one more thing. It's made a major difference in my life.

Financial Question 4:
Why Do You Work?

You need to ask yourself that question . . . seriously, candidly, and thoughtfully. Why do you work?

Most people will answer, "To survive." They are working just to make money to pay their bills.

The Bible says that our motivation for work must be "as unto the Lord"—and not unto people. We aren't called as Christians to work solely to please someone else. We aren't even called to work solely to please ourselves. We are called to work "as unto the Lord"—to please Him as our senior supervisor.

If you don't work in that fashion, you'll ultimately be disappointed with every job you undertake.

You may be a professional person with your own clinic or office. You may work for the city and drive a truck. Either way read what Colossians 3:22–25 says to you.

> You slaves must always obey your earthly masters, not only trying to please them when they are watching you but all the time; obey them willingly because of your love for the Lord and because you want to please him. Work hard and cheerfully at all you do, just as though you were working for the Lord and not merely for your masters, remembering that it is the Lord Christ who is going to pay you, giving you your full portion of all he owns. He is the one you are really working for. And if you don't do your best for him, he will pay in a way that you won't like—for he has no special favorites who can get away with shirking (TLB).

Word hard and work cheerfully! What great virtues.

Note especially three things in this passage.

1. The Lord Christ is going to pay you a "full portion of all he owns." Friend, when you work for the Lord, you work for a company that has unlimited financial resources. Talk about backing up your company with assets! Talk about a vast fortune!

2. You are working for God, no matter who your earthly employer is. Look yourself in the mirror today and say, "I am working for God. He's my employer."

"But," you say, "I'm not a slave, and this passage is for slaves."

You are a slave. To the Lord Jesus. Paul wrote that again and again. He is a slave to the Lord Jesus Christ, who purchased his eternal soul with the blood He shed on the cross of Calvary.

3. You will also be paid for slovenly work, but you aren't going to like the wages.

"But," you say, "I work for a local mechanic shop." Or "I work for the government." Or "I work for the university." Or "I work for a company."

No, you don't. You work for God. He has given authority to those who supervise your effort on a daily basis. But all authority comes from God.

You may say, "Well, Larry, you don't know my boss. He doesn't act anything like Jesus."

If you could see with your spiritual eyes the position of authority that God has placed that man in . . . for your sake and over your life . . . and God's higher purpose in placing you exactly where you are working daily, . . . you might begin to see that boss with new eyes. Your boss or supervisor—no matter whether he or she is a Christian—has been put in that position over your life by God.

God is not testing your boss in your work environment nearly as much as He is testing YOU. How will you work under authority? How will you stand up to the demands placed on you? How loyal will you be? How will you work when your boss isn't watching? He isn't testing your boss in relationship to you as much as He is testing your boss in relationship to HIS or HER boss! God wants to see how we will respond to authority.

I get up every morning knowing that I work for God. I do my work with an attitude that I want to please God in the work I do.

Financial Questions 5 and 6: Do You Sow Regularly to God's Work? Do You Give in Faith?

I've grouped those two questions together because they are so closely related.

Let me run quickly through God's principles about giving.

First, you are commanded to give to God's work, and the standard for giving is the tithe—10 percent.

Malachi 3:10 says clearly that we are to bring our tithes into the storehouse. It is our responsibility. It's a commandment for our lives. And when we do it, God says, "Prove Me now in this. . . . If I will not open for you the windows of heaven and pour out for you such blessing that there will not be room enough to receive it."

Second, you are commanded to give generously, willingly, and cheerfully.

Second Corinthians 9:6–7 says: "He who sows sparingly will also reap sparingly, and he who sows bountifully will also reap bountifully. So let each one give as he purposes in his heart, not grudgingly or of necessity; for God loves a cheerful giver."

Sow a little. Get a little.

Sow generously. Receive generously.

Third, you will receive in like kind what you sow.

Galatians 6:7–8 says, "Do not be deceived, God is not mocked; for whatever a man sows, that he will also reap. For he who sows to his flesh will of the flesh reap corruption, but he who sows to the Spirit will of the Spirit reap everlasting life." Many people think that this passage relates only to spiritual things. It doesn't. Galatians 6 discusses supporting the fivefold ministry of the church and bearing one another's burdens. The context is actually related to financial matters, although the principles can be applied to both material and spiritual areas of life.

Whatever you sow to the ministry, that you will also reap.

One of the foremost things I've noticed during the recent preacher bashing is that the devil is not solely after the leaders of the church. He is ACTUALLY after the flock—after the laypersons. The devil wants their faith to be utterly destroyed so they will quit supporting the work of the Lord, and, thus, the work of the gospel will not go forth.

I've heard a number of people say in skepticism, "Well, I'm just holding on to my tithe right now to see what happens."

I ask, "For whom are you holding it? That money belongs to the Lord anyway. It's not yours to hold on to."

The minute you get out of the rhythm of sowing your seed and expecting to receive from God what you need, you begin to look to yourself as the source of your total supply in life. And you can't be your own source. At least not a very good one. God alone is the ultimate Source of your supply.

Fourth, the Bible never talks about giving without receiving.

Never. Try to find even one passage that mentions giving in which receiving isn't also mentioned.

"Seek first the kingdom of God and His righteousness, *and all these things shall be added to you*" (Matt. 6:33, emphasis added).

"Whatever a man sows, *that he will also reap*" (Gal. 6:7, emphasis added).

"Give, and it will be given to you (Luke 6:38).

"Bring all the tithes into the storehouse. . . . and prove Me now in this. . . . If *I will not open for you the windows of heaven and pour out for you such blessing that there will not be room enough to receive it*" (Mal. 3:10, emphasis added).

Sowing always has an act of reciprocity in the Bible.

That's God's plan, not ours. That's God's principle, not some a human law of economics.

So I ask you today, "Are you sowing?"

Are you giving of your finances? It's God's wisdom that you do that.

And are you sowing in faith with an expectation that you will receive from God's hand everything He wants and desires for you to have—which is a blessing in every area of your life? Are you anticipating in faith that you will be blessed . . . so you might be a greater blessing? It's God's wisdom that you give in faith.

Financial Question 7: Will You Pray Daily for Wisdom as You Ask God Specifically to Meet Your Financial Needs?

I come to the Lord daily and ask Him for wisdom in how I should deal with the finances of the church and for wisdom in how I should handle my personal finances. (As a pastor, my responsibility is first and foremost to the church and to having wisdom in that area. If you are a pastor, I encourage you also to seek FIRST for the things pertaining to the kingdom of God, and secondarily for yourself. That isn't at all to say that you shouldn't seek God's financial wisdom for your own personal life and that of your family. You should! Just get your seeking of God's wisdom about finances in the proper order.)

When you ask the Lord for wisdom in this area of finance, you must be willing to change or to make adjustments to CONFORM to God's word and to His wisdom. You MUST be willing to change. Unless you are willing to change, there's no point in asking.

God's ways are higher than your ways (see Isa. 55:9). They are higher than my ways. And if you and I are to live up to His ways, then we must be willing to abandon our own lowly ways and move on to higher ground!

Are you willing to accept God's wisdom in your life today in the area of finances? Are you willing to make changes in your life to conform to God's wisdom as it relates to your money? Are you willing to EXPECT God's wisdom to become a reality in your life?

_____*Let's pray about it.*_____

Father, I come to You as my Source and my Provider of everything I need. You know exactly what I need in the way of material resources. You know my heart. I ask You today to forgive me for failing to follow Your wisdom about financial matters. I ask You today to give me the courage to work hard, to save, to live within my means, and—even more so—I ask You to renew in me a right spirit so I WILL trust You as my Source, I will work as unto You, and I

WILL be willing to sow to Your work and to sow in faith, expecting you to BE my Source and to provide for me. Help me, O God, to be a blessing and to be willing to be blessed by You. In Jesus' name I pray. Amen.

Chapter 10

Wisdom and Health

*Now may the God of peace Himself sanctify
you completely; and may your whole spirit,
soul, and body be preserved blameless at the
coming of our Lord Jesus Christ. He who calls
you is faithful, who also will do it.*
— 1 Thessalonians 5:23–24

So much is said today about health. You can scarcely drive down a freeway, read a magazine, listen to the radio, or watch television for even a half hour without coming across at least one billboard, advertisement, or commercial promoting a health club, a new diet plan, or a food product with high fiber, low fat, and no cholesterol! *Prevention* has become a key word in medical circles—an amazing fact since as recently as ten years ago *prevention* was a word linked more to forest fires than to human diseases. We are a fitness-aware, prevention-concerned people.

Indeed, we may be fitness-*crazed* people. Americans spend more money each year on medications, health products, and physician appointments of all kinds—including fitness, health-club, and recreational activities—than on any other single item except for the purchase of a home!

All that does not mean, of course, that we are a fit people. As one man said to me not long ago, "There's a big difference between knowing about oat bran and eating the stuff." The United States is still the nation with the highest average intake of calories per person, and more Americans are overweight per capita than any other people on the earth. We Americans seem to have two major obsessions: eating and dieting.

We are caught, it seems, in an age-old problem. When it comes to our physical health, we know what to do and how to do it. We just *don't* do it.

What is God's wisdom on this truly life-and-death matter? What does the Bible have to say about health and fitness?

I believe that the foremost key to God's wisdom about health lies in our recognition that physical fitness and bodily wellness are only one aspect of a much larger vision of health and wholeness that God has for us. Furthermore, our physical well-being cannot be separated from our TOTAL well-being.

God sees us as whole people. Again and again we read in the Bible that Jesus said to those in need, "Be thou made *whole*." He did not heal without saving. He did not save without healing. In fact, the same root word in Greek gives rise to both of our English words *save* and *heal*. Jesus saw a person's deliverance as total, complete, aimed at restoring WHOLENESS. He saw men and women as fully integrated individuals, albeit ailing in one area of their lives at a particular moment. Mind was not separated from body. Spirit was not separated from mind. Man was total man, woman was total woman—with any one part of a man or a woman related to the total well-being of ALL of that man or woman in any given moment or circumstance.

Stated another way, health relates to far more than our bodies because WE, as human beings, are far more than flesh.

At the same time, the Scriptures state plainly from cover to cover that persons have three functions or aspects of their being. They are triune beings—spirit, soul, and body—in the same way that the Godhead is God the Father, God the Son, and God the Holy Spirit—three in one, each operating distinctively and yet in total and complete harmony as one.

In Genesis 1:26 we read that God said, "Let Us make man in Our image, according to Our likeness." We have been created in the image and likeness of God, who is spirit. At the very core of your essence you are spirit. It is that aspect of your nature that communes intimately with the Most High God and gives rise to every other unique and distinctive quality in your life. Never lose sight of the fact that you are a *spiritual* creation.

In the next verses and chapters of Genesis we read that God molded the dust and made a man—and then a woman as bone of his bone and flesh of his flesh. Human beings are physical entities.

And then we read that God placed the man and the woman that He had made in a garden and gave them the mental authority to name all of the animals. He gave them a freedom of choice—to choose the manner in which they would subdue and replenish the earth. He gave them a free will—to choose to obey or disobey God. And God also gave them the capacity to feel—to know sadness and joy. Man was created with a soul, which we sometimes call mind, or will, or emotions.

God made man and woman unique creatures: spirit, soul, and body, blended as one.

The apostle Paul recognized this triune nature of persons when he wrote to the church at Thessalonica: "Now may the God of peace Himself sanctify you completely; and may your whole spirit, soul, and body be preserved blameless at the coming of our Lord Jesus Christ" (1 Thess. 5:23).

Note especially the order of Paul's words: *first*, spirit; *second*, soul; and *third*, body. So often we hear this verse misquoted in reverse order: "body, mind, and spirit" or "body, soul, and spirit." But Paul stated very precisely the true order of our creation. We are first and foremost spirit. Above everything else we are a spiritual creation. It is our spirit that will live on into eternity. It is our spirit that joins with the Holy Spirit in prayer to defeat the forces of Satan in this world. It is our spirit that bears the fruit that is good and lasting and most beneficial for life: love, joy, peace, faith, long-suffering, meekness, goodness, temperance, kindness, and gentleness.

Your spirit is the real you. Never lose sight of the fact that you are spirit. Not that you have a spirit. You *are* spirit. It is your lasting, unique, and ever-present nature.

Secondarily, we are created as souls. We have minds, wills, and emotions. Our souls are connected with our spirits in an intricate and awesome way to reveal the very nature of our souls and to give our spirits expression.

Perhaps the saddest words any person can hear a physician say about one they love is that the beloved one is brain-dead. The body continues to function, but the mind of the person has been impaired. No longer does that person exert control over his bodily expressions. The link between spirit and soul has been severed. Laughter and tears and words are gone.

On the other hand, we see those who, even with the most severe physical limitations—quadriplegics, the multiply disabled, the severely maimed—rise up in their humanity to become productive, joyful, and richly blessed human beings when they choose to remain alive and strong in their souls. Their minds are active; their wills are determined; their emotions are strong. The link between soul and spirit is intact and operating fully. What an inspiration such a person can be!

It is our soul that allows us to display different personalities, traits, skills, and talents and to speak in such a way that virtually every sentence we speak in our lives is an original string of words. Everything we know as communication—whether written, spoken, body language, dance, art—is an expression of our soul nature. Never lose sight of the fact that you are a soul.

Thirdly—lastly—we are flesh. It is our "weakness," according to Paul. As you read Paul's letters, you come across numerous references to the frailty and limitations of the flesh. The works of the flesh are corrupt; the lusts of the flesh war against the spirit. Physical prowess profits very little apart from the spirit and soul of a person.

To Peter, the flesh was associated with filth, corruption, and death. He likens our flesh to the fragile grasses that wither and die in the heat of the day.

In reading the words from these apostles, one might draw the conclusion that the flesh is worthless—something to be denied, beaten, and flagellated—as is done in many cults. Not so! There is a balance in the apostles' teaching. Time and time again we see these apostles praying for the physical healing of the saints. Paul's journeys were filled with miraculous healings of body.

Jesus Himself came "eating and drinking" (Matt. 11:19). He lived within the form of flesh. The incarnation—God in flesh—is the very hope of our lives that we, too, might be a reflection of God resident in human form. Jesus could just as easily have manifested Himself as spirit only or as soul only, but He came as a baby—a living bundle of flesh, thus validating the value of our bodies as we live life on this earth.

Our bodies are not to be worshiped. Neither are they to be considered as worthless. They have a function, and that is to carry out the will of the spirit and soul—to express ideas; to show emotions; to create and procreate; to complete work; to engage in prayer, praise, and worship. Our bodies allow us to relate our inner selves to one another and thus to build up the greater body of Christ and to establish the kingdom of God.

How different that view of our bodies is from the picture of humanity that we get from advertisements for get-thin-overnight diet pills and commercials for running shoes! To the secular mind today, the body is everything. And if not everything, the most important thing. From God's perspective the body is a valuable tool for carrying out the will of God on this earth.

Furthermore, God has structured our humanity so that our triune nature functions from the inside out. Our nature, our identity, and our uniqueness flow from the soul outward through the spirit, which then expresses itself through the body. If we diagramed human nature in very simple terms, the illustration might look something like the accompanying drawing.

Finally, it is important to recognize that God intended for all three aspects of our beings to function in harmony. That is wellness. That is health. That is fitness. When one part of a person is sick or hurting or diseased, the TOTAL person is sick, or hurt, or diseased.

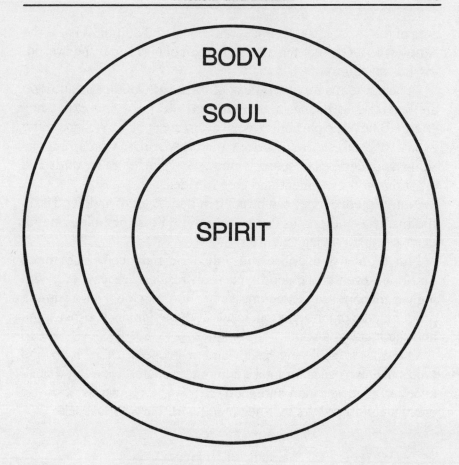

Have you ever had a bad hangnail? Your entire body hurts! In reality, you can sit down and analyze the situation and say, "Just this one finger hurts." But the pain somehow affects everything you do!

When you feel "down" in your soul, your body doesn't feel like moving. Extremely depressed people generally become bedridden because their bodies simply quit functioning with strength and energy.

To discover and experience God's wisdom for health, then, we must begin to think of fitness from the inside out, not the outside in. And we must think in terms of WHOLENESS, of all parts of our beings working in harmony.

I believe that another concept is vital for us to understand before we move into a more detailed discussion of health in each major area of our lives. It is the concept of intake and output. That is the simplest aspect of our function as human beings and is the overriding law related to our health.

In health terms we often speak of intake and output as nutrition and exercise as taking in the nutrients we need and expending energy. The principle holds true in every area of life. We inhale and exhale. We take into our beings pictures, songs, words, impressions, and all types of sensory input. We "exhale" new words and emotions and movement and creative ideas.

Nutrition, of course, can be good or bad. A lot of junk food is on the market—and not just for your body! The same holds true for exercise. Just moving isn't exercising.

Nutrition and exercise must also be balanced. Too much nutrition—even of the good kind—can result in excess, overloading, stagnation, self-centeredness, fat. Too much exercise without proper intake of nutrients can result in depletion; loss; exhaustion; and, ultimately, death.

Our goal in achieving health and wholeness, then, is to find God's divine balance for intake and output in our lives—God's balance for good nutrition and good exercise. We must seek this in every area of our lives . . . beginning with our spiritual self.

Spiritual Fitness

A number of years ago I found myself riding in the backseat of a car with one of my heroes in the faith: Dr. Paul Yonggi Cho, pastor of the world's largest church—Yoido Full Gospel Church in Seoul, South Korea. Dr. Cho was and is a spiritual giant to me, and my respect and awe of him were immense as we drove through the streets of Dallas that afternoon.

With great sincerity—for I truly wanted all of the wisdom and insight I could gain from that rare opportunity to be with him—I turned to Dr. Cho and said, "Dr. Cho, what is the secret of your success?"

He answered me quickly and succinctly: "I pray and I obey." And then he chuckled that distinctive "ha-ha-ha" laugh of his, and I, not knowing what else to do in that moment, joined him in laughter—although I readily admit that I didn't have any idea at the time just *why* we were both laughing!

Now I had expected some great and glorious exposition from Dr. Cho—something I could really grab hold of as a secret formula for ministry. I expected him to condense his years of experience and insight into at least twenty or thirty minutes of private counsel as we drove along. I was an eager recipient of all he had to say; I was waiting to hang on every word. And here it all was in one short sentence: "I pray and I obey." It wasn't that I was disappointed in his answer; it's just that it was . . . well . . . shorter than I had anticipated!

And yet, as I have thought about Dr. Cho's answer over the years, I have come to appreciate more and more what a tremendous answer rooted in God's wisdom he gave me that day. He truly gave me the key to spiritual fitness.

I liken it to spiritual breathing. Inhale. Exhale. "I pray and I obey."

To PRAY and to hear from God are inhaling. It is taking in all of God's nature, . . . God's opinions, . . . God's heartbeat, . . . God's desires. It is feeding on the word of God made alive in your spirit for that day, that hour. It is experiencing God in every circumstance, every situation. Talking to God and then hearing from God in prayer are tantamount to good spiritual nutrition. It is taking into your spirit the "right stuff" on which to feed and live and draw strength and energy.

Obeying God—following through to speak or do what God says—is like exhaling. It's expending your very life's energy toward being not only a hearer but also a doer of His word to you. Sometimes obeying takes great courage and great effort. It is truly the EXERCISE of your faith.

Good spiritual nutrition. Good spiritual exercise. "I pray and I obey."

The health of your spiritual self, which is central to the health of your total being, begins with prayer—not only a commitment to pray but actually to practice prayer on a daily basis.

We eat every day. In fact, most of us eat at least three meals a day, not to mention countless snacks between those meals. We easily spend an hour a day feeding ourselves. Why not pray every day? Why not pray an *hour* every day?

A number of years ago, as I was reading the story of Jesus in the Garden of Gethsemane, the words of Jesus to His disciples seemed to leap off the page to me and ring in my entire being: *"Could you not tarry one hour?"* (see Matt. 26:40). Jesus was experiencing the greatest spiritual battle of His life there in Gethsemane. His hour had come for the ultimate defeat of Satan for all ages. His disciples were with Him, and yet they weren't. They were there in body but not in soul and spirit. They were asleep. Twice Jesus called them awake. "Pray," He said. "Pray that ye enter not into temptation."

In that moment I saw with new insight that the Lord Jesus continues to wage a spiritual battle on OUR behalf today. Seated at the right hand of the Father and with all of the angels of heaven at His command, He is waging a war for OUR lives. And how might we engage ourselves in that battle with Him? Only through prayer! "Can you not tarry with Me for one hour?" He asks. With all of my being I responded in that moment, "Yes, Lord, I WILL pray. I *will* tarry one hour a day with you."

And I made that the pattern of my life. I challenge you to do the same. There's simply no substitute for setting aside an hour for spiritual intake, for spiritual nourishment in your life. There's no excuse for NOT doing it.

I will not begin to tell you that it's easy. Many mornings I've longed to roll over and spend that hour sleeping. But the battle the Lord is waging is a battle on MY account, on YOUR account, on the account of your children and family and loved ones. Can you not tarry one hour to wage that battle with Him? Can you not spend one hour with the Lord each day?

Immediately, I began to ask questions of the Lord that I'm sure are questions we all ask at one time: "What do I do for an hour? How do I pray for an hour? What shall I say?"

These are not impudent questions to the Lord. They are honest ones. In fact, "How shall we pray?" is a question asked by Jesus' own disciples (see Luke 11:1–4). His answer to them and to us is the prayer we call today The Lord's Prayer.

I personally don't see any way to improve on the prayer that Jesus Himself established as an outline. And so that is my prayer each morning. Here is HOW I pray. Here is how this great prayer becomes good SPIRITUAL NUTRITION for my wholeness, wellness, fitness, health, and well-being . . . and for those who pray with me at the Church on the Rock or in prayer meetings across this nation.

We begin by praying, *"Our Father in heaven, hallowed be Your name."*

Who is God to you? What has He done for you? What aspects of His nature has He revealed to you? Praise Him for His very nature!

He is the Most High God, the Creator of the heavens and the earth, the almighty One. He is YOUR Creator.

He is your Savior, . . .

    your Deliverer, . . .

        your Protector, . . .

            your Counselor, . . .

                your Comforter, . . .

                    your Source of total supply in life. He is the Vine, and you are the branch abiding in Him. He is your Friend of friends. He is your Righteousness. He is living Water flowing through your life, carrying away any impurities and cleansing you so you are as white as snow. He is your Way. He is the Truth. He is Life itself. He is your Rock, your sure foundation when the winds of change blow against your life. He is King of all that you own and have. He is the Lord over everything that attempts to lord it over you. He is your Healer. He is the One who makes you whole.

Begin to say aloud WHO the Father is to you. Lift up the name of Jesus. In these minutes you are literally setting your affection on the Father. You are giving Him your full attention. You are focusing on His name. You are declaring that He is your everything.

Give Him thanks for all that He has done for you as a loving Father. I stand and say, "Father, holy is Your name! You are my Father, MY Father. I draw my life from You. I draw my 'spiritual genetic traits' from Your fatherhood. I take into my being the fullness of You. I long to be Your son. Holy is Your name forevermore!"

Ten thousand years times ten thousand years times ten thousand years from now we will be praying that same prayer. We won't be concerned about our mortgage payments or what color dress to wear or what somebody said about us at work or about what kind of car to buy. We'll be crying out to God even as the angels shout around His throne today, "Holy, holy, holy is the Lord!"

"Our Father in heaven, hallowed be Your name."

And then we pray, *"Your kingdom come. Your will be done"* (Matt. 6:10).

What is God's will for your life? Do you know it? What are the attributes of His kingdom?

Begin to pray about those. Pray that they will be established in your life NOW . . . this day.

"But," you may say, "I'm not sure what God's will is for my life."

Let me tell you! God has made a fivefold covenant with those who love Him and seek to serve Him. That covenant is an expression of God's will for you.

First, it is God's will that you be saved and delivered from anything and everything that would attempt to destroy you or keep you from doing the work that God has set for you to do. It is God's will that you be free from the enemy's snare and safe from the devil's attacks on your life. It is God's will that you be saved and be saved totally—spirit, soul, and body.

Second, it is God's will that you be filled with the Holy Spirit and experience His comfort, counsel, and power every day of your life—not just once in the distant past and not just in theory. His will is that you experience His comfort, counsel, and power AS YOU LIVE YOUR LIFE each hour, each day, each week. It is God's will that your spirit be united with His Spirit.

Third, it is God's will that you be whole. God desires for you to live in health, with spirit, soul, and body functioning in harmony. He created you that way. It's His design. He said that His creation was good. It's His plan for your life to function as He created it to function. God wants you to be well and in good health.

Fourth, it is God's will that the work of your hands be fruitful and that your efforts be multiplied into a harvest of reward. God wants you to experience an increase in your life as you grow from grace to grace and from glory to glory. God's way is an upward spiral, not a downward spiral. God desires that you reap an abundant harvest from the good seeds that you sow in good soil. God desires that you prosper in all areas of your being, simultaneously and in harmony.

And fifth, God's will is that you fight spiritual battles and win. It is God's will that you defeat the devil and conquer your spiritual enemies. It is God's will that you confront evil and destroy it, thereby claiming yet one more piece of this world for God's kingdom.

That's God's will for you!

There may be other specifics that God has revealed only to you about what He would have you do, but these things are God's will for EVERY believer. The Bible is filled with promises and commandments and covenant statements that point toward these five things. You will find no place in the Scriptures where God denies these things to those who love Him and earnestly seek His face.

I stand in that confidence and pray aloud, "Father, let Your will be done in my life today! Save me, O God, from the enemy. Deliver me from the oppressor. Defeat the enemy in my life. Fill me with Your Holy Spirit and let me experience Your comfort, counsel, and power today. Make me whole, O God. Mend the broken places in my life. Heal me. Make me strong. Put my life back together the way You created it to be. Cause the things that I do to bear a good harvest of good fruit for Your kingdom. Work through me, O God, to defeat the devil today. Let Your WILL be done, Father. Let it be done in my life!"

And what is the kingdom that we are asking God to establish?

The kingdom of God is where joy, peace, and righteousness reign supreme. That is the very atmosphere of heaven. And our prayer is that this same atmosphere of heaven will become the atmosphere in which we live and move and have our being here on the earth. It is this atmosphere that we inhale into our lives as we pray.

God's kingdom is one of joy. Are you experiencing His joy in your family, in your job, in your church, in your relationships with friends and neighbors and colleagues? I pray, "Father, let me experience YOUR joy today. Let the atmosphere of my family, my workplace, my church, my car be one filled with JOY. I declare that Your kingdom WILL come to my life, and I will have joy."

God's kingdom is one of PEACE. Are you experiencing peace today? In your family, your job, your church, your relationships? I stand and put my foot down and say with all my heart, "Father, let Your kingdom and its peace come into my life. Let everything related to Your kingdom be magnified, amplified, exemplified, and glorified through my life today. Your kingdom come. Your will be done!"

And then we pray, *"Give us this day our daily bread"* (Matt. 6:11).

God invites us to pray for our needs and to ask Him for daily bread—which is a term encompassing everything we need in life. He says to ask, and so I do. I stand in prayer and ask Him to give me what I need to feed and clothe myself and my family, to provide a house for us to live in, to give me the resources I require for my children to have an education, and so forth. I pray for the things we need in the church. I pray specifically for certain people, for situations, for problems, for things. I pray for every need and every area of lack and want that I feel in my life.

A blind man in Jericho once cried out to Jesus with such intensity and perseverance that Jesus stopped His journey and called for the man to be brought to Him. When this blind man, whose name was Bartimaeus, stood before Jesus, the first thing Jesus said to him was, "What do you want Me to do for you?" (Mark 10:51).

It certainly was obvious to all the people there in Jericho, and certainly to Jesus, that Bartimaeus was blind. He was dressed like a blind man of that day, in a beggar's robe. He had to be led to Jesus. His eyes lacked luster and focus. Everyone in Jericho knew that he was blind and had been for a long time. But Jesus said, "What do you want Me to do for you?" Apparently, there was value in Bartimaeus' SAYING to the Lord what he wanted and needed in his life. And it was only when Bartimaeus said, "Rabboni, that I may receive my sight" that he was healed (Mark 10:51).

Many people say to me, "Well, God knows my problem, and I'm willing for Him to do something about it if He wants to." Friend, that isn't the way God set it up. He says to ask, and to ask specifically, for what we want. I don't know why Jesus set it up that way. But He did. It's up to us to do the ASKING. So I do.

And then we pray, *"Forgive us our debts as we forgive our debtors"* (Matt. 6:12).

The most important thing you and I can experience in life is God's forgiveness. Guilt is the greatest burden any of us can possibly bear. The weight of sin is intolerable.

I believe with all my heart that someday medical science will be able to measure the full damage of guilt on a person's physical health, and I believe that it will be enormous. Why? Because guilt and sin are the chief diseases of the spirit, and our spirit is the core of our being. It is impossible for the whole person to function in health and harmony if the spirit is suffering from disease.

Our number one prayer must always be, "O God, have mercy on me, a sinner. Father I have sinned. Cleanse me and make me clean!"

That is not just a once-in-a-lifetime prayer. That is a prayer for every day, because the sin of this world clings to us like dust on our feet as we go about our lives. We bathe daily. We ask God's forgiveness daily for the cleansing of our souls from this world's dirt and filth and smut.

And yet, there is something that can block the flow of God's forgiveness into our lives. What is it? It's our refusal to forgive others. The Scriptures state it clearly again and again: you cannot receive forgiveness from God if you do not forgive others.

We are forgiven AS we forgive. Unforgiveness is like a major blockage in the river of life flowing through our souls. It keeps guilt from being washed away. It keeps our spirits from being truly cleansed.

As Paul wrote to the Colossians:

As the elect of God, holy and beloved, put on tender mercies, kindness, humbleness of mind, meekness, longsuffering; *bearing with one another, and forgiving one another, if anyone has a complaint against another*, even as Christ forgave you, so you also must do (Col. 3:12–13, emphasis added).

In the words of Jesus, "Be merciful, just as your Father also is merciful. Judge not, and you shall not be judged. Condemn not, and you shall not be condemned. *Forgive, and you will be forgiven*" (Luke 6:36–37, emphasis added).

If there is one key to your spiritual health, it is this: forgive and receive God's forgiveness in your life.

How do we forgive others? We pray for them, and we do good to them.

I stand, therefore, every day and pray, "Father, I pray for my enemies," and I name them. "I pray that You will heal them. I pray that You will save them and fill them with Your Spirit. I pray that You will lead them into Your wholeness and prosperity. I pray that You will deliver them from the devil's snares. I pray that You will restore all the enemy has stolen from them. Father, I forgive them for what they have done to me, and I ask You to forgive me so I might be free of all sin and guilt. Let me be blameless in Your sight, O God!"

We then pray, *"Do not lead us into temptation, but deliver us from the evil one"* (Matt. 6:13).

The unspoken truth behind this phrase is that the evil one is after you. He wants your life, your health, your mind, your money, your family, your mission in life. He's out to steal, kill, and destroy whatever he can get his hands on. Temptation is all around us.

The great cry of victory, however, is that the evil one can and will be defeated if we will resist him! We can walk in God's paths away from temptation.

Psalm 37:23 says, "The steps of a good man are ordered by the Lord, and He delights in his way."

I stand and pray, "Lord, I believe that You are the good Shepherd and that You are going to lead me today as one of Your sheep in paths of righteousness for Your name's sake. I'm trusting You to order my steps."

And then I get armed for spiritual battle. How? I take up the whole armor described by Paul in his letter to the Ephesians (6:11–17):

- a girdle of truth for our loins
- a breastplate of righteousness
- shoes of preparation of the gospel of peace
- a shield of faith
- a helmet of salvation
- the sword of the Spirit

That's our spiritual armor! And every morning in prayer I put it on. I declare, "Lord, Your truth is going to dominate me today and be the nature of everything I create. Righteousness is going to be all over my heart. My feet are ready to walk in the Spirit today wherever You lead me. I'm picking up my shield of faith to quench every fiery dart the devil throws my way. I'm pulling down my headgear so that my mind is going to be focused on Your saving power. Your word is going to be in my mouth today and will go forth from me to penetrate the shadows of darkness. I'm ready to go in You, God!"

And finally we pray, *"Yours is the kingdom and the power and the glory forever"* (Matt. 6:13).

We conclude our time of prayer by praising God and worshiping Him and exalting His name on the earth! We lift Him up high. We declare that all we are and have and will ever be or do belongs to Him. We acknowledge that all power comes from Him and that all glory belongs to Him and that it is His kingdom, not our own, that we are trying to build.

The Bible says that God inhabits the praises of His people. The angels are present, too, anytime praise is voiced. The Bible also says that God gives His angels charge over us (Ps. 91:11; Matt. 4:6) and that God sends His angels to be "ministering spirits" on our behalf (Heb. 1:14). Do you know what happens when we sit back and refuse to praise and exalt God? The angels fold their wings and wait. They cannot operate apart from our praise. Their purpose is to praise God. Their purpose is to worship Him. And it is not until we have the same PURPOSE as the angels that they can fight battles in the spirit realm for our sakes.

Our praises to almighty God actually RELEASE the angels to do battle for us. Our praises release the power of God into our lives. Our praises cause His kingdom to advance and His glory to shine forth. What a privilege it is to praise the Lord!

And, friend, let me assure you that after you have prayed for an hour, . . .

declaring the presence of the Father in your life and that He is holy, . . .

declaring that His kingdom and His will ARE going to be in your life, . . .

asking for the things you need, . . .

forgiving others and receiving forgiveness, . . .

putting on your spiritual armor and preparing to walk in paths of righteousness, . . .

it will be no problem to praise the Lord! Your very soul will erupt with praise and worship. You will know as you can never know any other way that He is your all in all, that apart from Him you are nothing, but that with Him you can do all things.

When you pray like that, you are truly taking God's nature, His purposes, His direction, His forgiveness, His will, His hopes and desires and goals and dreams for you INTO your life and making them your own. You are feeding on Him. You are delighting in Him. Friend, that's spiritual nutrition of the highest order!

And your spiritual exercise?

It is the exercise of resistance.

John Jacobs and the Power Team are closely associated with the Church on the Rock. I meet with John periodically for great times of sharing in the Lord, and I've been to the gym with these great hulking guys of the Power Team to watch them work out. Along the way I've learned something about strength.

A weight lifter's muscles become strong through the process of resistance. It's not lifting a heavy weight that adds strength but letting down that weight ever so s-l-o-w-l-y. Holding the muscle against the weight—or resisting the pull of the weight—causes the muscle cells to get stronger.

The same is true in the spirit realm.

What are we called to do once we are fully clothed with our spiritual armor? Paul wrote, "Put on the whole armor of God, that you may be able to stand against the wiles of the devil. . . . Therefore take up the whole armor of God, that you may be able to withstand in the evil day, and having done all, to stand" (Eph. 6:11, 13).

We are to make a stand and resist. And we are to pray. Paul said that once we are fully armed, we should be "praying always with all prayer and supplication in the Spirit, being watchful to this end with all perseverance and supplication for all the saints" (Eph. 6:18).

We stand and we pray. That is the exercise of our faith. That is our RESISTANCE.

The Bible clearly says that when we resist the devil, He WILL flee from us (see James 4:7). He's got easier prey to pursue. He doesn't hang around those who put up a strong resistance.

The output of our spiritual nature, then, is to resist, to persevere, to endure to the end, to take a stand—and to pray in the Spirit. When we do that, we become stronger. We experience the value of exercise in our spirits.

Good nutrition. Good exercise. "I pray and I obey."

That's God's wisdom for spiritual fitness!

Fitness for the Soul

Where do we begin in our quest for soul fitness—health for our minds, emotions, and will?

As we discussed earlier, your soul is the seat of your will. It is within your power as a human being to make choices; to make decisions; to exert your will so that your mind, emotions, and, ultimately, your body must obey. That is a part of your God-given ability as a God-created soul.

Many people say to me, "I just don't have any willpower."

But you do. God gave you a will. He gave you the power to use it. The truth of the matter is that these people don't WANT to use their willpower.

God's health for our souls comes as we exert our will to make three key decisions or as we answer three key questions.

First, "WHAT WILL YOU TAKE INTO YOUR SOUL?"

We've all heard the phrase "Don't let them do your thinking for you." In reality, nobody can do your thinking for you. You alone determine what you will think about, what you will imagine, what you will dwell on in your mind. You—and you alone—decide what you will allow into your soul and what you will allow to grow there.

God's challenge to you—indeed, God's wisdom on this matter—is that you RENEW your mind. In Ephesians 4:21–24 we read:

> As the truth is in Jesus: that you put off, concerning your former conduct, the old man which grows corrupt according to the deceitful lusts, and be renewed in the spirit of your mind, and that you put on the new man which was created according to God, in righteousness and true holiness.

As we discussed in an earlier chapter, something is to be PUT OFF in the process of soul renewal. And something is to be PUT ON. The something to be PUT OFF often involves turning off or tuning out or walking away.

Think for a moment about all of the messages that are being carried on airwaves through your home or office this very instant. You can't see them, but they are there. How do I know that? Because if I walked into your home or office with a radio or television set, I'd be able to tune in hundreds of channels of information and input for your soul! Much of it would be "junk food" for your mind and emotions. Some of it would represent good nutrition. The messages are there. But it's up to you to tune them in or tune them out.

A big part of renewing your mind is CHOOSING not to take negative "junk food" input into your soul. You simply CHOOSE not to receive it.

You may say, "But what about those messages I can't tune out? The criticism from those at work, the angry shouts, and the swear words that come my way whether or not I want them to?"

You CHOOSE not to let them lodge in your spirit. You CHOOSE not to respond to them. You CHOOSE not to let them influence you or disrupt you or influence you in any way.

Can you make that choice? You can! In Philippians 4:8 we read,

Brethren, whatever things are true, whatever things are noble, whatever things are just, whatever things are pure, whatever things are lovely, whatever things are of good report, if there is any virtue and if there is anything praiseworthy—meditate on these things.

Paul wouldn't have told his readers to do something impossible to do! You CAN choose what to think about and concentrate on. When negative influences come your way, immediately make a choice to think a replacement thought that is something of GOOD report. You CAN do it. It's the renewal of your mind.

"But," you say, "my culture has made me a certain way. My family upbringing has taught me to think a certain way."

You can change that. The Bible says that once you are born anew in your spirit, you have the mind of Christ. You can begin to think the way Christ thinks. You can begin to speak what Jesus would say if He were on the earth today. You can react and respond the way Jesus would when confronted with problems and negative input. You can stand and declare today in the face of anger or blasphemy or hurtful words and actions, "I have the mind of Christ. I will not respond according to my old nature. I will respond according to my NEW nature. I will CHOOSE to think about things that are noble, just, pure, lovely, true, and of good report."

Is that denying reality?

No! It's choosing a HIGHER reality!

We know that the world and all that has been influenced by Satan and his minions are corrupt, filthy, and decaying. But we don't have to wallow there. We can CHOOSE to occupy a higher reality in our souls and to feed—nourish, nurture, develop—our souls with the good things of God.

You can choose what you will take into your soul. Choose RENEWAL!

Second, you must answer this question: "HOW WILL YOU CHOOSE TO RESPOND?"

The challenge of the Scriptures is to respond with REJOICING. That's God's wisdom for the health of your soul.

Recently, a woman came to me for counsel and started by saying, "I'm so worried, Pastor." She then proceeded to give me twenty minutes worth of reasons why she was worried and depressed. Finally, she stopped and asked, "What do I do?"

I said, "Rejoice."

She stared at me as if she hadn't quite heard me correctly. "Did you say rejoice?"

"Yes, rejoice."

"What good will that do?"

I said, "It's the only good thing you CAN do. There's really nothing else you CAN do that will make any difference. Rejoice is the only godly response you can make!"

When we rejoice, we are saying, "God, in the face of all this mess confronting me—these problems, these tragedies, these tough situations, these bad circumstances, this insufferable obstacle—I know that my only hope is You and that You WILL act on my behalf, and, therefore, I choose to have JOY because You will be the victor in this. I rejoice at what You are going to do!"

Depression and rejoicing cannot live in the same house.

Worry and rejoicing cannot live in the same house.

Hatred and anger and bitterness cannot live with rejoicing in the same house.

But again, you must CHOOSE to rejoice.

HOW do we rejoice? What does it mean to rejoice?

It means that we respond to the situation or circumstance with praise to God. Note especially that our praise is *to God*. We aren't praising the situation or the person causing the trouble. We aren't praising God FOR the negative circumstance. Our praise is directed away from the trouble and toward God. Our praise is TO GOD.

The same goes for our thanksgiving. We are not thankful FOR the problem or *for* the circumstance. We are thankful *in* the midst of the circumstance. We are thankful to GOD for His delivering power.

Hebrews 13:15 says, "By Him let us continually offer the *sacrifice of praise to God, that is, the fruit of our lips, giving thanks to His name*" (emphasis added).

Our rejoicing is voicing our praise and thanksgiving to God. We rejoice IN THE LORD. We rejoice because of the Lord. We rejoice at the victory that will come from the Lord. We rejoice because we belong to the Lord. We CHOOSE to have joy as the hallmark of our souls.

You can express many emotions when faced with a difficult time. God's wisdom is that you express JOY.

You can express many emotions when faced with a difficult person. God's wisdom is that you express LOVE.

You can express many emotions when faced with trouble and turmoil and change that you can't control. God's wisdom is that you express peace and faith.

These are choices you make. You can determine the response of your soul.

Third, you face the question "WHAT WILL YOU SAY?"

Again, the answer is one you can CHOOSE to make with your will. It's a decision you face.

Jesus faced the Pharisees one day and had some very bold, tough words for them.

> Brood of vipers! How can you, being evil, speak good things? For out of the abundance of the heart the mouth speaks. A good man out of the good treasure of his heart brings forth good things, and an evil man out of the evil treasure beings forth evil things. But I say to you that for every idle [not flowing from God] word men may speak, they will give account of it in the day of judgment. For by your words you will be justified, and by your words you will be condemned (Matt. 12:34–37).

Jesus was giving them the chain or hierarchy for our communication. We speak from our souls what is TRUE in our spirits. If our spirits are out of alignment with God, our words will cause pain, confusion, and alienation. If our spirits are in tune with God, our words will bring healing, unity, and peace.

We must make a decision that we will speak God's words into the situations of our lives and bring about God's reality even in the midst of problems.

You may ask, "Are you talking about name-it-and-claim-it theology, Larry?"

No. I see a great many problems arising when people name a blessing from God but don't want to fulfill the responsibility that God attaches to the blessing. Most of the Bible's promises are IF-THEN covenants. In other words, IF we do certain things, then God will act in a certain way. We can't have God's blessing unless we are willing to do our part.

I hear others who are naming and claiming what THEY want to happen. Their claims have nothing to do with the will and purpose of God. They are voicing their own private wishes.

This does not mean that I deny the power of a true biblical confession. Not at all! There is great power in speaking the words of God into a situation. The very means that God used to create a beautiful, productive, living world out of a dead, formless, meaningless void was the SPOKEN WORD. When we speak God's words in the right context and with full responsibility for fulfilling our part of His covenant, we can see great results. We'll see God's creative power manifest itself in ways that are in keeping with the nature of God.

The Bible teaches that often we have not because we either don't ask of God OR we ask amiss, seeking to use God's blessings for our own consumption and to fulfill our own lusts. Appropriating God's goodness to fulfill our own "lust of the flesh, . . . lust of the eyes, . . . and pride of life" (1 John 2:16) is the direct opposite of what God desires for us. His blessings are for us to enjoy and to pass on. We bear fruit in our lives so others might taste it and see that God is good. We produce harvests so that even as we are blessed, we BECOME a blessing to others.

Our words, our confessions must have two great overriding characteristics.

First, they must be what God says about the situation.

Second, they must produce a blessing that extends beyond our-selves to reach others.

That's a true biblical confession, and nothing can match it!

Certainly, the power of the spoken word cannot be denied. James had a great deal to say about this and about the importance of taming the tongue or of harnessing the power of the spoken word.

> We put bits in horses' mouths that they may obey us, and we turn their whole body. Look also at ships: although they are so large and are driven by fierce winds, they are turned by a very small rudder wherever the pilot desires. Even so the tongue is a little member and boasts great things. See how great a forest a little fire kindles! And the tongue is a fire, a world of iniquity. The tongue is so set among our members that it defiles the whole body, and sets on fire the course of nature; and it is set on fire by hell. For every kind of beast and bird, of reptile and creature of the sea, is tamed and has been tamed by mankind. But no man can tame the tongue. It is an unruly evil, full of deadly poison. With it we bless our God and Father, and with it we curse men, who have been made in the similitude of God. Out of the same mouth proceed blessing and cursing. My brethren, these things ought not to be so. Does a spring send forth fresh water and bitter from the same opening? Can a fig tree, my brethren, bear olives, or a grapevine bear figs? Thus no spring can yield both salt water and fresh (James 3:3–12).

How do our spoken words relate to the health of our souls? I believe that the connection is a very direct one. The number one person hearing the words you speak is YOU. You are your own primary audience. The words come out of your mouth, and, gener-ally, the closest set of ears to them are your own!

What you say recyles into your soul. The Scriptures say that "faith comes by hearing . . . the word of God" (Rom. 10:17). If your words are in line with what the Bible says, then those words will sink into your spirit and cause faith to develop. If they are NOT in line with God's Word, then they will sink into your spirit and cause doubt to grow. Faith builds you up toward wholeness. Doubt tears you down to defeat. It's that simple.

The Bible says that you are created by God. You are beloved by Him. You are worth something in this life because you are precious to Him. You are His child. You have talents and skills and abilities that He has given you. You are called according to His purposes, and eternal life belongs to you.

When you speak words along those lines to others and to yourself, you HEAR those words; and since they coincide with God's Word, they build you up. The Bible uses the word *edify*. You are edified, built up, encouraged, strengthened, and MADE MORE WHOLE by what you hear.

But when you criticize or pass judgment or slander, those words tear down and destroy. They give rise to bitterness and distrust and discouragement. And those, my friends, are the breeding ground for worry and depression. And those, in turn, are fertile soil for disease and sickness and pain.

You may say, "Are you talking about mind over matter, Larry? That I can 'talk myself' into better health?"

No. I'm saying that as believers in the Lord Jesus Christ, we are called to have our SPIRITS dictate to our minds and bodies what they should do. Nothing can damage our spirits more than feeding them with doubt, fear, and discouragement. And when our SPIRITS are defeated, then we are no longer WHOLE persons, and it's very difficult to stay healthy in either our souls or our bodies.

You have a choice rooted in your soul as to what you will SAY. God's wisdom is that you say what He says. You have a choice to make.

Now CHOOSING to renew your mind and to think with the mind of Christ, . . . CHOOSING to rejoice even when tough times come, . . . CHOOSING to speak the words of God . . . cause your SPIRIT to be exercised and nourished in good ways.

You are embedding the good thoughts, good emotions, and good words of God into your mind, heart, and spirit. You are exercising your will to EXPRESS only the good thoughts, emotions, and words of God into the world. A healthy balance is struck—a good bridge is built between spirit and body.

Some months ago I had a conversation with Dr. Larry Edwards, who was the dean of the School of Medicine at Oral Roberts University for several years. While we were discussing the relationship of disease to our souls and spirits, he said, "Larry, I have found in my practice that nearly 80 percent of all disease is caused by stress-related problems."

Stress!

We hear about it again and again and again. It's a killer. It's a destroyer. And it seems to be the plague of our age.

What causes stress?

Some people say, "Too much to do in too little time."

Some people say, "Too many pollutants in our environment."

Some people say, "An inability to let go."

Some people say, "My boss," or, "My job."

Some people say, "My husband," or, "My wife."

Some people say, "Being responsible for too many things at once."

All of those responses have *some* truth to them!

I believe that the ROOT of stress, however, lies in the spirit at those points where we fail to trust God. We may fail to trust God in very subtle ways—thinking that God's too busy or that God's unconcerned about certain areas of our lives. We may not even be aware that we are failing to trust God. But the fact is that we are no longer relying totally on God to meet a particular need or to provide for a particular area of our life. At that point we then try to do it on our own strength. We start STRIVING to make something happen.

STRiving leads to STRess.

We no longer seek to have God renew our minds, because we are operating in that area on our own mental ability. We no longer choose to rejoice in God's presence and victory, because we aren't looking for God to provide a victory in that area. We no longer are concerned about what we say, because we've counted God out of that arena.

The more we fail to trust God, the more we feel we have to do it on our own. The more we strive, the more stress we feel. The more stress we feel, the more convinced we are that God doesn't care and, therefore, the more we fail to trust God. A very negative, destructive cycle is established. It's as if we have set out on a course on which we constantly have to do more and be more to get more done and have more so we can buy more and be responsible for even more!

And that, my friend, can't HELP but affect our bodies.

The key to releasing stress doesn't lie in exercise—although that can help release tension in our muscles. It doesn't lie in our soaking in a hot tub or a bubble bath.

The key to releasing stress lies in our spirits. It lies in our souls' taking direction from and feeding the right things back into our spirits.

If Dr. Edwards's experience is true for all physicians, then we can do a great deal toward achieving God's wholeness and health in our lives by confronting stress head-on and by getting down to the basics of trust in our spirits.

But what about physical health? Is everything about health limited to our spirits and souls? No. There IS value in good physical habits. God's wisdom extends there, following the same principles that hold true for other areas of our lives.

Physical Fitness

The principles are very clear in this area. Watch what you eat. Watch your exercise. And strike a balance between the two!

Recently, a person came to me and said, "Show me in the Bible where Jesus exercised. I don't believe in exercise because I don't see it in the Bible."

The Bible doesn't have a lot to say about exercise because it didn't have to. The main form of transportation in Bible times was walking. And physicians today tell us that walking is the best form of exercise for most people most of the time!

Jesus didn't travel by chariot. He didn't ride a camel. It was rare that He rode a donkey into Jerusalem—and then to fulfill Scripture. Jesus WALKED virtually everywhere He went.

We live a sedentary life-style today. We get up from sleeping to sit at a breakfast table and then walk a few steps to our cars, where we sit on our way to an office or job, where it is most likely that we will sit much or most of our workday, only to walk a few steps back to our cars and sit in them on the way home, where after we sit at the dinner table, we plop ourselves in front of the television set and sit the night away until we go to bed.

God's wisdom is that His people be on the move. Do something aerobic every day. Get your blood moving. Give your lungs a workout. Stretch your muscles. I walk every day. I figure if Jesus did it, it's good enough for me. I pray as I walk. I engage my spirit and soul in exercise even as I exercise my body.

And what about good nutrition? I believe that the Bible supports two key principles in this area.

First, don't take anything into your body that will cause more harm than good.

Alcohol has the potential to do far more harm to your body than good. Cigarettes and other forms of tobacco do NO good to your body. Drugs—when not used precisely as prescribed by a physician—cause damage. Stay away from these things! Simply refuse to take them into your body.

(Prescription drugs are actually chemicals from God's earth. God has given scientists wisdom about what can be used for our good. I'm not speaking about that kind of drug here. I'm talking about ABUSING those drugs or about taking illegal and dangerous drugs into your system!)

The same principle holds for too much fat or sugar in your diet. It does more harm than good!

Recognize that some common things have more potential for harm than good. During my seminary years we called coffee "Baptist beer" because so many students were high on caffeine! If you find that you are taking four or five "hits" of coffee a day to have energy or to function well, consider yourself hooked. You can get off that stuff by cutting the caffeine in half (half regular and half decaffeinated) and gradually eliminating the caffeine or by cutting down the number of cups you drink a day.

Second, do GOOD things in moderation and with self-control.

At the beginning of this chapter we talked about balancing intake and output. No place is that more obvious than in your physical habits. Too much food and too little exercise result in fat. Fat is a burden, slowing you down and sapping your energy.

The key to maintaining the right amount of intake can usually be summed up in these two verses: "Let your moderation be known unto all men" (Phil. 4:5 KJV). "The fruit of the spirit is . . . self-control" (Gal. 5:22–23).

My mother-in-law moved to Texas, where we lived, in 1974. Within a matter of weeks I gained thirty pounds as the direct result of eating her wonderful pies and cakes. Now that wasn't her fault. While it is still true today that nobody can bake like my mother-in-law, the problem didn't lie with her. It lay in the fact that I didn't know when to say when. I didn't have a stop button when it came to her pies. I had a difficult lesson to learn. Sugar is directly related to fat!

It was a tough lesson—and one I've had to relearn a couple of times—but I'm gaining in my ability to use moderation in that area. Eating sweets is now a reward I give myself once a week. No longer is it a life-style. I don't live on sugar or WANT to be on a sugar high as I walk through life.

Recently, I faced the fact that I had gained more weight than I should carry for my frame and height, and I discovered an important key to losing weight: prayerfully agree about it with other believers! I had three hundred people agreeing and praying with me to lose weight, and those twenty-five extra pounds came off quickly and more easily than any weight I've ever lost! Try it.

Finally, ask God to give you specific wisdom about your particular metabolism. Nobody is made just like you are. You are a unique creation. Your body works in the same GENERAL ways as the bodies of other human beings, but every person's body works in PARTICULAR ways that are unique to the individual. Ask God to reveal to you just HOW wonderfully He has made you and also to reveal to you just what YOU can do to achieve and maintain the best level of health He desires for you.

Never forget that God wants you to be a WHOLE man or woman. That is His desire for you. You are never outside His wisdom by wanting for yourself what He wants for you!

God has made you a triune being with spirit, soul, and body. Your spirit is the core of your being. It is the key area for health in your life. Your spirit expresses itself through your soul (mind, emotions, and will) and outward through your body. Approach your health and fitness from the inside out.

• Develop a healthy spirit by praying daily and exercise your faith as you resist the devil's attacks.

• Develop a healthy soul by choosing to guard carefully what you allow into your mind, how you choose to respond to life's situations, and what you say. Renew your mind. Rejoice. Speak God's words.

• Develop a healthy body by taking in only GOOD nutrients for your physical being, in moderation and with self-control. Exercise your body daily.

God has designed you to live your life with harmony in spirit, mind, and body and with balance between intake and output (or nutrition and exercise). Seek God's balance. Seek God's wholeness!

Finally, I encourage you to repeat to yourself every day those words from 1 Thessalonians 5:23–24 and to make them personal. "May the God of peace Himself sanctify [ME] completely; and may [MY] whole spirit, soul, and body be preserved blameless at the coming of our Lord Jesus Christ. He who calls [ME] is faithful, who also will do it. I believe that He who is faithful WILL do it . . . for YOU!

_____Let's pray about it._____

Father, I ask You today to lead me into wholeness. I ask You to heal my spirit. I ask You to heal my soul—my mind, my emotions, my will. I ask You to heal my body. I ask You to give me the strength to achieve Your healthful balance of intake and output in every area of my life. I want to be whole and to have the most strength and energy I can have as Your servant in building Your kingdom on this earth. I trust You, O God, to be MY Healer today. I pray in Jesus' name. Amen.

Chapter 11

Wisdom and the Workplace

Be diligent to present yourself approved to
God, a worker who does not need to be ashamed,
rightly dividing the word of truth.
—2 Timothy 2:15

I stand in amazement as I read the business sections of our newspapers and magazines today. "How is it," I ask myself, "that America has gone from being the biggest creditor nation in the world to being the biggest debtor nation—and in a matter of only a decade? What has happened to the American workplace, . . . to the American worker, . . . to the American employer, . . . to American ingenuity and productivity? Where do we go from here?"

Perhaps the more basic question for us to answer as believers in the Lord Jesus Christ is this one: "Does God *really* care about what happens to me at work?"

Most of us are pretty much convinced that God cares about what happens to our families and to our churches, but do you REALLY believe that God cares about what happens to your company, your job, your firm, your career, your work?

I believe that God does care in a deep and vital way about the work you do, the job you hold, and the company you work for! Why? Three great reasons.

First, the average person between the ages of twenty and sixty-five spends more time on the job or at work than in any other activity in his or her life, including sleep. The average worker spends more than twice as much "awake" time each week with work colleagues or colaborers than with his or her family. The average worker spends more than ten times as much time each week with fellow workers than in church, including all church-related activities. God is concerned about where you are and about how you spend your time. He meets you where you are, . . . and for most of us, that is likely to be WORK!

Second, the workplace is the number one mission field in the world. It's the place where most of us are placed to manifest our Christian faith. Most believers are called to boldly share their faith in their everyday workplace. Our toughest spiritual challenges often come on the job. The workplace is a spiritual battleground for the Christian worker—a place to win souls, defeat the works of the devil, and claim territory for God's kingdom. No other place requires as much of us or allows us greater opportunities to lift up the name of Jesus.

And third, the workplace is the means of financial reward for most of us. It's where we earn our money. It's the way we participate in the overall commerce and ebb and flow of resources that extend beyond just our jobs and companies to our entire community; the nation; and, ultimately, the world. God wants His people to be prosperous and to be blessed so they can BE a blessing. That includes earning money! I believe strongly that Christians should be among the top money earners in the world so they can USE that money to evangelize the lost, preach deliverance to the captives, teach all nations the gospel, and see this world won to Christ! Your job is the means, the vehicle, the method that God uses to TRANSFER wealth to you so you can use it for His purposes and glory.

Yes, God is concerned about your job because He is vitally concerned about you and about your witness and your finances.

So we may ask, "What is God's wisdom about the workplace?"

I believe that ten key principles govern the life of the believer in the workplace—whether as a worker or as an employer, whether as a person in white-collar management or a person on the lowest rung of a blue-collar work force. These are principles that relate to all kinds of jobs.

Before we go any further, however, let me say one more word to those of you who may be reading this and don't believe that this chapter is for you, because you don't work at a job outside your home. Perhaps you are retired, . . . or perhaps you are a home-maker, . . . or perhaps you are self-employed and work out of your home and, therefore, don't feel that you have a workplace. I challenge you to reconsider your position.

When you stop to look at your situation more objectively, you'll no doubt come to the conclusion that you are working. You are expending effort. You are reaching goals. You are involved with other people in the process. You are receiving some type of rewards in order to be able to live.

I, frankly, do not know a person today who doesn't work in some fashion. And that includes women who work in their homes caring for their children, managing the household, and working as co-laborers with their husbands.

Recently, I talked to a woman who came to me for counsel because she felt worthless. She said, "Pastor, I don't contribute anything. My husband brings home the check, and I don't feel as if I'm providing anything for our home."

I asked her, "What do you do in an average week?"

She started talking about her schedule and the various tasks she did; and as she talked, I started making a list. When she finished, I had listed twenty-one jobs that she held: cook, housecleaner, meeting planner, chauffeur, swimming teacher, child-care worker, business manager, investment broker, laundry expert, landscape designer, bookkeeper, secretary, tutor, counselor, professional shopper, delivery service, repair service, practical nurse, party planner, yardworker, and budget supervisor!

If you are retired from a job, chances are you still have plenty of work to do. Your job has just changed, and your workplace has a different look to it. The same is true for those who are self-employed. You still are a worker, and you still encounter people and work problems as you go about your job.

You *are* a worker. Recognize that fact. This chapter *is* for you.

And secondly, you HAVE a boss. Every person has a human supervisor or boss of some type. We are all under authority of some type. Furthermore, every Christian has an ultimate divine "boss," and that's the first principle of God's wisdom for the workplace. . . .

Principle 1: Recognize Your Ultimate Boss
As Being the Lord Jesus Christ

As a Christian, you are a worker employed ultimately by Jesus Christ. The apostle Paul wrote from a Roman jail cell: "Paul, a servant of Jesus Christ, called to be an apostle, separated to the gospel of God" (Rom. 1:1).

Paul was a prisoner of Rome, guarded by Roman guards and shackled by Roman chains. And yet Paul never thought of himself as being a true prisoner of Rome. From his perspective Rome didn't determine whether he lived or died—His life belonged to Christ. Rome didn't determine whether he was well or sick. Christ did. Rome didn't dictate his emotions or his ideas. Christ did! Paul was a slave, or a bond servant, only to the Lord Himself. And as such, Paul regarded everything he did or said as being done "unto the Lord."

Today you and I are challenged to live our lives in the same manner, with the same outlook. We work "as unto the Lord." It may be scrubbing floors or forging the latest corporate alliance. The nature of the TASK really doesn't count for much in the light of eternity. That floor or that corporation isn't even likely to exist one hundred years from now, if the Lord delays His return that long. The importance of the TASK is how we do it and for whom we do it! It's not so much that we do the task but what doing the task works in US. The jobs that we do and the positions that we hold are actually God's tools for molding our lives for eternity.

We may think that we are doing a job, even doing a job for God. In fact—from the perspective of God and eternity—that job is doing something in us. It's affecting us, changing us, challenging us, and doing a work in us that is divinely ordered and directed by our ultimate boss, God almighty.

Never lose sight of that fact. You may be employed by company X, doing Job Y, in Office Z. But you are ultimately a worker—a slave, a bondservant—of Jesus Christ, called by Him and set aside by Him to extend the gospel and to build His kingdom on this earth!

Principle 2: There's No Substitute for Good, Old-Fashioned WORK

Recently, I met a man in our church, and although his words of greeting seemed friendly and upbeat, I could tell in his eyes that he was down about something that day. I asked him, "What's wrong?"

He said, "Pastor, I can't seem to find anybody who will work for me."

I said, "Well, surely with all of the unemployed people today you can find someone to hire. Have you checked all of the local employment agencies?"

He responded, "Oh, I can find somebody to hire, all right. That's not the problem. In fact, I can hire LOTS of people. I just can't find someone who will really WORK."

I immediately knew his problem. He wasn't just talking about work as a job position; he was talking about the effort, the energy, the work of doing a job. He was talking about the WORK behind the work.

As a Christian, you are commanded to work hard and to give your best effort. The Bible says plainly, "Those who don't work don't eat." Paul put it this way:

But we command you, brethren, in the name of our Lord Jesus Christ, that you withdraw from every brother who walks disorderly and not according to the tradition which he received from us. For you yourselves know how you ought to follow us, for we were not disorderly among you; nor did we eat anyone's bread free of charge, but worked with labor and toil night and day, that we might not be a burden to any of you, not because we do not have authority, but to make ourselves an example of how you should follow us. For even when we were with you, we commanded you this: If anyone will not work, neither shall he eat. For we hear that there are some who walk among you in a disorderly manner, not working at all, but are busybodies. Now those who are such we command and exhort through our Lord Jesus Christ that they work in quietness and eat their own bread (2 Thess. 3:6–12).

In Haggai 2:4 we read, "Be strong . . . and work."

There are no ifs, ands, or buts about it.

No matter what your job, God challenges you to give it your full effort. And then, when you've done that, He challenges you to go a second mile. In Matthew 5:41 we read these words of Jesus: "Whoever compels you to go one mile, go with him two." To whom was Jesus speaking? To Jews who were living under Roman occupation. A Roman soldier could stop any Jew he encountered walking along the road and command him to carry his personal load for one mile. Jesus was saying, "Don't stop then. Go a second mile. Give him TWICE the effort he requires of you."

My—what would happen in America today if every worker gave DOUBLE the effort to his job that his employer or supervisor requires of him? What would happen if you required of YOURSELF twice what you are requiring now?

"But," you say, "I'm already so busy, Larry. I already have so much to do. . . ."

"Having a lot of things to do" and "doing things with a lot of energy" are two different things!

Have you ever seen how quickly a teenager can clean his or her room if it means getting a special treat or reward or if he or she will be left behind if the job isn't completed? A teenager can double his or her effort in a hurry if properly motivated! The same is true for almost any job you face. The problem isn't the amount of work you have to do—it's the amount of energy and effort you apply to it that counts!

The greatest thing you can do today for yourself and for your employer and for your job is to make a decision that you will give your work a double effort.

Most people today are concerned about getting ahead. To them I say, "Then get going." In all thy getting . . . get moving!

Principle 3: Work Honestly

Most people I know—Christian and non-Christian alike—would list honesty as one of the greatest virtues a person can have. It's right up there with not lying or cheating or stealing on the "good behaviors" list. And yet, . . . most people aren't honest.

I read a poll recently in which workers actually admitted that they frequently took business equipment and supplies home for their own personal use, they sometimes cheated on their taxes, they regularly took breaks from work that weren't authorized, and they often left work early or arrived late (or left for lunch early or returned from lunch late). These same workers ranked honesty as one of the best traits an employee can have!

What does it really mean to be honest?

Various Bible versions translate the word *honest* or *honestly* in a number of ways. Here are some of them.

• *Pure.* We are called to work in a clean way, with no dirt swept under the rug. Our motives are pure. Our intentions are pure.

• *Honorably.* We are called to do our jobs in a way that brings honor to the Lord Jesus Christ—so that there's nothing about which we would be ashamed if it came to light. We don't try to sneak anything by. We don't cheat.

• *Just.* We are called to do our jobs in a way that is fair and equitable. If we say that we are going to do something, we do it. If the price is $.89, we charge only $.89. If we are hired to work from 8:00 A.M. to 5:00 P.M., then we WORK from 8:00 A.M. to 5:00 P.M. We give a full day's work for a full day's wages.

• *Good.* We are called to do a thorough, complete, accurate job. We don't take shortcuts. We don't skimp on quality.

These traits—good, just, honorable, and pure—are often limited in our thinking only to what an employee or a worker would do. How much more important that employers and supervisors manifest these qualities. Let the employer also have pure motives, not intending to "pull something over" on his or her employees. Let the employer deal justly and honorably with those under his supervisory care—giving promotions when they are due, giving credit and praise when it is earned. Let the employer be concerned with the quality of his product, the quality of his service to both customer and employee. Often employers consider it their right and privilege to use people toward their personal ends, when the godly approach is to become a "slave of all" (see Mark 10:44).

Honesty is that which rings true. It's being genuine.

Honesty is also letting others know the truth about you as a believer in the Lord Jesus—not only by what you SAY but also by what you DO. It's living your life in the workplace in such a way that what you SAY about the Lord matches what you do!

Perhaps no greater witness can be made in the workplace today than for employers and employees to be HONEST about themselves and their work.

Principle 4: Pray for Those in Authority over You

Paul admonished Timothy in this way:

I exhort first of all that supplications, prayers, intercessions, and giving of thanks be made for all men, for kings and all who are in authority, that we may lead a quiet and peaceable life in all godliness and reverence. For this is good and acceptable in the sight of God our Savior, who desires all men to be saved and to come to the knowledge of the truth (1 Tim. 2:1–4).

Certainly, your earthly bosses are among those in authority over you. Pray for them!

I use the plural here with a purpose. Very few of us are at the top of the ladder in any workplace. Most of us have a boss who has a boss, who has a boss, who may have a boss. Even the top man or woman in a corporation today has a boss known as the stockholder. It's not at all unreasonable to consider a customer your ultimate boss.

Pray for all of your bosses! Pray for your immediate boss and then pray for the one in authority over him. Pray your way up the corporate ladder!

I encourage you to note several things about this exhortation. First, Paul said that we are to pray AND TO GIVE THANKS. When was the last time you thanked God for your boss and for your job? They are gifts from Him. Your boss is authorized by God for his or her position over your life. Thank God for that person.

Second, expect something from the LORD as you pray for your bosses. Expect God to move and work in their lives so your own work life will be quiet and peaceful and so you will be allowed to work in ways that thoroughly please the Lord. Now we don't expect that from these persons. We expect that from GOD. We expect Him to do that work in their lives.

I don't know of anything more enjoyable than going to work and doing my job all day without constant interruptions, petty grievances, and hidden innuendos. I believe that most people are that way. Most of us LIKE to do our jobs. And we especially like it if the environment is free of haggling and backbiting and quarrels.

Pray that God will move in the heart of your boss (and his or her boss and his or her boss) so that a peaceful and orderly atmosphere can be established in your workplace.

Furthermore, Paul said to pray expecting that your workplace WILL be a place where you will be free to express Christ. In very practical words, . . . your boss won't ask you to do something that is dishonest. Your boss won't ask you to spy for him or her. Your boss won't ask you to cheat or lie on his or her behalf or on the company's behalf.

Paul said that this is a "good and acceptable" thing to do. Your boss doesn't have to be a Christian to be influenced by your prayers. PRAY . . . and expect God to create a good work environment on your behalf as you pray.

I also believe that it is the Christian's privilege—and responsibility—to pray for the success of his bosses and for the success of the company.

Pray that your boss will have ideas that are profitable and productive. Pray that your boss will find more efficient ways for the company to work. Pray that your boss will be on target in his or her understanding of the marketplace. Pray that your boss will be in good health and will have sufficient energy to give to his job. Pray that your boss will be able to organize the company in the best ways to get the most done with the least number of obstacles to help the most people. Pray that your company will see great increases in profit and that you may be able to benefit from that.

Everybody wants to be part of a winning team. Are you doing your part to pray your team to victory?

Principle 5: Give a Good Report

This has nothing to do with oral or written reports, proposals, or presentations. It has to do with your attitude toward your work and your job.

Never underestimate the value of giving a good report or the destructive power of a bad report.

The Bible holds a vivid example of this in Numbers 13. The children of Israel had left Egypt under the leadership of Moses. They had cross the Red Sea and were well on their way to Canaan, their Promised Land. As they neared the borders of their divinely appointed homeland, God told Moses to send twelve men to spy out the land. One was to be chosen from each of the twelve tribes, and the men were given very specific commands. They were sent to learn (1) how to fight the victory and (2) how good the victory would be.

I believe that it's important to recognize that these spies were not sent out to determine whether they could take the land. They were not ordered to come back and conduct a political campaign and a vote as to whether they could defeat the enemy. They were simply told to gather information that could be used for strategy. They were on a reconnaissance mission.

The spies were told to bring back some of the fruit of the land to ENCOURAGE the people that this was, indeed, a land "flowing with milk and honey," as God had promised. They were sent in search of EVIDENCE OF A VICTORY.

But what happened?

Ten of the men came back scared to death. They didn't just return with a good lead on where the cities were located and how the people were armed. They came back with an OPINION about the situation that amounted to a negative report. They said,

> The land through which we have gone as spies is a land that devours its inhabitants, and all the people whom we saw in it are men of great stature. There we saw the giants (the descendants of Anak came from the giants); and we were like grasshoppers in our own sight, and so we were in their sight (Num. 13:32–33).

These men, the very personification of low self-esteem and a negative self-concept, convinced the others that the mission was futile.

Now this report was the exact opposite of what God had told them about the land. He had said, "I am going to give you a land flowing with milk and honey"—a good, fertile, prosperous land. He had promised the people, "You'll be able to take the land. It's yours. Don't worry about it. Just hear and obey."

The ten spies lost sight of the goal and the challenge of a victory. They gave in to a tendency in us all to see circumstances, problems, and situations with DOUBT.

The Bible simply calls their report a "bad report." What made it a bad report in God's eyes? It was a report CONTRARY to what God had already said about the situation.

What about Joshua and Caleb? They gave a ringing testimony:

> The land we passed through to spy out is an exceedingly good land. If the Lord delights in us, then He will bring us into this land and

give it us, "a land which flows with milk and honey." Only do not rebel against the Lord, nor fear the people of the land, for they are our bread; their protection has departed from them, and the Lord is with us. Do not fear them (Num. 14:7–9).

In other words, they were saying, "God said that we can take this land. He said that it's ours. He said that He doesn't intend for us to wander around in this wilderness and never reach our goal, our potential, our home. So let's go and get with it!"

They had the right idea! God had said "life" and "blessing" to them about the land of Canaan, and they were giving a report in line with God's message. The other ten spies were giving a report of "death" and "cursing."

The result? The people believed the ten instead of the two. They bought the bad report. The Bible says that they "lifted up their voices and cried, and the people wept that night" (Num. 14:1) and that they took up stones as if to stone Joshua and Caleb to death.

Those who believed the bad report never saw victory. They wandered in the wilderness for an entire generation, and God allowed their children to enter the Promised Land, along with two great old men—Joshua and Caleb!

"But, Larry," you say, "are you saying that we should never give a negative report, even if the situation is a bad one?"

I'm not saying that you shouldn't be realistic or that you should ignore the information that's readily available about your business or work. God didn't ask the people of Israel to enter Canaan on blind faith. He SENT them to get the facts.

What I'm saying is that as you gather the facts about your idea— as you conduct your marketing research and get price quotes and talk to various persons about your proposals—gather the facts with the viewpoint that these are the obstacles that we must overcome. View your end result as BEING an overcomer. Don't approach facts as reasons we shouldn't try but as pitfalls we need to circumvent and directions we should avoid taking.

Tell the truth, but tell the truth WITH FAITH.

An accountant does his boss no favor by withholding accurate facts about the firm's current financial status. But the facts aren't the total story. They don't tell where the company MIGHT be six months from now. Offer a way OUT of the problem; encourage your boss that he CAN find a way through this struggle.

You may be facing a situation in which you MUST improve productivity just a percentage point or two to be truly competitive in the marketplace. Approach the challenge as a SOLVABLE PROBLEM. Gather the facts with the intent that you ARE going to succeed. You ARE going to get through to the other side with a solution that works, is equitable for all, and holds promise for your company!

Be a man or a woman who gives a GOOD report, one filled with life and blessing, one aimed toward a positive outcome.

I asked a man one time where he and his wife had gone on their vacation. He said, "We didn't go anywhere because we couldn't decide where to go. Terrorists seemed to be active in the first area we chose, the weather was bad in the second, the exchange rate for the dollar was unfavorable in the third, and the flight was too long to get to the fourth. The week was over before we got out of town!"

I could think of at least a dozen wonderful places nearby where these folks could have gone, where terrorism, weather, and the exchange rate of the dollar were no factors! The fact was that they got themselves bogged down in "negative reports."

Use facts to guide your direction. Don't let facts keep you from moving forward.

Principle 6: Be an Encourager

Build up your fellow workers. Build up your supervisor or boss. Let them know how much you appreciate them as human beings.

I'm not speaking of blind flattery. Giving untrue compliments results in the very opposite of encouragement, because it is rooted in falsehood and manipulation. I'm speaking of genuine truth speaking to others about who they are and who they can be in the Lord Jesus.

You can always find something genuinely positive to say about someone. It may be an appreciation for their appearance . . . or their ideas . . . or their work performance . . . or an action they took. Your encouragement may be expressed simply with a SMILE. How much brighter and more cheerful most workplaces would be if the employees smiled!

Give a pleasant "Good morning." Give genuine praise when you approve of something that has been said or done.

I'm not advocating that you be a constant gusher of compliments. Not at all. That can be disruptive and become so annoying that people won't take anything you say seriously. To be encouraging, a word of uplifting encouragement must be sincere, and the person receiving it must believe it to be sincere. Overstating your case only decreases your perceived sincerity.

The Bible's word for *encouragement* is *edification*, a word not common in our everyday business vocabulary. *To edify* means "to build up." An element of instruction is involved. Give a word of encouragement to indicate approval and instruction. A supervisor may say, "Bill, I really like the way you typed this report. It was set up on the page just the way I like for it to look." That's a word of genuine encouragement even as it instructs Bill as to what is appreciated or approved.

A worker may say to his supervisor, "Mary, I really appreciate the clear instructions you gave at the last meeting. It helped us all to know what was expected." That's encouragement even as it instructs Mary that it's good to give clear instructions!

More important than the words of encouragement that you speak is your attitude of encouragement. Your attitude speaks volumes. Your attitude is what truly builds up the morale of your workplace. As Paul wrote to the Corinthians, "We know that we all have knowledge. Knowledge puffs up, but love edifies" (1 Cor. 8:1).

Do you have a genuine love for your coworkers? If you don't, ask God to give you one. Ask Him to give you a glimpse of your fellow workers as He sees them. Ask Him to bathe your heart with compassion toward them. Encouragement born of LOVE contributes most toward building a work team with a true team spirit.

"But what if my boss isn't a Christian?" you may ask. "What if he or she is a really difficult person to be around?"

How much more important to encourage that person with genuine praise, born of genuine love.

I recently heard of one woman who worked as a secretary for an extremely demanding, difficult, and often rude man. She determined that she was going to maintain her good attitude, no matter what he said or did. Believing strongly that God had put her in that job, she served this man "as unto the Lord." And once a week she found an opportunity to say to him, "Mr. Jones, I'm just sure God has something good for you in this."

Usually, he would just respond with a gruff "Hmphhh" and ignore her. Months went by with no visible sign of change in this man. But one day he became so exasperated that he responded, "And just what makes you so sure about that?"

She said simply but boldly, "Because I know that God loves you and that He wants only good things for those He loves."

"And how do you know that He loves me?" he roared back.

"Because he put a little piece of that love in me for you."

The man became silent. He knew that had to be true. No other secretary had put up with him for that long. No other person in his company had maintained such a cheerful attitude around him. And something changed in that moment. His outlook about God and about his secretary changed ever so slightly, but it was in a direction toward God, instead of away from God. A healing was birthed in that moment, and over several months this man came to a saving knowledge of the Lord Jesus.

You can always speak the truth to persons about who they are in God's eyes. God loves them. God values them. God has given them talents and skills and unique abilities. God has provided for them.

Speak to a person who he or she is in Christ Jesus! Be an encourager! You'll be amazed at the change that can come about in the atmosphere of your workplace over time.

Principle 7: Pray for God's Answers to Specific Problems and Situations

Make prayer your first resort, not your last one, when you are faced with what appears to be a brick wall.

So many times it seems that we lock God out of our decision-making, researching, developing processes in the workplace.

You may not know where to turn next in your scientific research. You may not know what to do to find the answer to a problem. You may not know how to deal with a certain person or how to approach a certain potential client.

Ask God about it.

In Exodus 31 we read encouraging words for workers everywhere. Moses had been given a detailed list of things to prepare for the tabernacle and all its components. Here in this chapter we see God's answer to HOW the work is going to get done.

> Then the Lord spoke to Moses, saying: "See, I have called by name Bezaleel the son of Uri, the son of Hur, of the tribe of Judah. And I have filled him with the Spirit of God, in wisdom, in understanding, in knowledge, and in all manner of workmanship, to design artistic works, to work in gold, in silver, in bronze, in cutting jewels for setting, in carving wood, and to work in all manner of workmanship. And I, indeed I, have appointed with him Aholiab the son of Ahisamach, of the tribe of Dan; and I have put wisdom in the hearts of all who are gifted artisans, that they may make all that I have commanded you" (Exod. 31:1–6).

Note three things about this passage. First, God had a person prepared to do the job. God gets His work done on this earth THROUGH people. In this case, He had two very special men—two very specific men—ready for the task. If you are an employer looking today for men and women to do the job, trust God for the precise man or woman of His choosing. He's got somebody prepared to help you!

Second, God is the Source of the talents that Bezaleel and Aholiab possessed. All talents and abilities come from God. God has given YOU specific talents. Trust Him to find a way for you to be expressed to their fullest.

Third, the WORK that these men were to lead is linked with wisdom. God expected His wisdom to shine forth in very practical, tangible ways. God's wisdom was about to be expressed in metals, jewels, woods, and fabrics. Don't ever exclude an area of your work from God's wisdom. He can show you a better way to take out the trash!

I mentioned Michael Cardone, Jr., earlier in chapter 6. He is one of the leading young industrialists in America, especially in the automotive industry. He and his father started a company in the early 1970s with just their own family members working in a basement, rebuilding automotive parts. Today he oversees a company with several thousand employees and more than a dozen plants. They've built a company of tremendous financial value, with an outstanding reputation in their city.

I asked Michael one day about their company's philosophy as I toured their great factory. He said, "Larry, those of us in leadership here consider this to be our ministry. It's a business, yes, but it's really a ministry to those who work here."

As we talked further, I learned about their chapel services held weekly before the workday begins. They start every workday with five minutes of inspiration and input from employees and a time of prayer. The vice-presidents meet regularly and begin their meetings with prayer. They approach every new product line, every new challenge with prayer FIRST.

Michael said, "A couple of years ago we realized that the market for rebuilt automobile computers would grow. All of the new cars had them, but you couldn't buy a rebuilt computer module. Because the replacement computers were very expensive, we believed that the consumer would want a less expensive alternative. We also knew that for some reason, which we didn't really understand, the big automobile manufacturers hadn't come up with rebuilt electronic components. We took that on as a challenge."

"What did you do?" I asked.

"First, we got the team together and presented the challenge.

We talk about opportunities here, not problems. We look at things as if they are challenges, not obstacles. And we put together a team committed to finding an answer. They refused to back away from the problem or to say no. These guys are yes people—not in giving in to whatever anyone says. They are yes people in believing that they can get a job done. They become committed to it. And then we prayed. We asked God to guide their hands and their minds as they took on the challenge. They continued to pray, day after day, as they worked on the problem. It was one of those things that just couldn't be done naturally. But within a matter of months they had the problem solved, and we started gearing up for production. I believe that God gave them direct insight into what to do BE-CAUSE they asked Him for it."

Then he added words that are still ringing in my heart: "Larry, we don't claim to be the most brilliant people in the world. Not all of us have a series of fancy degrees after our names. But we are willing to work hard—make that *very* hard—and we desire to put God at the center of our work."

Friend, that's the key.

I believe that it is the key to finding cures for seemingly impossible medical problems. I believe that it is the key to solving financial problems. I believe that it is the key to scientific breakthroughs.

Put God at the center of the process. Ask Him to lead you only in paths of righteousness for His name's sake. Ask Him to guide your research. Ask Him to guide your business decisions.

Are you stuck today with a problem in your lab? In your clinic? In your office? In your factory? In your store? Ask God to give you the specific answer to your specific need!

Principle 8: Be a Finisher

God loves a finisher. It was His own nature to finish. Jesus did the FULL work that God sent Him to do, all the way through the Cross and the resurrection! At one point in His ministry Jesus said, "My food is to do the will of Him who sent Me, and to finish His work" (John 4:34). Finishing was what motivated Jesus. It kept Him going even when times got tough and persecution mounted. The final three words that Jesus spoke on the cross before He died were these: "It is finished." He accomplished what was set before Him to do. He got the job done.

The apostle Paul also had the spirit of a finisher. He said, "None of these things move me; nor do I count my life dear to myself, so that I may finish my race with joy, and the ministry which I received from the Lord Jesus, to testify to the gospel of the grace of God" (Acts 20:24).

Being a finisher is another way of saying, "Be loyal."

I believe that one of the major problems in our American economy today is that we have lost the principle of loyalty in the workplace. Employers are no longer loyal to their employees. Too often they shrug their shoulders and say, "Well, I'll just get somebody else and probably cheaper."

Employees—not surprisingly, in light of that general employers' attitude—are forever "job hopping." When things get the least bit tough or when a new job opportunity offers even the slightest advantage, they are quick to move.

What happens? In the big picture millions and even billions of dollars are spent each year in our economy on training new people for jobs. Productivity is less; efficiency is less. Income margins drop. Less money is available to invest in growth and in rewards for employees. And a very negative cycle is established. The less people are rewarded, the less they feel appreciated, and the more likely they are to find a new job, leaving behind a position that will be filled by yet another person who needs to be trained.

One of the greatest examples of loyalty in the Bible is that which David displayed for King Saul (see 1 Sam. 24:4–7). Even when King Saul went mad and seemed to be consumed by his hatred for David, David refused to take revenge. He spared the king's life when he was within killing range. He refused to speak evil of the king or to allow those around him to speak evil of him. He chose to flee rather than to fight the king, who held God's authority over the people.

And the reward for his loyalty was a "promotion" of leadership and his own victorious, prosperous reign as king.

Loyalty operates in all directions. Employers must be loyal to their employees. Employees must exhibit loyalty to their employers. Workers must be loyal to one another.

What does it mean to be loyal?

To be loyal is to be faithful, and to be faithful is to be FAITH-FULL—to be full of faith that God's purposes are going to be fulfilled in a situation, that God's promises are going to be manifest, and that God is going to be unwavering in His faithfulness to the purposes He has established and the people He has called.

We can be truly loyal only when we understand that God is eternally loyal to those who seek to follow Him. The key to becoming a finisher is to become assured that God is going to finish within you all that He has started. As Paul wrote to the Philippian church. *"being confident of this very thing, that He who has begun a good work in you will complete it until the day of Jesus Christ"* (Phil. 1:6). Be confident! Jesus IS going to finish in YOU the work He has begun. A part of that work includes the lessons you are going to learn in your workplace.

In Psalm 138:8 we read, *"The Lord will perfect that which concerns me; Your mercy, O Lord, endures forever"* (emphasis added). Jesus IS going to finish the growth in you until it comes to fruition in due season. He is going to stick with you. He is going to endure by your side and never leave you. He is going to be supremely faithful and loyal to you. From that flow of loyalty you, in turn, can find the enduring strength to COMPLETE that to which He has called you.

"Are you saying, Larry," you may ask, "that I should never leave a job?"

Not at all. But I do believe that you should use a twofold criterion to determine whether you should leave a job. First, are you leaving a job that the Lord led you to TAKE in the first place?

I know many people who are employed by companies and in positions where they are miserable primarily because they didn't ask the right questions BEFORE they took the job. How can you tell if it's the right job?

Ask yourself these questions.

Will I be unequally yoked? In other words, will I be yoked into harness with people who are pulling in a direction that I don't want to go? Are they providing a good service that is helpful to people? Are they providing a product that is well made and useful to people for their ultimate good? God says that we are NOT to be yoked in agreements with unbelievers who are pulling toward evil. He calls us to pull toward good.

Will I have the opportunity to be rewarded? God is a rewarder (see Heb. 11;6). He is a God of blessing, . . . of harvest, . . . of promises, . . . of uncountable riches, flowing from the windows of heaven. Rewards come in many forms. Some of them are tangible—raises, promotions, benefits, bonuses, and so forth. Some of them are intangible—appreciation, praise, a sense of being fulfilled and of having purpose. It is not God's desire for you to enter a position where you are continually trampled on, denied, mistreated, or ridiculed UNLESS He has sovereignly and very specifically called you into such a place so that His power and love might be manifest.

Have I sensed in my spirit that God has called me to this place? You can know this only if you have prayed and sought God about your employment. Was there a quickening of joy in your soul when you first heard about the job, when you first met the people you were going to be working with, when you first learned of the work that you would be doing hour after hour, day after day? Doing the will of God is not drudgery. The psalmist wrote, "I delight to do Your will, O my God" (Ps. 40:8, just one of many, many examples). God is not going to call you into a place of work—which is also a place of ministry—where you will be miserable.

This does not mean, of course, that every hour of every day on a job is ever going to be joy. As God works out His purposes in you and in those around you, you may experience pain, even discouragement.

In Hebrews 12:11–13 we read,

Now no chastening seems to be joyful for the present, but grievous; nevertheless, afterward it yields the peaceable fruit of righteousness to those who have been trained by it. Therefore strengthen the hands which hang down, and the feeble knees, and make straight paths for your feet, so that what is lame may not be dislocated, but rather be healed.

You may encounter some rough moments in your job. But these aren't signs that you should quit. Endure . . . and see if this is a chastening time in which God is actually HEALING something in you. Be encouraged that God loves you enough to use your job to refine your soul and spirit!

Many people miss God's greater blessings because they leave their positions in the workplace too quickly. They turn tail and run the minute things get the least bit awkward or troublesome. A plant undergoes watering, pruning, cultivation, and fertilization many times before it brings forth blossoms and fruit. Don't miss the full blessing just because you feel a little pruning of your branches or scraping of the soil around your roots!

This leads us to the next point: if you are certain that God did, indeed, call you to your position, then you must be certain that God is now leading you AWAY from that position and to a new challenge.

Ask God about it. Ask . . .

• *Lord, is my work here finished?* Is there more You want me to do? Am I leaving undone something that should be done before I move on?

• *Lord, search my heart. Am I leaving with the right spirit?* Am I leaving because I'm angry, frustrated, or bitter? Heal me, O Lord, so that I might leave with a clean heart and clean hands.

The Lord may very well lead you into a new path, but it will be His highest desire that you finish the work you had begun for Him in your previous job and that you leave with the right attitude, in the right timing, and with the right results!

Bear in mind, too, that your loyalty to people extends far beyond your loyalty to any one company or organization. The Lord will hold you responsible for the way you treat people, no matter what else may happen along the way. Can you still be a brother or a sister in the Lord to those you are leaving behind? You MUST be! That is your highest calling. That is the ultimate loyalty.

Principle 9: Learn to Give and Receive Criticism in the Right Ways

Receiving criticism is one of the toughest challenges any of us ever face in life. Why? Because criticism calls for us to change, and change is against our human nature. Criticism can have in it elements of rejection, and it is our human nature to desire love.

How can we know whether a word of criticism is justified?

Ask yourself these questions.

Will the desired change bring about more growth for my ultimate good in the Lord? If so, the criticism may be something God is allowing for your edification and development in Him. It's tough to be honest with yourself, but try to be. For example, . . . perhaps someone is correcting your grammar because, ultimately, it is part of God's plan for you to speak to groups of people about Him, and poor grammar may be a stumbling block to some in your audience. Bad grammar is a difficult habit to reverse. It requires a genuine EFFORT to make a change. Yet such "criticism" could well be some of the best advice you ever receive.

Does this criticism cause me to doubt God's love toward me? Does it cause me to feel fear? If so, you can be certain that such criticism is NOT of God. I've had struggles with doubt in my life, and many times the enemy has come to say, "If you were saved, you wouldn't have thought that thought" or "If you were truly delivered from sin, you wouldn't have done that." I didn't even need to get criticism from another person. The devil threw enough criticism at me on the inside to take the place of one hundred people!

One day I had enough of that harassment. I began to resist the enemy by saying, "Spirit of doubt and spirit of fear, I resist you steadfastly by the blood of Jesus. I belong to One who bought me with His own blood. I belong to Jesus. I'm valuable to Him. I AM redeemed because He did the work. Therefore, I do not belong to doubt and fear, and in the name of Jesus, doubt and fear, you must go OUT of my life!"

Do you have the authority to do that? YOU DO!

You see, criticism may come through a human vehicle, but, ultimately, criticism is either a chastening from God or a destructive blow from the enemy. It's one or the other. If it's something that can yield your ultimate growth and good, it's a chastening from God. If it's a blow aimed at destroying you or causing fear and doubt to grip your spirit, then it's an attack of the enemy.

The agent of criticism is generally a person, however, and that's something else you must deal with. We will all face some type of persecution in this life, . . . and, generally, persecution is linked directly to a persecu*tor*. PRAY for the persons who are persecuting you. PRAY that their hearts will be changed or that God will remove them from your workplace. PRAY that your heart will be changed toward them and that you will begin to feel and to manifest genuine love in their direction.

At times you may need to confront those who are agents of the devil's criticism toward you.

You may need to stand up and say, "Stop it; that's enough." If they don't even recognize that they have been falsely accusing you, you may need to let them know that you are carrying something negative against them and try to clear the air. But again, . . . as we discussed in chapter 6, PRAY it before you say it. You can do far more damage than good by speaking from your own limited wisdom.

Principle 10: Expect to Be REWARDED by GOD

God has rewards for you that far exceed anything a boss, supervisor, customer base, or stock market can give you. The Bible says that God "is a rewarder of those who diligently seek Him" (Heb. 11:6).

God has ways and means of rewarding you that go far beyond

your job or your salary. Look for His rewards! Desire His rewards! Expect His rewards!

This does not mean that you should constantly be looking for a raise from your supervisor. Neither does it mean that you should NEVER ask for a raise. It DOES mean that any raise or promotion or increase or benefit that you receive *ultimately* comes from the hand of God. God rewards those who diligently seek HIM.

How can you put yourself into a position of being rewarded?

First, *seek Him as your first priority.* "Seek first the kingdom of God and His righteousness, and all these things [which includes every material thing you need] shall be added to you" (Matt. 6:33).

Second, *give of yourself.* That's really what the first nine principles we've discussed have been about. You are planting yourself in your work when you do your work with the full strength of your ability, when you do your work honestly, when you plant PRAYER to your work and for those in authority, when you give words of encouragement and a good report, when you accept the pruning work of good criticism, and when you choose to endure and persevere until the goal is achieved. Your very life is becoming a good seed planted in your workplace. And from that, God promises a multiplied harvest!

God's desire for you is always increase. He wants to bless you so you can become a blessing, and out of your giving yourself and your resources to bless others, you in turn will be in the right position to receive EVEN MORE from His hand, and so the spiral continues in an upward, not a downward, manner! God causes you to GROW from grace to grace, from glory to glory, from increase to increase, from reward to reward. Your life is EXPANDED through the work and ministry that you GIVE.

God's rewards are not only for the by-and-by. They are for the here and now. Expect God to give to you. Receive all that He gives. Use it wisely and be a good steward of it, giving generously into the good soil of His work.

The ultimate word on God's wisdom for the workplace is that God WANTS the work of your hands to succeed. He wants to do a good work in YOU through your job. He wants to touch others THROUGH you in the workplace.

Make yourself available as HIS employee on the earth today!

Let's pray about it.

Father, I ask for Your wisdom about my work. Show me what to do. Show me how to do it. Show me the people with whom I should work to get the job done. Give me the strength and motivation to work to the best of my ability and to go a second mile.

Father, I ask Your forgiveness today for the things that I have done in a dishonest way in my work. Show me how to set things right.

Father, I pray for those in authority over me . . . every one of them. I ask for Your good to come into their lives. Give them insights and ideas that will lead to a better workplace and greater rewards for every person in their employ.

Father, I thank You for the work You have given me to do. I praise You for the things You are doing in my life through my work.

I ask You now for Your rewards, even as I plant myself in my workplace. In Jesus' name I pray. Amen.

A Few Concluding Words

My greatest desire—and prayer—as you finish this book is that you will WANT God's wisdom in your life.

Even more than want, that you will CRAVE God's wisdom as your highest desire.

When that desire for God's wisdom takes root in your soul, I have no doubt whatsoever that—

• *you will find wisdom*. God will liberally impart to you that which you seek from Him.

• *great things will begin to happen in your life!* Furthermore, great things will happen in all areas of your life.

Your health will improve.

Your mind will flood with new ideas.

Your family relationships will deepen and strengthen.

Your financial situation will improve dramatically.

Your work will blossom into a greater harvest.

Your soul will be flooded with joy and peace. And your spirit will soar!

Everywhere I look I see two kinds of people in the world: winners and losers. They have something in common. They both feel like quitting every day. What is the difference? Winners don't quit. Losers do.

On most days I find that the devil throws at least ten good reasons at me to entice me to give up my faith or to operate in my own strength and not seek God's wisdom. The Bible says that "he who endures to the end shall be saved" (Matt. 24:13). The pursuit of wisdom takes endurance.

Wisdom is for doing. Wisdom is for LIVING, and living life to its fullest. I admonish you, "Don't live life without it!"

The words of my admonition, however, imply something very serious and direct. You CAN choose to live life without wisdom. I know of nothing sadder. So many of God's blessings will never be yours if you choose that path. I also know of nothing tougher. To attempt to live life in your own strength and knowledge is not only very hard but also ultimately futile. But perhaps of greatest concern to me is the fact that you really don't have to DO anything to choose a life without wisdom. You only have to sit where you are, maintain the status quo, and pretend as best you can that everything is as wonderful as you'd like it to be. Living WITHOUT wisdom takes no effort.

Let my final words to you on wisdom, then, encourage you to make the effort to have God's wisdom.

You CAN experience God's wisdom.

You DO have the strength it takes to seek diligently and to pray fervently for God's wisdom.

And NOW is the time for gaining wisdom as never before.

Friend, I promise you this: having God's wisdom operating in your life is worth every effort! It's the secret to having it ALL from God!